The Vine Garden

Alex Dingwall-Main

EBURY PRESS

First published in Great Britain 2005

1 3 5 7 9 10 8 6 4 2

Ebury Press, an imprint of Ebury Publishing.
Random House, 20 Vauxhall Bridge Road, London SW1V 2SA

Random House Australia (Pty) Limited
20 Alfred Street, Milsons Point, Sydney, New South Wales 2061,
Australia

Random House New Zealand Limited
18 Poland Road, Glenfield, Auckland 10, New Zealand

Random House South Africa (Pty) Limited
Endulini, 5A Jubilee Road, Parktown 2193, South Africa

The Random House Group Limited Reg. No. 954009

www.randomhouse.co.uk

A CIP catalogue record for this book is available from the British
Library.

Cover design by 2 Associates
Page design by Dan Newman
Typesetting by Textype
Illustrations by Don Grant

ISBN 0 091 89758 0

Papers used by Ebury Press are natural, recyclable products made from
wood grown in sustainable forests.

Printed and bound in Great Britain by Bookmarque Ltd

For Jan and Lorn

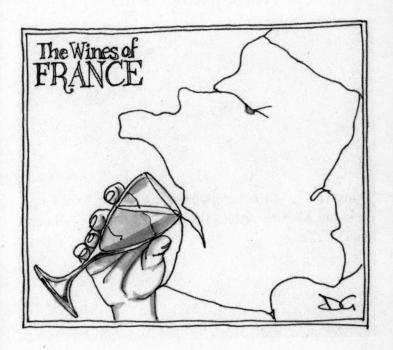

Acknowledgements

Thank you to: Lélia Leyris, Steven Spurrier, Don Grant, Dick and Martine Aubin, Isabelle Bachelart and Hannah MacDonald.

Chapter One

It was just a little over seven years since my young wife and I had packed up our home and most of our life, moved out of the centre of London and arrived in the Luberon region of Provence, where we had bought a dilapidated but charming old farmhouse heavily in need of renovation. It had approximately seven acres of land, of which three-quarters was put down to vine, with orchards of cherry, apricot, fig, plum and quince making up the balance. There was no garden at all, apart from a few decorative trees and a handful of misplaced oleander bushes. Coming from Britain, it seemed quite magical to be surrounded by row after row of burgeoning grapes, and reassuring to realise that the climate was warm enough to ripen the fruit.

However, the immediate challenge for me as a gardener

was to figure out how to incorporate the vines into a garden design. There were so many vine plants that the best idea seemed to be to clear them out in certain places and make a series of cultivated gardens linked by vine walks. It would be a garden within a small vineyard. Of course, certain economic practicalities had to be considered. If we were to pick the grapes, or let a neighbour pick them for the wine co-operative, we would need to leave room between rows and include turning circles for the little tractors. The basic methods of viticulture and the more sophisticated methods of horticulture would need to be carefully executed. But just as the concepts were being discussed, rough plans drawn up and preliminary marking-out started, any ideas of a vine garden came abruptly to a halt.

We had returned to our house one spring evening – we had been in Aix all day – to witness a tractor systematically working its way down the lines of vine, ripping them out by the roots. The driver, who we had never seen before, had nearly accomplished his mission, leaving a wake of terrible destruction. We finally caught his attention by standing suicidally in front of his monstrous machine. Rippling with indignation at his audacity, furious about the mess and horrified at the uninvited intrusion, we demanded he stop immediately and announced our intention to seek legal advice. Did he not know that we now owned the land, that any work to be done was to be ordered by us, that he had wrecked our landscaping plans and would be sued, prosecuted and probably executed? As we ranted and raged, he turned his engine off, removed his cap and scratched his head. After a few more minutes of being attacked in English-accented French, which he probably didn't understand, the poor chap climbed off his tractor, spread his hands, heaved his shoulders and walked away with a bandy-legged gait.

We surveyed the devastated land, the piles of dark wood roots, the muddy troughs and, worst of all, the suddenly open space that surrounded the house. We felt violated. That evening, in a more rational mood, we rang the people from whom we had bought the property to see if they could shine a little light on the situation. They certainly could.

It transpired that, prior to selling the house, our vendors had taken advantage of a government-backed initiative wherein the smaller co-operative wine farmers of the Luberon region, and other areas for all we knew, were being encouraged to stop growing vine. It was considered uneconomical. To increase the quality and thereby the profitability, it would be necessary to decrease the quantity. To this end the Ministry of Agriculture paid – and handsomely – those farmers who would give up, or radically reduce, their quota. And yes, our vendor, the sneaky old pigeon, knowing he was about to sell his property, took full advantage. But in order to receive the compensation, the land had to be inspected when the vine had been dug out. No roots pointing in the air, no dosh.

I think the old boy who sold us the land (I thought of him as 'the old boy' because he seemed so frail and nervous when I first met him; actually, and deeply alarmingly, he was a year or two younger than me) should have warned us of the impending rape or commissioned the removal of the vines before putting the house on the market. It was, at the time, a cruel blow.

Moving home, as most of us know, is an impassioned business; moving country even more so. It took time to settle, but with determination, nearly enough money and blind faith, we had turned our farmhouse into a pretty smart place to live. We spent two years stitching up the house and another two to shake the grounds down into some kind of a garden. After the destruction of the vine fields, we planted a lavender river – 2m by 150m – which flowed into a circle of old vine plants we had managed to save (the wine lake). The rest was put down to rough grass and cherry orchard.

Re-inventing my landscape design practice and establishing a reasonable word-of-mouth client base took a while longer. The first landscaping job I was offered was on condition that I designed it for nothing and then, if the client liked my proposals, I would get commissioned. Needless to say, we were duped. Of course they didn't like the designs, of course there was no job and of course they ripped off most of my ideas and got a local nursery to install it. I suspected it at the time and had it confirmed when I drove past the property again a couple of years later. After that if a client wanted to see my ideas they paid for it. Not much to begin with, admittedly, but enough for me to retain copyright and dignity.

When everything is new there is no time to dwell on shortcomings. At the beginning my wife and I pushed and pulled together, united by a little boy, Theo, whose birth had taken us somewhat by surprise. There were no smart cars, and flying back and forth to England needed careful planning. Then, as each year passed, our house became better organised, the puppy went to school and my land-scaping business continued to expand. We established residency in France and introduced ourselves to the French Inland Revenue. I travelled a lot, working in Scotland, Ireland and England as well as filming with the BBC in Europe. My learning curve of designing gardens in the South of France started to flatten. I had established trade suppliers, built up relationships with various contractors and attracted commissions by reputation. Going to the markets was still an exciting exploration, making new friends seemed easy and being happy at home quite possible.

But with the flattening of the curve came a flattening of life, and now it seemed that the seven-year itch of living together in the South of France was on the verge of becom-ing a nasty little rash – one that looked like it would require more than a tube of quartazone cream and a few antibiotics to fix. So much had been achieved in a relatively short time that when things started to level out it felt startlingly mun-dane. Not for us the life of monotony – why, we had far too much to do! Almost without it being noticed, a fatigue of tedium crept in under the back door and dispersed itself silently and slowly around us like slow-release bacteria. Perhaps because the preceding years had been such an enormous adventure our thresholds for normality had been ruined. Perhaps this and perhaps that. Perhaps, perhaps.

Friendships built up from the legends of a shared lifetime slip easily into that comfort zone in which they remain intact even though separation may have spanned huge drifts of time. But making new friends in a relatively unknown country is a whole new cauldron of conundrums. You need to search out like-minded people and start over-doing your best to avoid the grim and chronics. If you happen to be a pretty girl with a baby, are married to a man umpteen years older and missing your girlfriends back in the city, the challenge of settling in is even tougher. The majority of newly discovered friends tended to be older and their children well on their way to becoming parents themselves if not millionaires.com.

However, Provence is arguably easier than, say, Spain, where expensive little compounds in the south sweat with clubby perversity. In Provence people tend to come and go. You might even miss them and look forward to their return. Their beautiful houses remain in a ghostly limbo as they slip off to make movies, publish books, rattle share prices or simply see more of the planet. At least the anecdotes are fresh.

Getting to grips with another language was taxing, too. To begin with it had all been a bit of a hoot, chuckling with neighbours as you tossed hopelessly inaccurate phrases and sayings into fledgling conversations. But as the day job pulled on long trousers, the game raised its stakes, and speaking French passed from foolery into a deadly business. Making sure I was understood became obligatory. Big money was riding on it. Realising that it was unlikely that I would ever get my French up to full speed – enough that is, to handle legal confrontations with contractors, spread eloquent projections across the bank manager's desk and debate the Third World War with French clients – I had to payroll the business with a core of bilingual people. There is a good team now and between us we manage to pull it off. But finding young people to employ, trained or otherwise, is difficult. Like the countryside everywhere, the young tend to moth it for the bright lights, perhaps returning later in life to pick up the pieces and live contentedly in semi-repose. Although around these parts property prices are becoming prohibitively expensive and the returning generations fewer and fewer.

As the winter months approached, an unforgiving melancholy wove itself into our lives, gnawing away at the roots of our comfortable existence in the South of France. The suddenly cold weather froze ponds and basins, cracked branches and destroyed plants, closed roads and frightened the elderly. By November, it was clear that the malaise was here to stay.

It all began with a duck.

Deronda was much more than just a duck. She swam with Olympic agility both on and beneath the water, waddled with great charm, and had a most resonant voice. She made hens look one-dimensional, game birds neurotic and peacocks merely vain. But then her lover, Georges, died. For a year Deronda sat resolutely on his grave – we had buried him near the pond – refusing to eat or move, until one night when she froze to the ground and became an easy target for a local fox. All we found the next morning was a paperchase of blood-stained feathers, which petered out in the misty woods. A sobering guilt and misery hung around us all.

But it was as nothing compared to the next blow – the death of my father-in-law. This loss completely annihilated the fragile well-being of my wife, and caused a major reappraisal of her own life. Nothing quite highlights one's own mortality as a family death. It bluntly focuses attention on what has or hasn't been achieved. And out of this chrysalis of introspection emerged a changed woman.

Then one of my sisters, who had been diagnosed with breast cancer, was forced to surrender to its atrocious treatment. She accepted it – and went on to manage it – with inspirational aplomb, never allowing it more than a nod of recognition.

On top of this an old school friend, with whom I consistently enjoyed an irreverent sense of blather, emptied life further by bowing out prematurely. He too had been attacked by the malignant beast, but the speed of devastation was breathtaking. It took him from fine to finished in a fortnight.

Because of, or perhaps in spite of, these events – which all took place that autumn – the matrimonial strings were becoming more and more out of tune, and our lives in France more discordant.

Earlier in the year, a new book of mine had been published.

Various journalists came to Provence, with photographers, to 'do' me and the garden for various British publications. It usually meant that they wanted some shots of the family as well so we had to rise to the occasion and put on a united front, even though by that point all the derring-do of leaving Britain, the novelties of a different culture and the gimmick of making these new friends had already lost much of its gloss.

'Just how close to heaven can you get?' a radio reporter asked, looking dewy-eyed at the surroundings. '*And* you manage to make money living here.'

'You're in paradise!' was another journalist's view. 'Wonderful old house with an incredible location, a pretty young wife, an adorable child and a job that is making you rich.' She was picking cherries off the tree and holding a glass of local pink wine. Nearly choking, she added, '*And* weather to die for.'

I muttered something along the lines of it might not be quite as perfect as it seems, that difficulties are difficulties wherever you are, that there might be cracks under the surface, there were always taxes to pay, and so on, but it fell on closed ears.

Being told how ideal your life is when you know it isn't can feel rather sickening, but to protest sounds churlish and disingenuous. In any case, my feeble remonstrances were met with: 'Well, it beats rush hour on a wet Friday night in Shepherds Bush'; or 'You should try living on the wrong side of the tracks in Wolverhampton.'

But Provence is not a weather bank, nor a pool of

perfect calm; it can throw up the same saddened wrecks you might find on any city street. I appreciate that the lifestyle we had been living was perfunctorily glistened in a golden light, but for us it was by then already losing its sheen.

So what were my expectations of moving to France? In truth, I had never really given much thought to that beyond a simple hope that it would work out. There had been no feasibility reports as to the viability of starting a landscaping business, no crammed French lessons or in-depth studies of French history and culture. I arrived with only a layman's knowledge of the country. The fact that, years before, I had been married to a Frenchwoman may have given me a slight advantage, and, historically, the Scots and the French had always enjoyed an accord. Certainly, when the idea of moving to Provence had first been mooted, I didn't reject it as I might have done had it been Bavaria or even Andalusia.

It had been a low time in the UK. I had been fighting and losing against a depressed market. Recession was snapping at the heels of creative practices and only the wily weasels of property development seemed to be scoring by buying cheap and holding until the market rose. Glad to be out of the race, spurred on by the challenge and still green enough to believe that anything was possible, I held hands with my young wife and jumped with extraordinary confidence.

But running a business in France is even more convoluted than it is in the UK. The bureaucratic system is quite unfathomable to anybody who isn't French, and very nearly so to anybody who is. Whether it's to do with banking and borrowing procedures, tax and property laws, or employment and accounting, it seems to be wrapped up in so much red, blue and white tape it confounds belief. A lively black economy infiltrates the process from top to bottom. The more punitive the taxes the more the people begin to look to the black market. Then the more the black trading, the harder the legitimate players get hit with tax to compensate for the deficit. There is even a tradition of reward from the government to anybody who reports the dastardly behaviour of neighbours, friends and even family who might be avoiding their tax payments. It is sinisterly Orwellian, and must bring terrible pain to small communities if a squealer is caught in their midst.

Nevertheless, I am sure that even if my wife and I had worked late into the night listing the pros and cons, we might have hesitated but would still have gone ahead. There was a mutual confidence, and it suited us both to move. But what exactly our expectations were, beyond a better climate and a different lifestyle, remain hazy. Perhaps there was a gut feeling that it would be better for us, a blind faith and a sense of destiny.

But here I was, seven years later, suddenly facing another great leap into the world of the separated.

I needed a break in order to come to terms with this, and, if I was honest, to fuel my creativity, which had begun to feel increasingly lifeless. Creative fuel can come, I have discovered, from many things: falling in love, absorbing art, listening to Elvis or even reading. It can also come from travel. A change of landscape often animates a limping mind.

Perhaps a French road trip was the answer, I told myself that miserable November as the winter approached. I could at once make myself scarce, recharge my batteries and, in a sense, test out France, to see if I really wanted to go on living there. Had my passion for the country been poisoned or had it simply deflated as the air escaped from my marriage? The mere thought of a Tour de France lifted my spirits. Perhaps, I thought, I could visit some of France's famous gardens, even attend some annual flower shows and exhibitions, see what the climatic variations produced and discover some new growers and dealers. I couldn't afford to stop working but I could at least get away and put it down to research. Not only that, but there might even be *châteaux* that had cultivated both garden *and* wine – thereby indulging two of my great passions.

Being hopelessly in love with my little seven-year-old boy, I decided such a journey of discovery would have to be made up of a series of short trips rather than any Kerouac-type black-topping. I simply couldn't manage very long without seeing him.

But what, I asked, was I really pursuing? Happiness and spiritual well-being? I never stop believing. To heal from the emotional mayhem (not forgetting the wrenching loss of my garden when I eventually moved out of the family home)? I hoped so. To unfold the secrets of the French countryside? To a degree. To taste some fine wines? Certainly. To be uplifted by some beautiful French gardens? Yes, please.

I was enthusiastically preparing to map out my itinerary when it all, rather unexpectedly, fell into place.

Chapter Two

The pounding bass notes seemed to bully the wind out of all other noise. No birdsong, no tractor splutter, no frog burps or leaf shake – just a thumping, repetitive invasion, like a mobile Voodoo unit. Then, onto the lane that leads out of the woods and down to our house, came a small white van, which stopped outside the gates.

It shuddered with oversized clefs and appeared to leer in through the pillars, as if trying to decide whether it should ease forward or abandon its mission. I could just see the shadow of a face through the tinted glass of the windscreen, and a cropped head guarded by big black sun glasses. To my great displeasure, the van then slunk onto the driveway and slid to a halt. The door opened.

A tall, well-built girl unfolded herself from the driver's seat. She was covered in black lycra, and a generous smile spread itself across her fine, Hepburnesque features as she removed her dark glasses. 'Hi. Are you Mr Dingwall-Main?'

'Who wants to know?' I asked, slightly off balance. The music was still too loud and troubled my nerves, but I didn't want to admit to this good-looking young girl that I was an out-of-touch old relic.

The music stopped. 'I have a delivery from the Château de Passet,' she said; then with a slightly conspiratorial aside, 'A case of wine.'

'Are you with a courier service?'

'No. I'm working at Passet.'

'Making deliveries?'

'Amongst other things. I recently majored in viticulture at UCLA and now I'm having a year out.'

'Why Provence,' I said, curious, 'rather than Bordeaux or Burgundy?'

'Oh, I'll get to all those places for sure. But the owner of Passet is a friend of my parents, or my father anyway.'

'Tom MacArthur? Mine, too. Where are you from?'

'Savannah, Georgia. And I'm twenty-six and Aries in case you're gonna ask.' She laughed and said, 'Next?'

'Well, if this case of wine is for me I'd better take it in,' I said, smiling.

I picked it up and found it weighed nothing. There certainly wasn't any wine in there. Removing the wooden top revealed only an envelope addressed to me and marked personal.

I thanked the easy-going delivery girl for her bizarre assignment, which she seemed to find amusing, and asked her to give my best regards to Tom. When she had gone I took the box onto the terrace and opened the envelope.

Inside were two sheets of paper, the first of which was a list of French *châteaux* – I recognised some of the names – and a second that read:

Dear Alex

Thank you for your help with the trees. By way of showing my appreciation I am sending you an empty wine case together with a list of *châteaux* I know have gardens. Some are nearby, others further afield, but as you were talking of discovering France through its gardens and your obvious propensity for a fine wine, I thought you might like to join the two. Why don't you fill this vacant case with some bottles you think to be worthwhile, choosing from the list? I'll pay and we'll meet again in the autumn for a tasting of your 'vine garden'. Some of the *châteaux* have better wines than gardens and vice versa. But above all, have a good journey and remember – don't drink and drive; it can shake the sediment.

Tom

In his semi-retirement, publisher Tom MacArthur had bought a small vineyard, Château de Passet, to indulge his somewhat capricious idea of making wine. This was built on a deep affection for the grape and a lifelong interest in fine wine rather than any kind of economic necessity. He was well aware that it was unlikely if not impossible for him to produce a *grand cru* in the Luberon, but it gave him enormous pleasure, occupied his time and allowed him to indulge in his own label. The Château de Passet had about 20 hectares and produced 5,000 bottles a year, mostly distributed to Tom's friends, acquaintances and business cronies. 'An unpretentious young fellow just finding its legs' was how he often described it.

A round man with a big moustache, Tom was never more content than when he was tipping a glass of wine at an angle, rolling it, sniffing it and then tasting it. He would then sagely offer his opinion, whether you wanted it or not. In his late fifties and divorced, Tom seemed to be supported on most social occasions by his adolescent son James, or Jiminie, as Tom fondly called him. Jiminie was already talking of making a career in viticulture, much to his dad's approval.

Tom and I had met at a book launch earlier that autumn. The latest thriller by a local English author was being published in French. The party was held in the gardens of a restaurant and Tom was busy rolling and sniffing his host's selection when some enthusiastic hack fighting his way through to the bar practically knocked him flying. Tom was carrying an elegant silver-topped cane, which dropped out of his grip. I picked it up and handed it back to him. It looked at odds with his fisherman's jersey and old brown cords. He emerged from his glass with his moustache dripping and his nostrils flared. Taking his handkerchief out of its breast pocket and dabbing his mouth, he said with a deep chuckle, 'It must have more body than I thought. Hi, I'm Tom MacArthur.' He was American.

We walked together across the garden to find somewhere to sit; he had a limp that slowed him down but the cane helped. 'I was Santa Claus one Christmas and ringing a bell outside Saks on 5th Avenue,' he explained, 'when a yellow cab mounted the sidewalk and knocked me over. The driver yelled some kind of unfestive insult and left me with a broken leg that never mended properly. That was nearly forty years ago.'

Finding an old bench, we sat in the fading evening light and talked of publishing, wine and gardens. He told me about his little corporation and how he was beginning to find retirement very seductive. I in turn found myself telling him about my rumblings of discontent and my plans to take a garden tour through France. He listened intently. When he realised that I was 'in the gardening racket', as he put it, he told me that having finally got his hobby under control he was turning his mind to some landscaping around his house, 'tree planting, to be more specific'. He was in a quandary, he said, because the quote he had for a few mature trees seemed excessively high. He admitted that he knew nothing of costs but reckoned he ought to seek a second opinion and asked if I would be interested in bidding.

I said I might be, providing he told me what price I needed to beat. I didn't want to spend a lot of time sorting out costs for him only to discover his quotation had been perfectly reasonable. 'I would need a copy of your estimate with exact specification of numbers and sizes, types, details of the guarantees,' I said. If I thought I could offer the same order for less I would let him know.

A few days later his estimate arrived in the office. 'A few mature trees,' he had said. It was in fact a substantial roll-call of huge planes, cedars, cypress, evergreen oaks, olives and assorted fruit trees. It had been costed by a salubrious local garden centre, a place that has quadrupled its size and prices in the last ten years. It made my eyes water to look at the total. They really started leaking when I realised that the price didn't include transportation or planting. I could see nothing about guarantees either, although it was unlikely that they wouldn't have some kind of insurance.

There is a big trade in supplying mature trees and shrubs. People don't want to die waiting for the shade, and Tom MacArthur was happy to join the club. As he said, 'They are not just for my grandchildren.'

After a week I had a firm offer on all the trees – supplied, delivered, planted and guaranteed, including an assurance of watering for the first three months, if necessary. It was substantially less than his other quote even with our handling charge, and he sent a deposit the next day. His trees were planted by October.

As I sat on the terrace looking at his list of suggested *châteaux* that day in mid-November, I realised that Tom had not only wanted me to know that he appreciated the saving we had made on the trees, but more importantly that he had also understood my desire to get away. With his perceptive and elegant generosity, Tom had figured out a way to blend the two, as well as working in my love of gardens and wine, and tackling my pervading unease about France, my adopted country. He must have spent some time thinking about his vine garden list, and I appreciated that. It was also an irresistible idea.

The first time I got drunk was at school during a summer term with a friend. We were both fourteen. We had talked a lot about this baffling phenomenon, trying to understand just exactly what 'being drunk' was like. We knew it came from alcohol and that our fathers were always drinking it, but we struggled to rationalise what it actually did to you. We realised it was popular and therefore must surely be a good thing.

We decided that an upcoming school walk would be the ideal occasion for us to investigate the secrets of inebriation, and were determined that by the end of the afternoon we would be legless. But what to buy and where? It was all very well saying with bravado that we'd just nip down to the off licence and buy a bottle of whisky, but in reality it was more tricky as it was unlikely that shopkeepers would risk their licence for a couple of pre-shave adolescents. In the end we worked out that a bottle of cooking sherry bought under the auspices of an elderly aunt would have to fit the bill.

The next day we detached ourselves with determined regularity from the main body of the march, slugged back great gulps behind juniper bushes and hurriedly fell in again. Each time our rejoining was more erratic. It was not long before the deed was done, our little glass instrument was sherryless and my light-headed crony had thrown the bottle with heightened disrespect over the stone wall that surrounded the local kirk. Feeling increasingly wretched we managed to join the troops for the long haul back to the school yard, only now we could see twice as many school children and felt iller than we could ever have imagined.

It didn't put us off, however. Quite the contrary. We seamlessly moved from sherry to wine, although it was a good few years before I fell off the perch again.

My father always kept a few special bottles of wine in his cellar and, in his self-appointed role as educational wine-master to his son, he had taken great pride in showing them off to me when I was in my early teens, explaining their heritage and ancestry, their qualities and differences. He was good with his tales of Burgundy and Bordeaux, often producing photographs of his arrival at private airstrips somewhere in the venerable vinelands of France. He was also good at telling me how drinking was part of our culture, from cavemen to Communion, from Aborigines to Zombies and he was particularly good at encouraging me to taste.

So encouraged was I that one night when one of my older sisters had some friends over for dinner and the old boy was out, I thought I would help jolly up the party by producing a few of his specials. I carefully uncorked, decanted and sniffed as I had been shown, and spent the rest of the evening generously pouring out the wine to one and all, including myself. Predictably, everybody quaffed the stuff as if it were a supermarket special offer, hardly noticing what was in their glasses – they were all far too busy flirting and fighting. But I was aware for the first time that I was drinking something decidedly different, and my toes curled with the new-found pleasure. It was so good that I quickly realised there was going to be a nasty paternal reaction. Having never tasted fine wine before, I hadn't really thought it through. I suppose I must have thought that he wouldn't mind too much. But the colour of his face when he discovered the absence of his little cumulus was rosé. His only consolation was when my mother pronounced me drunk. The boy at least showed promise.

From that day forth, and with considerably more respect, I have loved wine generally and good wine specifically. I have been treated in my time to some great classics, but have never become anything approaching an expert. I have wasted lots of money on misguided purchases, still do, but have also felt my senses spiral to giddy heights when getting it right.

I have a close friend whose religion excludes alcohol. Much of his denomination's philosophy is easy for me to grasp, but one stumbling block is the earthly joy of fine wine. Despite our discussions and deliberations, I am glad that my God condones it.

When I rang Tom to thank him for his generous and insightful proposal – and, of course, to take him up on it –

we agreed that home territory should be the start of my journey, a short recce before venturing further afield. With my previous idea for a road trip in mind, I asked him about the possibility of combining wine *châteaux* with gardens in Provence. He warned me that many of the local producers would most probably not have gardens per se: 'They are far too busy making wine to fuss about a garden. Except, that is, some of the very grand estates.' As things would turn out, this would be true of all France, not just Provence.

Rather than concentrate on the big estates, however, Tom suggested visiting some of the less well-known venues. His Provence picks, for instance, offered a choice of Château d'Astros and Château de Beaupré for Coteaux de Provence, and as a maverick, the Château Brillane for Coteaux d'Aix. It also mentioned the famous Domaine Tempier if I reached Bandol, not far east of Marseille. It is an area with an AOC – *appellation d'origine contrôlée*, a guarantee of a wine's quality – and possibly the greatest reputation of all Provence's *appellations* for its red wines.

'You have to train before you go out in earnest,' Tom added, when I reminded him that he had sent just one case. 'Get a few bottles, taste them, choose one and that's the first in the box.'

'This is going to be tougher than I thought,' I said. 'Not only will I not be sober for months, I'm going to end up with dozens of bottles of delicious wine.'

I planned to embark on this first trip at the end of the month, so asked Tom to provide me with some intelligent-sounding questions, catchphrases and buzzwords in advance. I didn't want to want to be a complete greenhorn in this red and white world.

And so, as November came to a close, I headed out into Provence.

The first mention of the Astros estate is found in the records of the Knights Templar, who founded the *commanderie* of Astros in the twelfth century. In the fourteenth century the *domaine* became the property of the knights of Saint Jean de Jerusalem before the Maltese took over. They stayed until the end of the eighteenth century. The Maurel family bought Astros in 1802 and built the *château* in 1860. The word Astros is of Greek and Provençal origin, and is thought to have been allied to the nearby village of Vidauban, which was called *Vitis Alba* by the Romans. (This translates rather prosaically as 'white wine'.)

There are 45 hectares at Astros, which produce both red and white wines. The current *producteur* there, Bernard Maurel, is the seventh-generation wine-grower and the second generation to be a banker. He works with passion, and balances his two hats with great acumen.

Château d'Astros itself is a fine Italianate building situated on a hill with a grand view out over the valley and on to the mountains beyond. Tall, floor-to-ceiling windows are arranged geometrically on three floors, and two turrets peak up from the back of the building, just visible from the formal front terrace, which is descended via spectacular double stone staircases. On either side of the steps a pair of bronze gundogs with partridges in their mouths look down from stone pillars.

Walking away from the *château* down a long, wide, gravel pathway, you pass through palms, pillars and parasol pines. At one stage the path breaks for a crossroads and, at each point of the intersection, a heavy stone lion guards the exit. Down the slope and through the woods a large pond reveals itself. The space is tranquil and simple. The planting is kept to a minimum but what there is maintains a high sense of style and history. It is quintessentially French and fans of the writer Marcel Pagnol might have seen a film version of his delicate story '*Le Château de Ma Mère*' in which Astros is cast as the building of the title.

The sales and promotion co-ordinator at the castle was an Englishwoman called Carol, who is married to a Frenchman. She had been designated to show me round the castle and grounds. There is no official recording of the garden, I was told, and, although it complements the *château*, there has never been a plan to create a complicated garden that might affect the labour needed for the wine production.

The site must have originally been cleared to make way for the castle's construction, as a residue of old-timer trees surrounds the area. Walking through the trees on paths beaten by generations of family, visitors and workers, a lingering feeling of changelessness haunts the woods. Business practices may have advanced, global awareness increased and communications exploded, but inside the simple garden of Astros, time was standing still. The intrusion of vehicles was minimised by strictly organised parking, and, as most of the cars, vans and farm equipment belonging to the *château* were from a different age, they didn't seem to matter anyway.

Two wines are produced here, I learned: Les Vins de Pays des Maures and Les Vins AOC Côtes de Provence. Some 120,000 bottles are produced every year. A tasting session was soon under way, carefully instructed by Carol, who helped me overcome my slight inhibition of swirling and spitting. 'You must let it attack your mouth, alerting your taste buds to the tannins and fruit,' she said. 'Swirl it around, suck and squeeze it between your teeth, then spit it out with force.'

Quite. I bought half a dozen bottles and left, a better-educated man.

As Tom had suggested, I headed next to Bandol. However, when I arrived, it was stricken by dark, argumentative-looking thunderclouds. The squawk of the battling gulls was drowned by the waves, which were breaking hard against the protective barriers and pummelling the shoreline. The town's promenade was deserted and all the little booths and boutiques were firmly closed. It was out of season, out of sun and out of sorts.

But one brave or foolish restaurant was open, cavernous and bursting with empty tables except for one where a couple, who looked intriguingly mismatched, sat gurgling at each other. I sat down and ordered fizzy water, with garlicky fish and chips. Behind the bar the attendant was tapping the work surface out of beat to the music with a pair of knives. The waiters were charming and attentive, all eight of them, and before I left to look for the renowned

Domaine Tempier, several of them had pulled out maps, pencils and bits of paper. None of them could agree exactly where the place was, but they collectively endorsed the first 5km.

Bandol is one of the longest-established *appellations* in France. It has, almost single-handedly, established the growing, international reputation of the wines of this *appellation*. Its full-bodied wines were popular at court in the sixteenth and seventeenth centuries, and were supposedly credited by Louis XV, who said they provided him with 'vital sap and wits'. Like Bordeaux, Bandol benefited from being a port, and probably shipped more wine under its name than was produced from its vines.

But despite the maps, drawings and car navigator, I couldn't track down the Tempier estate in the torrential rain. The garage assistants I asked next made it sound easy, and a dawdling old tractor and its young driver pointed it out across the valley, but still I couldn't find the wretched place. A beaten and exhausted man, I slunk off towards the small hotel that I had booked for that night. I decided to rest up then go straight on to the Domaine de la Brillane the next day.

To my chagrin, I later discovered that the Tempier estate lay about 15km from the Château d'Astros.

As you reach the end of the long driveway to Domaine de la Brillane, you come face to face with a vast and rather heroic newly built *château*. It is constructed with grand proportions and sits on top of a rise with great aplomb.

Confident in a daring, pink plaster overcoat, it announces in no mean fashion that it is open for business.

After gaining a history degree and spending a couple of decades in investment banking, forty-something Rupert Birch decided to give it all up and pursue a long-standing dream – to produce a wine that would give pleasure to all who drank it. He hunted far and wide for an existing winery to buy but kept arriving at dead ends. Somewhat frustrated by the lack of enthusiasm from locals, he decided instead to tackle the mammoth task of starting from scratch. He secured some fine land that promised a reasonable *terroir*, even if there were no production facilities or cellars. Almost immediately, an inexpensive wooden chalet was bought from the local DIY centre and Rupert established his *domaine*. Later came exciting expansion in the shape of a series of hoops with green polythene stretched over them. They are still there as a monument to struggle. Now, six years later, he has not only added a cellar and a state-of-the-art winery, but also the whopping *bastide*, or *château* as it should be rightly called, and is watching his fifth harvest mature in large Burgundian casks. Domaine de la Brillane *est arrivé*.

With a financial battering incurred after his divorce, and three children to care for, it was always going to be difficult for Rupert. On top of which, his neighbours had been slow to applaud his efforts partly because they suspected change, partly because he was a foreigner playing their game and partly because he had gone 'bio'. Being sensitive to the hard-working countrymen, Rupert avoided the hard sell in the immediate region, preferring instead to conduct his business a little further afield. Later, when he felt a little more secure in the area, he diplomatically led in the locals slowly by offering his wine up for tasting. 'Then they were hooked,' he says confidently. To prove his point he recently 'landed' a two-star restaurant, something that all viniculturists want. It rewards them with status as well as profit and self-assurance.

The new caves at Brillane are a wonder. The attention to detail, and Rupert's certainty that working the vineyard on an organic basis is the only way forward, ensures such delicacies as using only chestnut beams to support the roof. Other types of wood have usually had some kind of treatment, the chemicals of which, by symbiosis, could affect the ether of the cave, thus tainting the contents of the casks. Now that's really being bio.

It takes a lot of hard work to be officially recognised as an organic viticulturist and, at the time of writing, Brillane is about halfway through the all-important process of gaining a certificate from Ecocert. It means that all chemical fertilisers and pesticides are avoided, and sulphur is used as the main preventative against disease. Encouragingly the *domaine* is already being noticed, written about and given awards. Rupert has named his premier wine, the best of three *cuvée*, 'Flora', after his daughter, so before going out and about the estate a small sampling was mandatory. It was very good. I took a case.

Outside, the rain had packed up, leaving behind a glorious view over towards Aix and the Mont Victoire mountain range. The garden at Brillane is young but determined like the owner. A huge catchment basin has been cut out in the land beneath the *château* and the fill has been used to pump up the terraces that surround the building. Banks have been planted with lavender, which is still shy but settling in contentedly. To one side of the house, but retaining the view, a sympathetic swimming pool has been installed. Set against a strong imposing retaining wall, water gushes out of several heads with satisfactory dramatic effect. In fact, the pool looks more like an old watering basin for animals than anything you might find in a newly constructed home. With reclaimed stone capping, it melts into its environment perfectly, and when the shrub planting has grown up it will be a simple but graceful support act.

'I love the idea of having a garden,' said Rupert, 'but as I am already the picker and producer, the blender and bottler, the secretary and the salesman, I don't get much time to indulge in the subtle world of horticulture. So viniculture it is, for the moment at any rate. If there was any time left over, which there isn't, and even before gardening, I would be daring and try to start some kind of social life.'

Being as I am a descendant of two grand old families – the Earls of Middleton (father) and the Earls of Derwentwater (mother) – and despite dilution over the years by some watery marriages, I still retain an affection for the aristocratic system, and was brought up in a family that lived very much by its old-fashioned foibles and follies. There wasn't much money but that didn't mean we didn't have tailors make our clothes, and although the houses we lived in seldom belonged to us, they were rather august.

When I was about ten I discovered a book in my father's study which was written by an aunt. It was, I saw, called *Charles the Second, Earl of Middleton*. I nobly boasted to my school friends that I was in direct line to become King one day. Then the aunt pointed something out. 'No, dear child,' said she. 'You are putting the comma in the wrong place. It's *Charles, the Second Earl of Middleton*.' I weathered the disappointment but stoically held on to my misplaced Royalist title even under interrogation from some Hanovarian pretenders in the school yard.

The aunt's book was not particularly easy to read. Historical facts of the first Jacobite uprising unfolded around the career of Charles, who spent nearly half of his life in exile following King James to France. (Maybe genes have won through and that's why I'm living here.) Anyway, the book fell short of the somewhat racier story written about part of my mother's family, *Devil Water* by Anya Seton, which tells the story of James, the Earl of Derwentwater, first cousin on the wrong side of the fence to exiled James Stuart, the Catholic son of the deposed King James II of England, who had seen his crown usurped by his Protestant daughter Mary and her husband William, Prince of Orange. A romantic novel based on historical events, it vividly describes the struggle of the Stuart dynasty in trying to regain the throne of England through the ill-fated Jacobite uprisings.

Whether the two earls knew each other is uncertain but

they were both opportunists who fell foul of the winning side. Down through the years, the titles disappeared either through a lack of the male line or because of irate kings deciding to deplete the honours with abstentions. A few generations later two direct descendants from both sides coincidentally met each other at a petrol station near London, fell in love and subsequently married. They produced me and my two sisters.

And so I felt a familiar feeling in the next *château* I went to, Château de Beaupré, which is owned and run by the Baron Doublé, a hard-working, quietly spoken French aristocrat. The patina of generations lay about the place like a friendly old scarf, and I felt a sense of peace as I sat in the vast, wood-panelled hallway talking to the Baron.

Built in 1739, the *château* is considered one of the most beautiful eighteenth-century Provençal manors. But Beaupré is also a working wine farm, which manages 200,000 bottles a year. It is surprising that anybody has time to look after the garden at all. None the less, it is open to the public and is cared for with some skill. Although you wouldn't necessarily guess, it is kept up to scratch by just one gardener and even he gets requisitioned at harvest-time. Nothing is more important than getting the grapes in at the right time.

Beaupré is essentially parkland but, typically, near the house are several attractively cultivated surprises, such as a pair of cast-iron urns on turned legs planted with oleanders. They would, I thought, probably only do two or three seasons before the roots needed to be liberated and new smaller plants installed as replacements. Meanwhile they look well balanced and the feathery leaves help the composition. The iron gates opening out of the courtyard support the coat of arms scribed into the metalwork like a family signature, and an old fountain has been decorated with dolphins (the symbol of young Louis XV) whose poor tails were said to have been damaged during the revolution of 1789.

French and Italian gardens often display long avenues of cypress trees marching regimentally away from the house. Beaupré is no exception. Falling in to the east of the *château*, these elegant 'pencil' conifers had been grown to draw the eye to a small timber building in the distance, which looks like a cross between an English summerhouse and a French seaside villa. It had recently been carefully restored, the Baron told me, and his son, Maxime, now lived there with his wife.

Almost as ubiquitous in Provence as the Florentinian cypress is the equally traditional plane tree. A versatile and hardy specimen, it is cultivated as much for its ability to withstand extreme pruning, or pollarding, as it is for producing a strong landscape statement. It is regularly found in courtyards, near swimming pools or on terraces, creating much-needed shade. At Beaupré, however, the plane has been staged differently. Head south from the villa and behold a field some 90m by 60m hosting a vast arboricultural rectangle of planes. Mature and graceful, they summarise the beauty of these classical trees in a completely original display of grandeur. Grown up in near perfect harmony, their great arms reach out to touch one another in a collective camaraderie. So successful is this particular example of tree planting that people visit the gardens of Château de Beaupré just to walk amongst these giants.

In what I realised was already emerging as a standard routine, I finished the garden tour and went like a well-trained hound to the caves for some more tasting. Already gaining a little bravado, I swilled merrily and muttered openly about the merits of the Château de Beaupré, Coteaux d'Aix-en-Provence, Collection 2000. Here was a good balance of an evolutionary fruitiness and evocative nose coming from a blending of 90 per cent Cabernet and 10 per cent Syrah grapes. I was getting the hang of things now and instantly flung a case into the back of the car. I was beginning to look like a travelling wine rep.

Chapter Three

It was now December, and although I was keen to put my Provence trip to further use, European vineyards were, for the most part, fast asleep, and better visited in May or June the next year. What to do? I couldn't just sit back and wait.

I found myself discussing this wine-and-winter problem with Ed Austin, a South African who had recently bought a property in Provence and had invited me to help him with some landscaping. As the project had developed so had our friendship and we now had no difficulty spending a few hours over lunch sitting in the shade on a restaurant terrace.

'You don't have a problem,' he said instantly. 'All you have to do is come to South Africa and we'll go wine-tasting in Stellenbosch.'

As South Africa has emerged from the shadow of Apartheid, its wines have begun once more to make an impact on the international market. The style of wine coming from this reborn nation seems to straddle the New World and the Old, combining the ripe fruit of the former with the elegance and restraint of the latter.

Stellenbosch is responsible for probably the Cape's finest red wines, harbouring a diverse range of styles. Although responsible for less than a fifth of all wine production, it is undoubtedly the centre of the South African wine industry. Many leading estates have their headquarters there.

Ed went on, 'If you come in the next couple of weeks I can introduce you to a chap who works closely with the de Rothschilds, as he'll be in the area. I am sure he'll arrange a tour of Fredericksburg for us.' Warming to his idea Ed immediately rang the man in question, Fernand Riboulet. After a few minutes of jovial conversation Ed stuffed the phone back in his pocket. 'Fixed,' he said, and smiled broadly.

South Africa sounded ideal. Lovely summery weather, gentle vine-growing valleys, gardens and wine. I booked a ticket the next day.

There was a frosty silence in the garden as I left home at dawn, and although the early wind was strong it seemed to clean my eyes. With no direct flights from Marseille to South Africa, I checked onto the breakfast run up to Frankfurt to make the connection. There was not much time allowance between flights so stress was already muscling in like a pathological condition. But as it transpired, the main flight down to the Cape was delayed by an hour so I had time in the corporate lounge.

I sat with orange juice and hard biscuits, listening to German voices. Quite unexpectedly, I suddenly missed France. I had only left the place a couple of hours earlier but the hardened accent, the cold northern weather and the businessmen in their uniforms flexing for a day of deal-squeezing and taxing negotiations had already made me almost homesick.

The Luberon is not a bitter land, I reflected. It is sometimes too cold in winter and too hot in summer. It gets over-subscribed in August and the restaurants close in November. But there are, as the English journalists who had visited that March had said, no tube trains, no struggling commuters and precious few screaming sirens of the emergency services. Instead there is the cry of the quail, the scent of pines and the soaring hawks. It has a comfortable rhythm and is, objectively, a fine place to live and work. Until that year I had never regretted moving there.

Recently, however, things had definitely been out of kilter. I believe, without being a signed-up Buddhist, that many of the problems churning inside us are mostly of our own making. To understand Karma is to acknowledge that this life is one of the successive states of existence, in which the before is as much an issue as the after. We have to deal with the previous existence, the present and the next. Hard work. It was this equilibrium, I thought, that had been elusive of late. Perhaps this journey to South Africa would help to restore it before I returned to tour my adopted country.

The Lufthansa jet hauled itself up into the night sky, dipped a wing and started its migration towards the southern hemisphere. As the sprawling, multi-runwayed enterprise at Frankfurt shrank away, its lights twinkled through the rain and bade a seasonal farewell.

In comfortable class, the German hostesses were soon passing around glasses of champagne as if their passengers depended on it, which they did. The man next to me pumped back his chair, adjusted his leg rest, slipped on a black Zorro mask, removed his shoes, wrapped his feet up in a complimentary pair of 'cozy-sox' and was asleep before I had finished my drink. Had to be sleeping pills, I thought.

In order to get to George, a small town about five hours up the coast from Capetown and the nearest airport to the Austins, I needed to fly to Johannesburg first. The journey went smoothly enough, apart from feeling wrung-out in a night-flight kind of a way, and it was thrilling finally to arrive in South Africa.

At Johannesburg there was an emotional meeting with my clever luggage, and, hand in hand, we started off in search of the correct check-in desk. From a bank of burly, eager and determined porters emerged one who ran up to me, hand outstretched in greeting, exclaiming, 'George!' I don't know what it was about me that advertised I was heading for George, but I commissioned Lunga to help me (he wore a helpful name badge). He heaved one of my not inconsiderable bags atop his head, wedged the other one under his arm (I have never been good at travelling light) and marched out of the building. From the main international terminal to the domestic flight shed was a long walk and my man earned his crust. Being unfamiliar with tipping practices in South Africa, I gave him what I thought to be fair. He diplomatically took the money without looking at it and put it straight in his pocket. His gentle smile revealed nothing so I assumed it was all right.

The flight attendant on the small internal flight was a personable chap. 'Good morning, women and men,' he said happily. 'My name's Ronnie and I am here to give you instructions on what to do when the aeroplane crashes.' In his hand he held a discoloured safety jacket whose toggles and whistles had long since fallen off. He pointed to the emergency exits adding, 'The captain says when we crash you must open these doors as quickly as possible. Which door you open depends on which way the aircraft hits the ground.'

Thankfully, the flight didn't take long and, with the mid-morning sun shining brightly on the Indian Ocean, we flapped into George pretty much on time, where, to my very good fortune, Ed and Christine Austin stood waiting for me.

Ed, a three-quarters retired businessman who successfully sold his company, spends most of his time enjoying himself. With an easy sense of humour and an engaging ability to get on with people, he seems to balance the act of living in a manner appropriate to expectation or custom. Christine, his elegant wife, is a keen photographer, quick wit and able sportswoman. The children from previous marriages are grown up and live mostly in Europe. Ed and Christine live about half an hour down the coast from George on the wild banks of a beautiful lagoon called Knysna, an inlet from the Atlantic Ocean.

Apart from the convenience shopping that the small harbour of Knysna offers, there is, Ed and Christine told me, little available in the immediate area other than essentials and expensive luxuries. They tended, therefore, to take advantage of any trip to George to catch up on the intermediaries. So the first stop on the way out was Woolworths! It was, I soon discovered, not the rusty old nickel and dime store of yesteryear but a slick supermarket hybrid.

Loaded with magazines, food and a few things to wear, we eased out onto the carriageway and headed for home. It was a fitful experience as our natural progression was constantly being interrupted by traffic-cameras monitoring our speed. As the threat of heavy fines and the removal of your licence for six months is very real in South Africa, people obey by going flat out between the cameras, hammering the brakes when one pops up, then letting rip again into the next section. It made France feel quite loose.

Knysna lies alongside the famous Garden Route, which is a little misleading and should not be construed as a walk through the Elysian Fields of garden fantasy. The area has a

Mediterranean maritime climate with moderately hot sum-
mers and mild to chilly winters. It is one of the richest rain-
fall areas, most of which occurs in the winter months,
brought by the sea-winds from the Indian Ocean.

Knysna's history began in the year 1804, the year that
saw the arrival of George Rex, rumoured to be the illegiti-
mate son of King George III, hence the name of the town.
He purchased the estate known as Melkhoutktaal on the
shores of the lagoon. The name Knysna is a Khoi word
meaning 'Straight Down', a reference to the Knysna Heads,
two great sandstone cliffs, which must be one of the most
striking geological features along the entire South African
coastline. They flank a deep but potentially dangerous
channel through which the sea pours into the wide and
breathtakingly pretty lagoon at the mouth of the Knysna
river.

Arriving at the Austin estate was enthralling. Having
trundled up a hillside track, (or what was a hillside track
before it was laid to brick), you then triumphantly turn off
the road and behold a view out over the lagoon that leaves
your repertoire of superlatives dangling somewhere
between prose and poetry. Bought about seven years ago,
the 50-acre hillside property has been cleverly reorganised.
About half has been cleared, leaving enough 'bush' to give
cover to a variety of wildlife, while the rest has either been
built on or landscaped.

The timber-clad house is comfortably proportioned and,
in keeping with the local vernacular, has a corrugated tin
roof enhanced by a veranda that travels the perimeter of

the building and is calmly painted in soft colours. Designed by a Capetown architect, it is a classical structure that hints gently of colonialism and Cape Cod. Tennessee Williams would have approved. Up behind the house, semi-hidden in the bush, nestles a guesthouse for extended family or friends with kids.

The gardens ramble through courtyards covered in bougainvilleas where pots brim extravagantly with marguerites, petunias and the indigenous marigolds. The retaining walls of the terracing, built strong enough to hold back a marauding tank, are cleverly hidden behind split wooden poles and tumbling plants. Further out the swimming pool perches on top of a grassy bank with an uninterrupted line out over the bay and bordered by some indigenous stinkwood, black ironwood and yellow wood trees. Guinea fowl who have flown in uninvited peck their way round the borders followed by groups of their chicks not much bigger than a 10p piece. As they dig, scratch and uproot the plants, little do they know how consistently close they are to seeing the inside of a cooker. An elderly Staffordshire with a sweet disposition and irritating arthritis occasionally makes a proprietorial effort to catch them. A slightly grumpy old Labrador sometimes joins in half-heartedly but it is all bravado and in the end nobody wins or loses. In the breathing heat of the afternoon, huge grasshoppers the size of a small child's shoe stick determinedly to the lawn. They seemed idiotically unperturbed as I stuck my camera lens up against their insect faces. By evening the lawns were cleared, the heat had abated and a couple of bush buck had slipped silently into the arena. Alert as deer, they grazed with twitching ears and anxious eyes, their muscles shivering with vigilance. There was, I thought, an edgy truce between man and beast here, but clinking glasses and popping corks soon disturbed them.

It was like stepping into a 'wish-you-were-here' postcard. Down on the beach a wooden-slatted jetty marches out into the scene. A vast lagoon decorated with islands of emerald-green sea-grass stretches across to the harbour. A small motorboat tied up to the board walk lies on the still, turquoise water, disturbed only by the wash of bigger boats. Up behind the house, semi-hidden in the bush, nestles another building in the same style. A guesthouse for extended family, or friends with kids. Even further up the hill, a third much smaller house is surrounded by horses and accommodates the groom and her husband, presumably the bride.

The time change of only two hours belied the complete transformation of climate and culture. I was deeply pleased to be away from an unhappy home and as it was only for about ten days I thought I could manage without getting child deprivation, although I kept thinking what fun Theo and I would have here.

That evening Fernand Riboulet – Ed's de Rothschild contact – arrived with his wife. Both young – compared to me – they were easy to get along with. They lived comfortably in Switzerland, and Mme Riboulet was about to give birth to their third child. Fernand's English was wonderful. Not just fluent, he had a colloquial accent that was as out of date as the Ealing comedies. Taking as good as he gave, he was an endless target for leg-pulling from me, but his humour never flagged. He had been with the de Rothschilds for most of his working life and was as close to being part of the family that any outsider was ever likely to be. He held a senior post that included international marketing and property development. Still only in his mid-forties it seemed he was likely to be busy with 'the Firm' for quite some time to come. He knew everybody and had contacts to dream of. By the time dinner was over Fernand had fixed a date for us to be shown round the de Rothschilds' vineyard, Fredericksburg, in Stellenbosch.

The next few days were made up of a whirlwind of activities that included visiting the colourful local markets, walks along the sandy beach and examining the ribcage of a crashed whale that had been pecked clean by gulls, afternoon naps, horse riding, evenings watching DVDs on an enormous screen and, of course, tasting some fine South African wines.

We spent the last but one day power-blasting out in the Atlantic in Ed's boat. The two great sandstone cliffs that guard the mouth of the lagoon connect the estuary with the sea and is a challenging strip of water for sailors to negotiate. You are not permitted to exit or enter without checking in with the control tower that monitors the conditions, and it is because of this mean streak of sea that Ed has attached the muscle of a thousand horses to his boat. A snorting, deep-sea-going craft with enough power to blow your nose inside-out, its twin Mac 500 engines are, as Ed was the first to admit, way over basic requirements, but extremely useful to pull him out of trouble if the currents or winds get too feisty. He was an old sailing hand with plenty of experience and had the appropriate licences that allow him to manoeuvre big and powerful boats. The lighthouse or 'life turrets' know he wouldn't try anything risky. He bobbed the boat slowly towards the yawning gap of the Knysna Heads, signalled to base that he was about to go, then throttled back and hurtled out of the lagoon and into the raging sea like a teased champagne cork.

Being out in the boat was an exciting experience, but most of my time was spent feeling as ill as an adolescent in Ibiza. While all around me the others gaily drank and laughed and Fernand caught fish, I felt wretched and watery-mouthed. I would have been embarrassed by my sea legs deserting me if I hadn't been well beyond caring. 'It's probably the medication I'm taking,' I managed between bouts, but Christine soon saw that things weren't settling and kindly encouraged the captain to pull the monster round and head back to the genteel waters of the lagoon.

'What medication's that?' asked Ed later when we were safely ashore and I had changed from green to white.

'Oh, just something I take for my heart,' I said nonchalantly.

The Austins must have taken this seriously, because the next morning, Christine cautiously called me for breakfast with the kind of concern one reserves for lost dogs.

On my last day at Château Austin, Ed took me out to lunch at the Knysna Oyster Company. Unfortunately a small problem raised its head. A few years ago I had had dinner at some chi-chi fish restaurant and had shucked back a quick dozen oysters while making up my mind about what to eat. It was a good evening with fine wine and good company. Things didn't really start to go wrong until I had been in bed for a couple of hours. Then suddenly through the murky fog of my uneven dreams came a pain that spread out from my stomach, twisted its evil way into my intestine and breathed liquid hell into the very ether of my being. I threw my head into the loo pan and convulsingly retched out my soul for six hours until dawn. The agony and distress of the physical attack introduced me to first division pain for the first time: oyster poisoning. They may have exceptionally high levels of vitamin B12, zinc and magnesium, but if they are an aphrodisiac then I'm a snake-venom Viagra tablet.

Knysna, however, has enjoyed a unique oyster reputation for years, and I gingerly agreed to try a couple, provided they were deep-fried.

Records show that in 1896 a certain George Firth, supposedly an Irish remittance man who settled in Knysna, was a hawker who marketed and sold oysters to anybody who wanted them – and probably just as many to those who didn't. In the 1920s an oyster club was formed by a chap named Swan, or Swannie, who came from England as a qualified telegraphist. His prodigious appetite for these crustaceans made him just the man to head up the club.

The oyster-pickers at that time were meant to be licensed but as none of them could read or write, and often had no fixed address, the forms remained uncompleted. There was nothing stopping you picking oysters for yourself, but if anyone started to cash in on the crop then the magistrates' office was likely to send round the dreaded 'collector'. By all accounts, oyster-gathering was a miserable, difficult and dangerous job at the time. The pickers worked hard and long in water, sometimes up to their necks, during autumn, winter and spring, prising oysters off the rocks with crow bars then loading them into sacks that they would haul up the hill and take into town to sell.

The Knysna Oyster Company was started in 1949 and with its formation came the first commercial oyster farming in South Africa. There are about fifty species of these edible creatures in the world and five of them hang out on the African coast. Of those only one seems to be really commercially viable – the *crassostrea margaritacea* or 'wild oyster'. There is a runner-up known as the red oyster, *ostrea algoensis*, but numbers are too low to be properly useful.

Our host was the restaurant's owner, Mr Oliver, a portly fellow with the sheen of a man who enjoys dining well, and who showed no signs that he might be tired of eating his crop. Quite the contrary, he slurped them down like it was a new-found treat – shell in one hand, chilled white wine in the other. He had bought the restaurant in 1999 on its fiftieth anniversary.

'Do you know the difference between an *ostrea* and a *crassostrea*?' he said.

'Sure,' I said. 'One fertilises its eggs internally, the other releases its sperm and eggs into the water and fertilisation takes place there.'

He stopped mid-mouthful and gazed at me with suspicion. Raising one eyebrow, he leaned forward and hissed, 'Yes, but which is which, eh?'

He had me there, of course. It's only because I loathe the damned things so much that I ever learned this bit of useless information. I took a guess. 'It's the *crassostrea* that fertilises internally and–'

'No!' he exclaimed, clearly relieved that he was able to put the upstart back in his pram. 'Wrong.'

The next morning the maps were out. Ed and I would be taking the scenic route down to Capetown. We were booked into the Cape Grace, a smart hotel right on the waterfront complete with complimentary limousines and intergalactic conferencing capabilities, and would head to Stellenbosch the following morning to visit the de Rothschilds' vineyard.

With a stack of CDs and plenty of luggage, Ed's silver Benz purred out of Knysna. Once off the motorway the five-hour journey down to the Cape produced some fine landscape with impressive passes and valleys, grazing herds of zebra and packs of ostrich. There was one nasty moment when a confederation of tortoises decided to cross the road. The car lurched, the tyres squealed and my heart beat faster than a headmaster's cane. We missed them – but only just.

The last couple of hours or so were spent in the company of mountains. Craggy escarpments, meandering streams and dangerous valleys stretched over a vast landscape. Pass after pass – usually engineered by Scotsmen in the 1930s, Ed informed me – uncovered tough beauty, but none more spectacular than the open country panoramas of the Stellenbosch plains and Franschhoek Valley. We didn't stop as we were due back in Stellenbosch the next morning, but seeing cultivated nature thriving so harmoniously with its wild counterpart was to forget momentarily the terrible scars that South Africa has suffered in its sad struggle for equality and recognition.

On arrival in Capetown, it transpired that our hotel was also the venue for the launch of the much-heralded new MacLaren Mercedes. A number of the hybrids stood right outside my bedroom window being slobbered over by motoring hacks.

That Capetown is a beautiful city is not in doubt. Displayed between mountains at its back and an ocean in front, it has inherited a protected existence with an unlimited outlook. The mountains – Table Top is the best known, supported by Devil's Peak, Lion's Head and Signal Hill – are, at 260 million years, the oldest in the world. Everest for example, might be much taller, but is just a young rock at 70 million. Table Top itself flattens out at about a thousand metres and, because it stands next to the sea, every bit of it is highly visible. Its characteristic shape looms to passing ships as they travel one of the planet's principal trade routes; the sea lane around Africa links east to west. To make it even more distinctive, nature often provides it with an unique cloudy tablecloth, a strange and beautiful phenomenon created by the action of the south-easterly wind, which carries a heavy load of moisture picked up in its passage over the warm waters of the Mozambique–Agulas current and reaches the end of its flow in the area known as False Bay. Condensation turns this moisture into cloud as the wind is forced to rise over the mountain top and then suddenly cools. Tumbling over the northern edge of the table, the wind falls immediately back down to a lower and warmer level. The cloud starts to evaporate, leaving a heavenly cloth of mist floating across the top and down the sides of the mountain.

Legend has it that Capetown emerged about two thousand years ago when both Phoenician and Arab sailors reached the mountain from the sea. The Phoenicians – circumnavigating Africa for the first time from Europe – are said to have landed at the foot of the mountain to rest, repair their ships and replenish food stocks by planting wheat. Not exactly in a rush, then. The Arab sailors – who were exploring the east coast of Africa as an extension to their slave, ivory and gold trading – also sighted the mountain and were immediately suspicious that it was a magical place and would draw ships to their doom. To both pioneering groups, Table Mountain became the absolute beacon at the end of Africa. The mountain streams supplied plenty of fresh water and meat was haggled over with the early tribes and their herds.

It wasn't until the beginning of the sixteenth century

that a Portuguese admiral lost his way and sailed into Table Bay. The sailors replenished water casks and argued with local residents over food, the first squabble between an African and a European, which ended in bloodshed with the Portuguese being driven back to their ships.

Apart from one or two further fracas with the Portuguese, nothing much happened at the Cape until around 1600 when the English East India Company was launched followed by the Dutch East India Company. There was, as a result, a considerable increase in the amount of shipping calling in at Table Bay. It became a welcome halfway break on what could be a terrible journey. The climate was healthy, the water sweet and the natives with their incomprehensible language (all clicks and clacks) were reported as being courteous. However, in time, the natives and the visitors began to irritate each other. Misunderstandings due to language problems, completely different cultures and the arrogance of the Europeans caused a divide that marked the opening of the turbulent story of South Africa. Apart from differences in music, eating habits and the apparent lack of education or parliament, there was the matter of land. The visitors saw no signs of enclosure, of cultivation or private title. The African concept of collective ownership was completely contrary to the European and Asian people who considered their homes to be their castles. Here beneath Table Mountain there seemed to be no such ideology. The whole land appeared to be wide open, ready for the taking.

In 1630 two English commanders laid a somewhat

spurious claim to the cape-annexing it in the name of King James. However, the government was surprisingly ambivalent about its ownership and, in 1647, a homeward-bound Dutch vessel was blown onto the beach at the northern end of Table Bay. Nobody was drowned but the ship was wrecked. Most of the crew made their way back to Europe either in Dutch or English ships, but sixty or so men stayed behind to salvage the doomed boat, encouraged by a valuable cargo waiting to be claimed. It was a successful time and the men flourished. They built a fort, cultivated vegetables, fished and hunted. They even went off to collect penguin eggs and beat the hell out of the poor unsuspecting seals for oil. They managed so well that they were able to supply meat and vegetables to all the ships that called in.

A few years later another fleet of homeward-bound Dutch ships arrived. The salvaged cargo, sixty healthy men and ample stocks of food were taken aboard and delivered in good order back to the Netherlands. The returning officers were so enthusiastic about the Cape and the possibilities of profit that the Dutch East India Company finally decided to establish a victualling station there. It was a defining moment in the history of South Africa.

After a good night's sleep at the Cape Grace, Ed and I descended to the restaurant the next morning and had a quick thirty-five-course breakfast on the terrace outside, so that Ed could smoke. In a crowded café I once asked a workman who had adopted my table as his own if he would mind if I ate while he smoked. It was breakfast after all.

'Nah, mate,' he said, 'I don't mind. 'Ere, why dontcha stir ya coffee wif me snout?' At which point he dropped his newly lit cigarette into my mug and sat there eyeballing me.

The problem with breakfast at these smart international hotels, where the food is piled high on a colossal table or two in the centre of the dining room, is that they try to cater for all tastes. If you're German, there are mountains of sliced sausages, the Swiss get a bouquet of cheeses, Sweden and Norway smoked fish, Scotland black pudding and oat cakes, bacon and eggs for England, maple syrup with everything for Canada, and waffles and cream for Americans. In the first few days it's impossible to decide which nationality to plump for, so I just snatch an obscene amount of everything and raise a multilateral flag. It is, admittedly, embarrassing as you head for the terrace with several plates aching with cholesterol, but it soon dies down and then you're back on what they witheringly refer to as a 'continental breakfast'.

The journey back to Stellenbosch from Capetown the next morning took about forty-five minutes. On the outskirts of the capital, sprawling townships gave way to new flashy shopping centres. We headed for the hills of the fertile Eerste river valley. At last the main reason for my trip to South Africa was about to manifest itself.

Many Protestant Huguenots from the South of France fled to Stellenbosch after Louis XIV revoked the Edict of Nantes in 1685, which had, until then, given the French Protestants political rights, religious freedom, and the possession of certain fortified towns. In effect, all protection of law was withdrawn. Although they were forbidden to leave France, hundreds of thousands did so. They carried French arts, manufacturing and culture to England, Germany, the Netherlands, South Africa and the British colonies of North America, and at the Cape of Good Hope 277 arrived by ship. Many were given land by the Dutch government in a valley called Oliphantshoek (Elephant Corner) – so named because of the vast herds of elephants that roamed the area. It was hoped that they would not only produce more food to supply the passing ships but also that these French farmers would provide further impetus to the local wine industry. Of course, they did, and their valley became know as De France Hoek. Of the 277 refugees a considerable number were from not only Provence but Lacoste, my local village.

Stellenbosch was the first town to be established after the Dutch East India Company had formed a settlement at the Cape. By the end of the seventeenth century, would-be farmers soon recognised that the area might provide thousands of acres of good land for grazing and cultivation. Fruit and vegetables could be produced for ships on the trade routes to the East. It didn't take long before the Stellenbosch farmers were planting vines. Each February and March the slaves picked the grapes and pressed them with their feet. By the first quarter of the nineteenth century the wine industry had expanded rapidly, encouraged by the presence of thousands of soldiers and sailors at the Cape. It led to a big demand that stimulated business, increased prices and, inevitably, introduced new taxes.

The golden years of wine production and high prices

collapsed when Britain reduced the tax on European wine but not on South African wine. It was difficult for the local growers but it made them concentrate on producing better wine and, in 1906, an organisation called the Stellenbosch Farmers Co-Operative Wine Company Ltd was formed. After terrible struggles, the company introduced Lieberstein in 1959, a semi-sweet white wine that, by 1964, had become the bestselling bottled wine in the world. Served cold on a blasting summer day, it makes a really good aperitif. Demi-sec has its place.

Back in 1945 a well-known viticulturist, Dr Anton Rupert, had established the Distillers Corporation with capital of 2 million Rand. The group also expanded rapidly and, under careful stewardship, merged with many of the best-known labels. At the beginning of the new millennium the two big names, Distillers and Stellenbosch Farmers, agreed a deal and a new company, Distelli, was officially listed on the Johannesburg stock exchange. It had assets of over 3,800 million Rand, a turnover of 4,600 million Rand and profits of 278 million Rand. It was into this big business that the de Rothschild empire positioned itself in the 1980s. You can see why.

The historic French Huguenot farm, Fredericksburg, where the Rupert & Rothschild partnership is located, lies at the base of the Simonsberg mountains between Paarl and Franschhoek. Life started here in 1690 with a simple white-washed two-roomed Cape cottage. Then, in 1711, a manor house was built, which was extended as prosperity grew. After Rupert & Rothschild took over the farm in

1984, it soon became a slick, modernised *vigneron*'s fantasy. Now the stainless-steel vats and brand-new French wooden casks stand proudly shoulder to shoulder. It is as hygienic as an operating theatre and rather soulless because of that. Soft air 'mists' automatically out of a thousand little holes in a suspended fabric that runs the length of the cellars, and the controlled temperature permeates the atmosphere with a gentle humidity. The two family coats of arms, screwed to the walls beneath the vaulted ceiling, stare at each other from opposite ends of gallery.

The courtyard and gardens have a simple elegance. White stucco walls with geometric water basins, vines growing over thick wooden posts and crossbars give shade to the metal tables beneath. Surprisingly, there are no grapes grown here at all. They are all produced on the local surrounding farms owned by the partnership, brought in and bottled. As the grounds stretch away towards the foothills, a swimming pool lies undisturbed by even the smallest ripple, and along the edge of low walls, masses of indigenous blue and white agapanthus ('aggies') are in bloom. There is a shadow of austerity hanging over the estate, compounded by a small house that sits forbiddingly in the grounds. This was home to Anthonij Rupert, son of Anton Rupert, who bought the farm and who died in 2002 at the age of forty-one. The house has been maintained as if he is about to return at any minute.

Somewhat dulled by the whole experience, Ed and I were next ushered into a shady inner quadrangle with sparkling white walls, neatly edged paths and tinkling water. The stage was set for a professionally conducted tasting session. On the table were three bottles, representing the three varieties of wine on sale from Fredericksburg: the Baron Edmond – named after the late Edmond de Rothschild – the Classique and the Baroness Nadine – in honour of Nadine de Rothschild.

A silver bowl to spit into, a bottle of fizzy water, a biscuit and a table napkin were laid out next to the press releases. A black man dressed in starched white linen stood to attention in the background, a pressed cloth folded over his arm. Our guide and instructor, Myfanwy, did the honours and explained in detail the different characters of the wines as they were poured, sniffed, swirled and pushed around the cavities and corners of one's mouth. The best, I thought, was the Baron Edmond, which was a blend of Cabernet Sauvignon and Merlot. Matured in new French oak, it had a velvety mouth feel and a long finish.

To be able to taste wine properly – that is, to recognise its character, identify tannins (preservative from the grape skins) and acidity, as well as knowing if it is good or bad – requires as much input from the nose as it does from the mouth. We get a sense of taste and flavour by smelling the aroma. A small region at the top of the nose called the olfactory area houses the flavour-sensitive nerve cells, which react to the volatile molecules of taste, transporting specific messages to the brain. That's why it is a good idea to swill the wine round in the glass before smelling, as it allows the molecules to dance around on the surface and then jump up your nose, alerting you to the taste. Of course, there are nerve cells in the mouth as well, about ten thousand of them. They are distributed all over the tongue and inside the cheeks, with a few desperadoes at the back of the throat. These mouth buds are much less discriminating than their olfactory cousins, however. Rather than distinguish between thousands of flavours they trade in the basics: sour, sweet, bitter, acidic and salty (although a salty wine must be unusual). Alcohol, of course, is omnipresent and part of the fun. It is interesting to note that the less alcoholic wines tend to come from the cooler climates and that sunnier climes make for a stronger potion. In winespeak, alcohol tastes sweet more than anything else.

Nobody ever seems to describe wine having the taste of a grape. It has to be blackcurrant, strawberry, caramel, marzipan, even tobacco or liquorice. A less than ripe Cabernet might be 'green pepper' whilst a ripe one is 'eucalyptus'. There are far too many superlatives to describe wine, and a lot of them sound like clichés or the work of a comedy writer, such as: 'An unstable little gooseberry with hot pencil shavings on the middle palate, but full bodied, well balanced and giving good finish.' Like all trades it has spawned its own language – just watch out for 'wet cardboard' or a 'struck match'. But none of this matters really unless you are intent on becoming a wine-buff. The rule of thumb should simply be 'I know what I like and I know what I don't like.' If you're indifferent then so is the wine.

For decades South Africa's wine industry struggled in the shadow of its oppressive apartheid regime. With vineyards focused on high yields rather than quality, and a strong emphasis on sweetish white wines, the country was out of touch and out of step with the rest of the wine world. However, now that full-scale democracy has taken root, and the doors of international commerce and communication are wide open, there is a great deal more interest in the wines of South Africa. They offer unique flavours, good quality and excellent value.

Because of having to battle so hard the wine-makers had a hundred worries on their collective minds, but gardening was not one of them. It wasn't until relatively recently that any kind of horticultural dexterity began to emerge and this was really born out of public relations more than a burning desire to grow plants. If the producers wanted to seduce people into their wineries then they had to make their places as attractive as possible and a little landscaping does wonders for pulling in the punters. With such a rich palette of plants to call upon and an easy-growing climate, the early gardens took shape quickly and effectively. Soon restaurants opened, with some even offering stay-over facilities. Nowadays the whole tourist industry is tuned into tours of the vineyards and their *châteaux*. It has become an enormous attraction and generates a lot of Rand.

After the clean commercialism of Fredericksburg I was somewhat relieved when Ed took me to see a completely different kind of *vigneron*.

We pulled off the main road and onto a decaying old track. After 500 metres we parked under a fine old copper beech and waited. In front of us a couple of tired sheds were being assaulted by weeds. The creaking doors hung from their hinges, watched by a couple of small, amiable mongrels. One lay out full-length on the ground while the other snuffled around our car, peed on the wheel and looked at us with a take it or leave it attitude.

This place belonged to Michael Hitherington, a sixty-something old Etonian, *bon viveur* and viniculturist extraordinaire, who was cajoling his enterprise along with great success. It was the absolute antithesis to the Rupert & Rothschild set-up. This was a scruffy dilapidated old pile with no PR blurb, no spare rooms for zealous wine buffs and no one in sight. The absence of slickness was charming. Here was the same subtle attraction that old-family homes have with nearly worn out carpets and dog hair everywhere. Sadly Michael wasn't there to lead us astray in his tasting room and, despite a number of phone calls, we couldn't raise him. But it was so peaceful we dwelt awhile in the shade, hoping the main man might reappear. But he didn't so we headed back to town.

It turned out he had been there all the time but was sleeping so soundly he didn't hear us or the phone.

Back in Capetown I decided to take the cable car up to the top of Table Mountain the next morning. The car with its rotating floor slid effortlessly up to the top. There are an estimated 22,000 different species of plant in South Africa, making up nearly 10 per cent of all the plant species on earth. It was good to see African marigolds growing in their natural state rather than in window boxes or royal park bedding-out schemes. Some plants, with origins in the mountains of central Africa, have evolved during the last 5 million years, and have multiplied into various species now recognised as part of the unique Cape Floral Kingdom. This complex collection of at least 8,500 species includes numerous bulbs, heathers, grasses and proteas. Locally these plants are known as '*fynbos*' because they have hardy wooden stems and fine needle-like leaves. In general they grow low to the ground and are extremely well adapted to high winds, long droughts, fire and wet, cool winters. South Africa is the only country that can claim to have one of the world's six floral kingdoms completely within its borders. The country is also home to more than 300 mammal species, over 500 bird species, in excess of 100 kinds of reptiles and countless insects.

There was a small film crew making an advert for the South African tourist board at the top of the mountain. The clearly amateur director-cameraman acted like a know-all from the local club while his two female assistants painted their nails and talked boredly to one another. It was my short straw that put them in the cable car on the way down where the Francis Ford Coppola of subsidised commercials held forth to his captive audience. 'Yes, this is a quick frame loop dispenser,' he said, 'that allows synchronised weaving without losing any consistency, particularly important if you want suspense without narrative. It's a multi-reflex cone lens with a polished Zeiss irritant remover.'

I wanted to push him out of the cable car, but tried instead to grin and bear it as we returned down to the town.

Like many old ports – Bristol, Leith or Marseille, for example – Capetown has developed its waterside into a tourist Mecca. Boutiques selling overpriced and mostly unoriginal wares compete with baying black boys hawking day trips in catamarans, or sea-edge restaurants serving predictable fare. Tucked away are some good Sushi bars and wine shops, but they are in the minority. How so many stalls manage to get away with flogging rail-art pictures of Table Mountain, tatty beads and badly carved elephants beggars belief. But if it generates income for the hard-done-by then it is worth supporting. I bought a picture frame made from recycled fizzy drink cans and a set of napkins printed with ill-proportioned zebras and dubious-looking lions.

On one side of the harbour there is a holding pen of sorts that some opportunist seals have sussed out. Here, for minimal effort, maybe just a honk or two or a slide down the steps, they can get overfed by the gawkers and gazers who wait to board the ferry to Robben Island, Capetown's answer to Alcatraz and the place in which Nelson Mandela spent twenty-seven years.

Suppressed and ignored, taunted and tortured, the ANC founders and principals suffered a shameful indignation here. A terribly unhappy place, it is now a ghostly museum that lingers as a reminder to the terrible misdeeds of mankind. To really understand what prisoners suffered, you need to see Mandela's cell, which is smaller than a letter-box. It boasts a tiny table and a 12in cupboard, a 2in-thick mattress and a neatly folded blanket. As I gazed into this box with the passionate explanations from our over-wrought guide ringing in my ears, I literally trembled with agitation and anxiety. One ex political prisoner described to me the pain of not seeing any children at all for eighteen years – let alone his own – but worse, not even *hearing* any children for those eighteen years.

I read Mandela's autobiography while in South Africa and was much impressed by the charm that pours out of this determinedly gentle soul, who has had to test his sensibilities in a way most of us cannot imagine. Injustice can be beaten. And when you see the shanty towns, you realise the total lack of education and opportunity, and understand the extraordinary ability of humans to believe that things will get better. The pride of the South Africans and their faith in the aspirations of their political leaders has been rewarded, but at what a sacrifice.

Later Ed took me out to lunch at what he referred to as 'the Curry Club'. A bunch of chaps who have known each other since university together still manage to meet three or four times a year to have lunch in the same curry house they used to visit when they were young and financially challenged. Nowadays the barristers, editors, politicians, judges and business reprobates still joke, do deals, argue and cluck contentedly together. That day the subject was rugby, enlivened by the guest appearance of a member of the Springbok Selection Committee.

But when I asked if there were any black players in the team, a stunned silence fell everywhere, and a terrible sense of social faux pas descended upon me. The judge next to me dropped his cigarette butt into his glass of water. One of the barristers came to my rescue with a story about somebody asking 'what that stain on Gorbachev's head was?'. 'It's a birthmark' his friend had informed him. 'Oh I see. So how long has he had that then?'

Anyway, there were no black players or managers, and that was all part of our friend's report. Only a few months later, the replacement manager was kicked out and the pressure to instate some black power has won through. The onward march of the new voters is irrepressible.

After a small zizz that night I headed for a bar. Friday night was *the* night for the hotel, and the weekly air of expectancy was tangible. No matter that I would be a hundred years older than anyone else – the music was good, the boats in the harbour sufficiently splendid and the kids all right.

Presenting yourself into a covert on your own, irrespective of age and experience, requires you to have had a good day and your confidence to be in place. You need to be able to stand at the bar and not look either pathetically lecherous or uncomfortably lonely. You mustn't look sad nor grin, but appear open enough to smile winningly when required, ready to move out of the way without fuss and at the same time wear a glow that says you might be with someone or you might not.

I was dreadfully out of practice. I felt clumsy and stiff, and, after a couple of shots, I was ready to leave. Perhaps, I thought, I'd order a little room service, undertake a lap or two round the mini-bar, puff up the pillows and call it a night by ten. Then I met Wendy – well, I met Wendy, Harry, Fiona and Mick, who were bright, pushy and assured, and into extreme sports. Their warm friendliness was hard to refuse. In the end, I didn't make it out of the bar and we all had dinner together where the buzzy conversation ranged from scuba diving to sky diving. Eventually I bade them goodnight – and good luck.

I ate my last breakfast in South Africa on the hotel terrace with a black friend that Ed had invited to join us.

Wozani Mugobbiana was a tall, smart chap in his early forties. A father of two and a lawyer, he was clearly socially aware and possessed a kind and utterly charming disposition.

I asked him if he felt that the blacks were gaining authority within the South African world of business, entertainment, architecture and sport. He himself was trained in law so I took it that professions like medicine, law and teaching already had some moral power.

'You're talking black empowerment,' he said. 'Nearly every day the papers carry stories of empowerment. Yesterday, for example, Sanlam the insurance giant struck a multi-layered billion-Rand deal with a broad-based empowerment consortium led by leading black business-man Patrice Motsepe. Just the other day in Johannesburg Stocks Building Africa (SBA), the unlisted construction company, reported taking on an empowerment partner. Then there is the three centuries old Franschhoek Valley wine estate that has just been sold. It belonged to an Anglo-American company and they have happily completed a deal with a consortium consisting of a Luxembourg registered company called Citation Holdings SA and a black empowerment group, Kovacs Investments, for something like 325 million Rand.'

'Ah, wine!' I said. 'The main reason I'm here is to taste the wine. Is this the first time black people have profited from an established wine farm?'

Wozani Mugobbiana smiled. 'On this scale, yes, I believe so. Have you been out to the Franschhoek Valley?'

'Sure,' I said. 'And Stellenbosch.'

'Well, you probably passed the place I am talking about. Franschhoek is the most beautiful wine valley in the world. There are well over twenty wine farms and you can still find the crested porcupines running free. You can even go wine tasting on horseback. If you like gardening you should visit Bien Donne Werf with its fruit research farm. There are lavender fields and herb gardens. That should make you feel at home.'

'I've seen enough lavender fields to last me the rest of my life,' I said. 'I suppose if you're a Huguenot descendant you can probably get your family tree drawn up there.'

'Probably. You can certainly commission a barrel of wine to be made under your own label. I think I am beginning to sound like a tourist executive!' he laughed.

'Why are there no black players in the Springbok team, then?' I asked. 'They surely could use a bit of empowering at the moment.'

Wozani smiled, sipped his coffee and, slightly apologetically, lit a cigarette. He looked at me cautiously, a little uncertain perhaps of the value of our exchange. 'The commissions will come,' he said with a sage's certainty. I felt a shadow of something deeper hiding behind the man, of stories not offered too readily to a politically guileless foreigner. 'Entertainment and sport will gain legal means and opportunity in due course,' he added with finality.

Before setting off for the airport I went for a quick walk through a park in the middle of town. It was lunchtime. Benches surrounded by phormiums, Judas trees, Magnolia grandifloras and giant proteas gave respite to hard-working denizens. Widely distributed in the southern areas of the Western Cape, the giant or king protea is the largest of its family and is South Africa's national flower, although for many countrymen the thorn tree is more representative.

Huge rubber trees, ginkgos and palms lined the paths bordered by 'birds of paradise' aloes, shrub roses, lavenders and 'swiss cheese' plants. Swoops of the familiar agapanthus gathered in swooping groups, splashing bright blue against the predominantly glossy green background. Occasional clumps of euphorbia shared space with gardenias, arum lilies and a mixed bag of pelargoniums. There were dusty, well-worn paths, but no grass or pigeons or, as far as I could see, dogs.

As I left the park I saw a young man snatch a woman's shopping, run twenty yards and then look in the bag. He shook his head with disappointment and returned the package to the poor old girl. She smacked the youth's face and shouted something familiar.

When I returned to the hotel I was given a message that my elderly aunt had died and that I ought to divert to the UK for the funeral. The world goes on turning.

Chapter Four

From the sun-drenched, ocean-lapped harbour hotel of Capetown to the rain-filled streets of a cold London was quite a jump. Gone were the yacht loops, galleries and promenading dollars to be replaced with tube stations, newspaper vendors and wrapped-up commuters.

I hired a car and drove to Westonbirt Arboretum to walk alone and think about my dear old dead aunt. The funeral was not for a couple of days and I had a pause before I started helping to sort through her deeds and affairs with my older sisters. She hadn't had children of her own so we were next in line to cope.

Westonbirt, now part of the National Arboretum in Gloucestershire, is cherished not just for its tree and shrub collection but also for its landscaped grounds. Incredibly there is a collection of over 18,000 numbered species covering some 600 acres of, excuse me, '*pinetum*'. Originally created in the picturesque style of Robert Holford, the arboretum is now managed by the Forestry Commission and open to the public most of the time.

The winter Westonbirt offers as good a show as it does in other seasons. Not as obvious perhaps, but in the quiet, short days it displays a brilliance of cold season colour. The last time I was there it was early autumn and the closing days of an international garden design exhibition. A selected group of garden designers from around the world had installed their designs, ideas and concepts ranging from extravagant nonsense to sophisticated simplicity. They were all, by and large, well worth seeing. It had been a hot day with hundreds of regular people in attendance not just at the exhibition but out enjoying the tree park on its own merits and finding solace in the dappled shade. All very therapeutic.

Now, in the cold sharpness of a winter's day with a chalky sun trying to lighten up a dingy sky, there were only a few of us walking and talking to the celebrated Westonbirt red dogwoods or watching the stylised marquetry of the upswept branches of the scarlet oak as it leant against the December wind. Further on, the naked conical crown of a liquidambar flashed at the sinuous Japanese maples. The hornbeam and beeches hung onto their dried leaves while the peeling bark of the birches and *prunus* gave occupation to an army of fidgety tits and finches. A starling was bossily refereeing a match between ravens, but apart from their agitated squawks all was quiet.

The journey eastwards and back into London was pure reminiscence for me. Since moving down from Scotland I had probably driven this road more than any other. It was the road to my aunt and to Cliveden House where we used to hang out in our early twenties. It was the road down which so many people who had second homes in the west of England travelled (myself included, as I had rented houses in Dorset, Somerset and Wiltshire). It was the way to Glastonbury and Reading, Bath, Bristol and South Wales, Eton, Windsor Castle and Henley. It was the fastest route out of London by car and train, and Heathrow airport was on the way. It had the River Thames as a companion and the whole commuter catchment area of the Thames Valley. It was, therefore, impossible for me not to think about my life in the UK as I drove.

It had been over seven years since leaving for France and yet, sitting in the Cromwell Road traffic, it was as if it had only been a dream. But the reality was I had moved on. I had no home in London, no office as such, and had lost contact with a lot of people here. As I waited at the lights opposite the Cromwell Road hospital, it not only reminded me of having ECG tests there years ago but it also rather morbidly made me think about where I wanted to die. France? Scotland? Did it matter? People jazz around the world, open up second or third homes, have international practices and never stay put in any one place for long, but when it gets closer to the final curtain the homing instincts tend to pull. Except, of course, for American artists who have discovered Paris.

There is a small graveyard perched on top of the cliffs in the very north of Scotland, not far from Wick, that is home to my paternal family's bones and ashes. After my father had died and been cremated in Edinburgh, my sisters and I were handed a very smart dark-gold plastic Grecian urn containing the ashes by the Presbyterian minister. It was about a foot tall and had proud handles with lots of swirly bits. Now you don't expect the Scottish church to be loose with its limited funds, but having avoided a plastic coffin we thought the holy man might have managed something a little more biodegradable for the ashes. Dad would never have drunk his dram from a plastic flask but what could we do?

Rather shamefully, Dad laid around my oldest sister's house in Edinburgh for a couple of months before we could organise a trip up to the north to bury, not scatter, his ashes in the designated cemetery as he had requested. In the meanwhile I expected to hear about him leaking from the magnificent urn like a genie and performing whizzical deeds dressed in a vinyl kilt.

The day we buried him it was grey and cold. Gulls yelled secrets on the breeze and early waves of nettles were elbowing their way up through the heather. The minister had thoughtfully organised a mini-grave to be dug. It was about two feet long by nine inches. My first reaction was that Dad would never fit in there. But it turned out that the Grecian urn was bog-standard issue and the 'pit' had been cut to fit the plastic.

'Jest pop it in theyre if ye'd be so kind,' said the man with the collar, 'an I'll sey a few wurds.'

I instantly resolved that when my turn came I would like to join the clan in Scotland, but it is in my Will that the urn must be High Empire and made of a carbon fibre/porcelain mix.

As I sat at the traffic lights watching the birds surfing the wind currents – old enough to read the sky, young enough to test its limits – I considered the familiarity of Blighty with its wonderful idiosyncrasies and comfortable corners, and asked myself if I was truly happy living the life of a Mediterranean.

A loud and aggressive blast from a Porsche behind brought me back from my reverie and alerted me that the lights were now green.

I had a whole new life now in my adopted country but was it a better one? That night I really wasn't sure. But instead of staying in to think about it, I took myself out. We had quite good fun. I bought all the drinks and I bought the food.

When I returned to France after my aunt's funeral, it was straight back into the process of moving out of the family home and buying myself another house.

There are at least five key components that make up the ideal country house purchase. If you want to buy a home in Provence nowadays for under a million euros it means that one or more of these will have to be deleted:

1. the great view;
2. the old stone house (rather than a rendered block construction);
3. the useful outbuildings;
4. enough land for a beautiful garden;
5. a location that is protected from any unlovely development happening on your doorstep.

In my case I had a sixth criterion; it had to be within half an hour of what had been the family home so that access to my fine little hooligan was as easy as possible.

No matter how I added up my post-divorce status, the million-euro residence was not on the agenda. Even more so when I realised how much would be needed to renovate and refurbish. I was never good at cutting corners or making do, and, after a protracted search, the terrible truth was soon sinking in: 90 per cent of the properties I was looking at were too depressing to contemplate and the remaining 10 per cent were still too expensive. In the end I went for a borderline compromise – a big little house built on three sides around a courtyard on the edge of a hamlet. About two hundred years old with first-floor terrace views out over vineyards and cherry orchards, it offered – potentially – three bedrooms and bathrooms, a huge barn-style sitting room, kitchen and dining room and – most importantly – four other rooms which could adapt themselves as offices. It had no further land on the deeds, however, and the possibility of development in the area remains a possibility.

Naturally enough, I had renovation ideas a little above

my station and the bank thought it a good idea for me to fill in a medical form for their insurance company before lending me the money.

The local doctor scampered through the usual knee-jerk, pulse-feeling and lung-listening rituals and declared me in tip-top order. The only thing he couldn't sign was the box relating to my heart. The ECG had to be carried out by a practising cardiologist. He made out an appointment card and said that from what he could hear through his stethoscope it was just another formality.

A rendezvous was made and I was soon whistling down the streets of Apt in search of the surgery where I was to be plugged in. I made a remark to the cardiologist that because my heart was not in love he might have to wake it up. I tend to make inane comments at times like this. Anyway he didn't laugh. In fact, he looked rather grim.

'It's irregular,' he said.

'A regular what?'

'*Non, monsieur,* your heartbeat is very irregular. I want you to have an anginagram. I will make an appointment for next week.'

'Is it serious?' I asked weakly.

'Anything to do with the heart is serious. We must find out quickly if the arteries are getting blocked. Previscan will thin the blood and make it move through the tubes more easily.'

He went on but I was barely listening. Was I *dying*? Drifting back into his conversation, I realised he was saying something about by-passes being ordinary surgery nowadays with a very high success rate. If I had one, I would be off work for months – that is, if the operation was a success. Income would dry up, insurance dialogues would ensue and take for ever to come to the meanest conclusion. They usually do. At the very least, it looked as though it was going to be a medical month.

It was a long week waiting to go into Avignon hospital for the tests. Ever since coming to live in France I had harboured a cloudy fear of being in hospital. Not so much because of the ailment but because of the idea of being in a potentially life-threatening situation without full language capabilities. They might cut something off by mistake because I couldn't explain my pain.

As Murphy's law would have it, my 'free' medical on the State came up two days before I was due to go for my heart operation. I was suddenly feeling very health-aware and vulnerable. If only I had done more exercise, stopped drinking, had more sleep. At least I didn't smoke. I decided to take the State up on its offer before going in for the heart tests.

Arriving at the Apt hospital as directed at 7 a.m. there was no one around except a cleaning lady. She was busy putting the paper cups from the previous day's business into black plastic bags along with discarded Kleenexes, and various bits of detritus abandoned by a malfunctioning congregation. She reappeared and stacked the coffee dispenser with sachets of coffee and piled up the tiny cartons of long-life milk. She shuffled around me like a tired warthog ignoring my '*Bonjour.*'

First up was an eye test. While the nurse filled in her forms I moved up close to the eye chart and memorised as much as I could. She got up and cheerfully led me to the back of the room and asked me to read the first six lines. As I finished with a flurry of e, x, f, d and o – which were blurring in 9 point – the nurse was clearly impressed and stamped a 20/20 on the card.

The hearing was harder because I had osteomyelitis as a child and as a result I have always been deaf in my left ear. I never walk next to anybody on my left side if I can help it and have to lip-read at rowdy parties. The nurse put me into a pair of earphones, turned her testing device right up and looked at me expectantly.

'What?' I said, and took the phones off.

'I didn't say anything,' she said.

She failed me, needless to say, but I scraped through thanks to a pretty perky right side.

Then, on my way to blood testing, I dropped off my urine sample, faeces specimens and sperm dose at reception. The receptionist didn't look too shocked so it must have been the right place.

A kind lady extracted gallons of blood, which I hope they kept to give to some needy soul, and told me to wait. I watched as she tested my urine with a kind of litmus paper, the resulting colour of which was then compared against a chart.

'You have blood in your urine,' she said. 'Could be a kidney problem. You'd better see a specialist.'

I was led out, dazed and suddenly thirsty, and straight

into the main man's surgery. After a few moments in walked the cleaning lady again. I smiled at her, silently sympathising with her about her miserable job. After all, who really wants to scavenge around collecting unpleasant waste? But this time she was wearing a stethoscope. She sat down at the desk and proceeded to ask me a lot of pertinent questions. She then told me with authority to take off my shirt and shoes and climb up onto the examining table. She prodded and poked, squeezed and fondled, and then told me about a few other things she had discovered were a bit shaky. She proceeded to write out pages of prescriptions, plus an address for a kidneygram.

Unceremoniously dismissed and unable to get my doubts under control, I rang my English-speaking doctor miles away to seek soothing advice. 'Probably stones,' he said. 'Get the kidneygram done tomorrow and don't think of flying anywhere. The pain can be so bad they would have to throw you out of the plane because you would be screaming so much.'

As if things weren't worrying enough, I now had to squeeze in another organ review. Happily my examiner was a treat. She must have been seventy, had a huge sense of humour, loved to speak English and teased me endlessly about being pathetic. 'There's nothing wrong with your kidney,' she said, 'nothing at all. It works as well as any I've seen.'

'Ah, thank God for that,' I said, relief sweating out of my skin.

'But the other one's useless. I would say it hasn't worked for at least twenty years.'

Talk about the good news and the bad news. I was a one-kidney kid.

'You will be OK if you look after the good one. Drink a lot. Of water.' Was she giving me a knowing look? 'The pills you are taking for your heart are thinning the blood so much it is permeating the kidney. Do you want to hear about your prostate?' she asked.

'Can't wait,' I said hopelessly. I was out of control now and wanting my mummy.

'Well, it's not too bad. Quite good actually. For a man of your age. How old are you – sixty-five?' I was about to indignantly protest when she squeezed my cheek and said, 'Only joking.'

A few hours later I was in the cardiology department at the hospital in Avignon. This time things moved quickly. I was directed into my room, which, because of two beds, I assumed would be shared. The lady told me to undress – 'come on, completely' – and then, as I stood there as naked as possible, she told me to go and have a shower. 'And make sure you wash properly,' she said, indicating the more sensitive areas with a gyrating hand. Indignation? Humiliation? Forget it. You are just a number and not even a single figure at that.

I returned from my deeply unromantic wash smelling of detergent and was told to get into bed. I was becoming institutionalised by the second. I obeyed orders with a slight thrill. I lay there wondering about what the next leg of entertainment might be, when in shuffled a bow-legged old boy in a cloth cap. He was supported by an all-female cast. The fussing one must be his wife, I thought, those two his daughters, and the fourth had to be his nanny. To somebody like myself who had committed to the programme without any seconds, I began to worry that this was a more serious operation than I had understood.

The gathering took no notice of me at all. I might as well have not been there. The old boy got undressed, aided by his pit crew, and, standing in the middle of the room wearing not much more than an anxious smile, proceeded to walk about looking for the loo. It was very close to my bed actually, just the other side of a skin-thin wall.

He emerged after five minutes – during which his party had cleverly connived at not spotting me and my permanent grin, slumped into the bed and fell asleep. His band of angels still didn't go. They didn't even leave when the same old nurse that had ordered me to shower came in with an electrical razor in her hand. Not one like you shave with in a normal way, but a commercial-sized clipper like you might use to help sheep to give up their fleeces in summer. She pulled back the covers, pulled up my 'nighty' and told me to open my legs. I did as I was told with a small flurry of panache. She moved effortlessly and with great experience. Three or four quick strokes and all the pubic hair I possessed had gone. Well, not counting the little exercise she negotiated with my testicles. With a final zoom she blew off the loose hair, pulled down the blanket, turned off the machinery and was gone. Mission accomplished.

A couple of hours passed. I nattered with my neighbour, who, it turned out, was a *maçon* who had built quite a lot of the walls near my now ex-house in Lacoste. At one point his watery old eyes seemed even more glazed than normal and then, quite unexpectedly, he pulled out from under the covers, like a magician, a bottle into which he had been widdling as we spoke, even though it hadn't been very long since he had spent a long five minutes in the loo. A warm rusty tang filled the air. Must have a shot bladder, I surmised.

Nothing much was happening, apart from an attractive nurse coming in and attaching me to a drip, but lunchtime arrived, and still no operation. In came a trolley that dispelled any stereotype about the French and food being on a higher level. The very same old girl who had so succinctly shaved off my pubic hair turned out to be the lunch lady as well.

An hour later an unexpected burst of activity invaded the tranquillity. A maintenance engineer burst into the room, grabbed my drip, attached it to the end of the bed and, releasing a brake, wheeled me out and into the traffic of the main corridor before I had time to finish my thought sentence.

He drove very fast, bouncing me off the walls like a dodgem car, as if I wasn't in the wretched thing. I pulled my elbows in and went with the ride. He then left me in a lay-by near the reception crossroads. Just as I was settling in to the hustle and bustle of corridor life, my mechanic came back and, with a swerve or two, drove us into the operating theatre. Again lots of *bonjours*, handshakes and *ça vas*. The surgeon and his assistants adjusted their masks, heaved me onto the operating table, checked instruments, tuned the closed-circuit TV and made ready to insert the tubes that would pump pink fluid round my hearteries. It was to be a small operation in which the fluid was monitored as it travelled around the bloodstream. On the television screen the surgeon would be able to observe how my heart was pumping, and whether there were any blocks building up. If he thought my arteries were closing up, he would, he said, insert little springs to keep them open.

He rubbed my right wrist with some kind of freeze jelly and before I could say anything I was coupled to the system. The lights dimmed, the crew pulled back into the shadows and the pump started pumping. Why on earth had they gone to all the trouble of shaving off the pubic hair around my groin only to stick the tubes into my wrist?

In the event my arteries were fine, but only a couple of weeks ago I had been trucking along thinking I was pretty fit. Now I knew I had a dodgy heart, which requires regular checks, was short of one kidney and in need of permanent blood-thinning medication.

However, I had at least managed to sort out the loan – the very thing that had begun the medical month – and I proceeded with the purchase of my new home.

Chapter Five

A few days after my return from hospital Theo got back from a skiing holiday. He was bubbling with pride as he told me that he had received a medal for 'ability'. Although it was fairly certain that most of the kids would have managed much the same thing, the wisdom of the ski school in awarding their students with some kind of recognition for their effort shone through.

His stories brought back memories of the last time I went skiing in Kitzbühel with my then-wife, who skied very well. Like learning to drive, husbands and wives should avoid trying to teach one another – it can only end in tears – so the queen of the black run and I decided that I should hire Herman for a few one-to-one sessions. A charming man, Herman led me through the rudiments of snow-ploughing and easy-does-it slaloms. 'Alex, you are a natural,' he would call, making me feel half encouraged as well as half annoyed at his fibs and pitches at extra remuneration. But every time he said anything positive, I noted to buy him another drink at lunchtime, when Herman and I would sit discussing the afternoon's objectives. As he blew on about runs we might attempt, tricks we could try and goals to achieve, I drank increasingly more in order to get the courage up to do it all. I would end up wishing hunky Herman a good afternoon while I settled down on the restaurant terrace and slept off all the morning's training.

On one of these afternoons I decided to swim instead of returning to the slopes. Naturally enough for a ski resort novice, I hadn't brought any swimming trunks with me, but the ticket attendant at the pool assured me I could hire some, strange as this might sound. She disappeared into a back room before returning to the ticket window and passing the garment to me. It only took up about a tenth of her little hand. A finer and tighter pair of G-string basketcrackers would be hard to imagine. I looked at the item in amazement. Was it disposable? Surely I couldn't wear that, could I? I'd seen such things in inappropriate adverts, but it wasn't quite me, frankly. I asked the lady for something a bit more subtle but she had nothing else.

In the changing room, however, nobody took any notice as I slipped the little jockeys on. I tucked the string into my bottom, puffed out my chest and headed out to the pool with as much conviction as I could muster, whereupon I broke into a playful run and rolled into the water as gracefully as a tall man wearing a thong can manage. Immediately powering up a flashy crawl, however, I found it difficult to move. My chest was grinding against the bottom of the pool. I stood up and found myself in about 20cm of water. Women were running around hurriedly gathering up infants. With horror, I realised I was in the children's pool. I had been concentrating so hard on coping with my horrid little swimming trunks that I had charged into the wrong place. In a frenzy of embarrassment I rushed back to the changing room. Next door to my locker was an elderly, overweight German. 'I went to the kid's pool,' I stammered. 'Yah Kitzbühel,' said my German neighbour, 'you like Kitzbühel?' 'Kitzbühel is fine but I was just in the– oh never mind.' There was nothing for it but to get to the grown up's area as quickly as possible. I strode out expecting instant arrest but all was calm. Never have I found a couple of meters of water more inviting than the beckoning deep-end. I let it swallow me up and I must have done fifteen hundred lengths underwater before surfacing a forgiven man.

'Honestly, Dad, you shouldn't be let out alone,' said seven-year-old Theo when I had finished telling him the story, and he went off to polish his skiing medal.

Later that week, I took Theo to see the Cirque de Paris, which had arrived with a fanfare in Apt.

With animal activists lobbying against the ill treatment of four-legged performers, the big tops of traditional British circuses are on the decline and have been for years. No longer do you see clowns on stilts marching through small villages announcing the upcoming event. They have, generally, become politically incorrect and too expensive. It is much the same for fairgrounds. But in France it is quite different. Here the circus lives on. No small town is overlooked by these huge events, which are wrapped up in smart-liveried, multi-wheeled articulated trucks networking their way across the country with army precision. A week before their arrival, posters and flyers are everywhere, sites cleared and the organisation is well under way. And there are still small shows – offering little more than a pony, a monkey, a ringmaster-cum-acrobat and his assistant – which continue to thrill the children of villages across France.

The sun shone brilliantly as we queued for our tickets with Theo's friend Andrew, who was also there with his parents.

'How much?' we all hollered incredulously, as the heavily made-up dame at the kiosk announced 30 euros each, no half prices for children over 3 minutes old. Half a bank account later we were at least sitting in a fine little box opposite the entry curtain. As we waited, I noticed the holes in the boards that made up the circle, the wobbly chairs and benches, the missing bulbs from the lights and the cheap loudspeakers, but it didn't seem to matter; we were ready to put any disapproval of animal treatment on hold, clap wildly and laugh with the clowns. As we were sitting outside a shaky cage it was reasonable to suppose that the lions would be first on the bill. It didn't do to study the structure too closely.

The lights dimmed and that circus music that has been played the world over a trillion times broke across the tent-mosphere. It was made that much more poignant by a dry mist that squirted from a machine on the side, hissing like an old boiler. With a few loud cracks of the whip the circus master announced proudly the opening act and, sure enough, in came a pair of disgruntled lions who snarled satisfactorily, threatened their keeper just enough to worry the children, did their corny old tricks with about as much enthusiasm as a junkie at the dole queue who's been told he's got a job. They were no sooner out of the tent when down came the cage in an impressive show of team co-ordination. It was strange to see the resplendent lion tamer shorn of his magnificent gold brocade and pillarbox-red uniform now in a house coat looking like an auction porter dragging huge sections of fencing out across the floor. But this 'all-hands-on-deck' was something we were going to get used to. There's a limit to the payroll even at twenty quid a kid.

There followed a fine juggling act from a fourteen-year-old (the sweeper-up of soiled sawdust), who was charming in the way he dropped his skittles, the clown made us cheer with his whistle and mime (strong man and lighting engineer), a skinny guy who had ripped off his shirt pumped himself up on some wooden chairs looking as if he was auditioning for a part in a circus, then, rather unexpectedly, in wandered a rather sleepy hippo with a little girl of about four years old balancing delicately on his back. He found this as irritating as we might find a fly on our neck.

He turned his great gaper mouth over a bulky shoulder and, with a heroic twist, lunged for the little girl, who leapt off in unrehearsed terror. As hippo was just about to exercise his supreme agility and gobble up the wee lass in one quick mouthful, his trainer come and whacked him one across his frothing lips with a polished hardwood cane. The little girl skipped gaily back on board and the parade continued, a big smile glued to the faces of both the trainer and the hippo.

'They kill thousands of humans every year, you know,' whispered Theo conspiratorially. 'Lucky the little girl escaped, huh?'

'Yes,' I replied sternly, knowing full well that my pup would much rather the hippo had consumed her in style.

The second half included a spurious Red Indian and his squaw, who war-danced themselves into the ring, firing arrows and hollering. After mimed rhetoric from the big Chief, the lights dimmed and the squaw attached herself to a wheel, which spun at a dizzy speed whilst the Chief picked up a batch of flaming tomahawks. A loud drum roll followed by a head-aching scream and before you could say Running Bear the axes were flying through the air and landing either side of her body, under her arms, skimming her hair and finally, with just a hint of hesitation, the last weapon zipped into place somewhere between the courageous girl's knees and crutch.

Soon it was finale time and, with blaring music, flashing lights and us all clapping enthusiastically, in came the entire portfolio of animals. Leading the parade was an oxen with gigantic horns, followed by two camels who looked like a pair of worn-out rugs, a donkey, llama and finally a horse. The hippo and lions were clearly above the parade. As each animal bowed down on their front knees, we stomped our feet and yelled for more.

As I recovered from the medical investigations of the winter, my mind turned to the approaching spring and the resumption of my wine and gardens tour. By March, I told myself that I could always taste the previous year's vintage even if the vines themselves were only beginning to think about stirring for the following season.

There can't be many villages, even in France, where so many of the inhabitants make their living from the same source. Châteauneuf-du-Pape, one of the most celebrated wine areas in the world, is a fine medieval town with a population of just over two thousand people, the majority of whom are either wine-makers or working in the affiliated trades.

Châteauneuf – which was the first ever *appellation d'origine contrôlée*, AOC, in France in 1935 – translates simply as Newcastle. But whilst the northern city in England has shipbuilders, beer-brewers and the River Tyne, its Provençal counterpart has a papal heritage, wine and the River Rhine. Situated on the side of a hill, guarded by the ruins of the ancient *château* towering above, the open views consist mostly of vineyards. To the south-east the river winds its way through the valley, glinting in the afternoon sun. Avignon shimmers in the background.

Built by the popes of Avignon as a weekend cottage to get away from the grand *palais* in town, very little of the castle remains, but what is still standing does so with great aplomb. The village streets are narrow and the buildings old, but restoration has hit big time. It is a tourist town with one thing in mind: to sell wine. If you are not growing it or blending or bottling it, you are probably tasting it, marketing it or wishing you had never met it.

A severe disagreement between Pope Boniface VIII and France's King Philip IV led to the election of a French Pope in 1305 and the seat of the papacy was moved from Rome to Avignon. The period has been called the 'Babylonian Captivity' by many Catholic writers and particularly by Martin Luther. It is a polemical nickname in that it refers to the claim by critics that the fabulous prosperity of the Church at this time was accompanied by a profound compromise of the papacy's spiritual integrity, especially in the alleged subordination of the powers of the Church to the ambitions of the Frankish emperor. Coincidentally, the 'captivity' of the popes at Avignon lasted around the same duration as the exile of the Jews in Babylon, making the analogy all the more convenient and rhetorically potent.

In 1378 the seat was moved back to Rome, although a disputing party continued to honour the bishop in Avignon as the head of the church. This is what was referred to as the papal schism, which caused parties to split within the Catholic Church. Although Avignon was abandoned as the papal seat in 1403 it wasn't until 1414 that the Council of

Constancy finally resolved the controversy and dismantled the last vestiges of the papacy.

Châteauneuf is known to have been popular with all the popes because they consistently knocked down or added to the building they inherited from their predecessor. There is no doubt that they imbibed most healthily. Proof being in the hundreds of hectares that they planted with the wine-vine.

With such a papal history, as well as the popes' dedication to the crop, it seemed manifestly on the cards that one of Tom MacArthur's bottles should come from the Châteauneuf region. Enjoyed by thousands the world over, the full-bodied reds and bold whites from the Côte du Rhône have a reputation that many outside of Bordeaux and Burgundy would smash bottles for. Having sniffed around various cellars on dozens of occasions and been turned onto one or two very good producers, it was with interest to see what Tom's choice of *château* offered. For the sake of getting under the skin of what makes this wine, with its heavily embossed coat of arms at the base of the bottle's neck, so famous and popular, he had deemed it best to head for one of its biggest producers and exporters.

There are two major wine-producers in the Côte du Rhône: Château Rayas and Château Beaucastel. The fundamental difference between the two producers is that Beaucastel is permitted by the wine lawyers to use all of the thirteen grape varieties available in the region while Rayas can only work the Grenache grape. Which is the easier? I wondered. Having over a dozen grapes to blend might prove inordinately confusing, or perhaps it opens up the possibilities to such a degree you can't fail to crack some kind of a result. Using only one grape may seem less complicated, but you need to know how to deal with it, and there are no support acts to take up the slack. The fact that both *châteaux* succeed so well says something for the game of making wine. Tom, however, had directed me towards Beaucastel, winner of many prizes, so that was where I went.

Beaucastel is approached across the flatlands where, in keeping with the spirit of the region, the vines seem to grow out of a strange carpet of stone. The Rhône flowed over all of the valley around 10 million years ago. The large pebbles that you see today are the same ones which were deposited when the river moved inexorably westwards all those years ago. They retain the heat of the day and eek it out to the roots at night. The stones lie some 50cm deep after which limestone gravel takes over.

My host was a bright and happy man called Fabrice Langlois. Trained as a sommelier and now in his early thirties, he was born within the nineteenth arrondissement in Paris but brought up in the Loire Valley and later studied for two years with the wine-makers of Tain l'Hermitage in southern Beaujolais. He was well grounded by his parents in food and wine appreciation, and despite extensive travel throughout France remains a fan of the Rhône wines. He was the in-house sommelier at the celebrated Michelin-starred Clos de la Violette restaurant in Aix-en-Provence and had known the Côte du Rhône wines well for ten years, since his training. When the previous sommelier at Beaucastel retired and left the *domaine*, Jean-Pierre Perrin, the master and co-owner of the *château* with his brother, knew about the passionate Fabrice through the restaurant. Having been impressed by the young sommelier's passion not just for wine in general but his love of the Rhône in particular, he asked him if he would like to join his team at Beaucastel. The young sommelier said he would.

It doesn't take long to realise that Fabrice is just as nutty about food as he is wine and talks of oenology and wine 'pairing' with such enthusiasm that it makes you hungry and thirsty all at the same time. I asked him if one is born with the ability to distinguish the fine shades of taste or whether it was acquired like scent-makers in the olfactory business. Were ordinary, untrained people able to develop all their senses: of smelling, tasting, hearing, feeling and see-ing?

'Personal reinvestment is needed to be a good taster,' he answered considerately. 'Women are good tasters, as genet-ically they are more sensitive. Men are more visual. It is a philosophical thing; you need to be aware of what is going on in your mouth and body. You are a part of the whole, at one with nature.'

To understand even the most basic secrets of gardening, it is essential to have a respect for the life force found with-in nature. It is not something learnt so much as something given, and it applies as much to plants as it does to animals and humans. The ability to give a plant or a grape, for example, the kindness and respect it needs to flourish, is enhanced by the experience and training of a grower, but the fundamentals are genetic and soul-sown to all of us, it's just that some people have to search a little harder than others. I try to assemble a cautious attention to the self and an anxious concern for all else around me, but it wanders sometimes. A day's gardening, especially planting, usually acts as a therapeutical fix – certainly more than sitting in the office sourcing and costing plant plans, for instance.

The Perrin brothers are the current owners of Beaucastel. With their three sons, they are one of the largest producers of Côte du Rhône. The average for a wine-producing *château* is 30 hectares; the Perrins have 100 hectares, which produces around 35,000 bottles per annum. Two-thirds of this is exported to the UK and the USA.

The Perrin forebears – Jacques and Pierre, the vine specialists – spent their lives rationalising the wine-making process and at the turn of the nineteenth century invented a unique heating device. That is, it heated the skins only and not the pulp, which meant a certain thermo-sensitive enzyme was killed, preventing too much oxidation of the wine. This heating process is the 'secret' of the Beaucastel, their patent, although there is no point in selling it as the method would not necessarily give the same result with grapes from elsewhere. It all depends on *terroir*, that strange combination of the soil, the lie of the countryside and the climate. *Terroir* is also someone's love of their land, or even an invitation to love someone else's land.

'How do you judge the length of time a wine needs to get to its best?' I asked Fabrice next. A naive question perhaps, but although understanding that most red wines improve with age I was still uncertain about the final judgement. One might think a particular bottle to be at its peak and drink it happily, only to be told a few years later by a buff that you should have left it to improve still further.

The expert had a ready answer. 'Wine always has something new to offer. If you buy a case of twelve bottles now, then drink one bottle per year you will have a completely different wine each time.' It didn't quite answer my question but I took his point; it is, after all, the same principle as a maturing garden. 'This year is going to be very good,' he added.

In anticipation of my visit, Fabrice had laid out a few glasses, a spitting bowl and an array of neat little bottles on a long oak table. He explained that the small bottles were '*cépages*' and were a collection of all their 'allowed' grapes bottled individually before being blended. We gurgled and spat our way through thirteen samples, muttering about the aromas and tastes of fur, leather, tripe and even meat. Like most people I preferred the fruity blended wine that we finished up with. But before any final conclusions could be drawn, we had to visit the cellars and taste the different years and vineyards there (they even have interests in the Napa Valley).

I tried to persuade Fabrice to release a couple of very special vintages into my appreciative hands, but he told me they were strictly kept for starred restaurants and

Beaucastel family members. However, I was allowed to buy one of their most expensive, limited bottles of wine. One bottle per person only, it is entitled 'Hommage à Jacques Perrin'. They have less than four hundred cases available and only make this special blend when there is a great vintage. It contains 70 per cent mourvedre grape and has been marked 100/100 twice by Parker, the wine expert – in spite of his 'new oak' ripe-taste preference, which is most unlike this particular wine. It celebrates the great grape which Jacques Perrin planted first on the *domaine* and which now makes up 30 per cent of all the harvests. Having forked out 150 euros for this baby, I was then told to leave it well alone until 2015 at least. Great. I shall have to leave it to Theo. There will be a proviso that if it is not stupendously good he must find Fabrice and firmly place the neck of the bottle up his bottom and demand a current market refund. But such is the confidence of the *château* I think it will be swellegant.

The recurring worry of a wine producer is a bad vintage or worse, disease. And they have all suffered or heard about both. But not the Perrins. Being thoroughly Mediterranean, they covered their backs by growing olives as well as wine. It was their cousins, the Tramier family (now a huge brand name in olives and associated products), who originally bought the *château*. Current owner Jean-Pierre Perrin's great-grandfather, an olive oil producer in Jonquières, acquired the vineyards at Beaucastel so he had somewhere to walk with his grandchildren on Sundays.

The tour came to a close with a confirmed order for a bottle of the big boy and a mixed case of less-expensive vintages. My overall collection was now up to three and a half cases.

While my order was being gathered, I took the opportunity to have a look at the garden, or, as it turned out, the extended courtyard. It was dominated by a vast, classically shaped basin, which was full to the brim with clear, clean water. Perfectly constructed to local tradition, which dictated that it should be half in the ground and half out, with a broad copping stone cut to shape in the manner of a bowl. The effect of a waist-high plateau of water big enough to skate on was as calming and tranquil on a bleak February day as it would be in July. Six giant grey conifers of nearly 7m in height and closely clipped into cylindrical shapes surrounded the water. Elderly parasol pines mixed in with plane trees – pollarded, as is usual, to within an inch of their knuckles – would later give summer shade.

The old olives planted on the stone paved terrace, surrounded by over-sized antique olive jars, gave reference to the family's involvement with the crop. A stately cedar regally watched over the gathering. Further down, another magnificent craggy olive protected a small fountain that nestled underneath it. In a far corner stood an ancient well, the design of which has been copied so often and mass-produced it almost looked out of place. At the far end an intricately designed pair of closed wrought-iron gates firmly fixed to their pillars gave a glimpse of the acre upon acre of well-attended vines. In the distance a silhouette of the village of Châteauneuf could be made out through the misty light of a February afternoon.

Châteaneuf hosts a wine festival every August. Over-subscribed and nearly throttled by tourists, it remains, nonetheless, a jolly event. A few years ago I was taken for the first time by an elderly friend of mine who had been brought up in the region. We parked high up on the hill and sauntered down to the throng below. As is customary, you buy a 'tasting' glass at the edge of the activities and from there on in you dive around amongst the *caves*, tasting. Music ensured that the festival felt like a festival and in the centre of the little town, men crowded and jostled round the old fountain. This ancient structure had a large upright stone in the middle which would normally have had water gushing from outlets on all four sides but at festival-time one side was spurting red wine instead and the boys were scrumming down to get their glasses filled free of charge. Rigged up in a plane tree above the fountain is a huge oak cask full of Côte du Rhône. Traditionally it flows all after-noon and is there for the taking. Skinny little guys and retiring girls needn't apply.

By mid-afternoon it was time to find somewhere to have a bottle of fizzy water to shake up the dulling taste buds and brighten the mind. From a terrace perched halfway up the village hill it was possible to discern below a parade of costumed players slowly integrating into the crowd. The summer sun was starting to dip out and the warm early evening took on an altogether calmer atmosphere. Trumpet music heralded the spectacle.

We wandered down amongst the throng, sought out a small *alimentation* and bought some sausage, bread and cheese, and found a table in a café that was being vacated by a pair of squabbling families. Children whooped with joy as the medieval troubadours danced and played down the streets, pretty girls showed off their traditional dresses, the handsome young men proudly jigged in their uniforms and the wine flowed on. As darkness won, the night candles lit up the streets and everybody partied. An uninvited English couple, worn out and emotional, decided they would join us.

'France is alwight and all that,' said the man, 'but it's England that's the dog's bollocks, innit? Know what I mean?'

His girlfriend giggled and gave him an encouraging shove. 'I 'eard you talkin' English and that, so I said to meself, I said, "I bet they are lookin' for a bit of company, like."'

He was not a big man but his belly made up for it. An old Arsenal vest hung off his midriff like a tent and his shorts only managed a few inches below his crutch. His little moustache twitched when he spoke and his hazy eyes battled out of a podgy red face. He went on, 'I mean, you wouldn't want to fuckin live 'ere, would ya? Know what I mean?' He belched, stuck up his hand and with menace flowing from his armpits shouted 'Oi, *garçon!*' continually until two rugby players who were part-timing as waiters appeared and suggested he and his *'amour'* push off. He got the hint and with a last 'See what I mean?' faded into the crowd with his short-skirted redhead tottering after him.

Every year there are wine 'shows' all over France. Jamborees for the aficionado, they are gatherings of growers, blenders, merchants, middle men and miscreants, and a chance for wine hacks to get legless again and write ever more reverberating reviews.

They are serious, of course. Wine is big business. But is there any other game where transactions are secured over so much alcohol? The spiritual world of brandy, whisky, vodka and gin is even more louche, of course.

This was the sixth international Mediterranean wine fare exclusively reserved for professionals but well supported by fringe beneficiaries. People like me.

Staged in Montpelier for the last six years it is ostensibly organised for the wine-growers in the South of France, or more specifically the south-west. Each year the fair gets bigger and better and now boasts support acts from Spain, Croatia, Germany and even Australia.

The acres of car park were filled to brimming with thousands of cars and it was only ten o'clock on the first morning. The parking sense of the French is quite unique. You try half-heartedly to find somewhere social to park, like a bona fide space, and if that doesn't turn up near to where you want to be, you just dump the car anywhere and let the rest work round it. The queue you find yourself in might easily be formed because a car up ahead has been abandoned, leaving little room for anything other than an Aixam to squeeze past it. (If you haven't met an Aixam, or quadricycle as they are known, they are little boxes on wheels that have a diesel Kubota one horsepower engine, or perhaps pony power would be closer, and that's not much bigger than a lawn-mower. They go so slowly as to be ten times more dangerous than a car going too fast and you need no license to drive them.)

Fortified by obscurity, I slid around the show and amongst the bottles like mercury on a polished table. It was clearly a very popular shindig. Like all shows or fairs there were big stands and little stands. The little stalls had a tiny bar with a café table at which four or five people sat tasting and chatting. Some of the less-wealthy producers had stacked a few cases on top of one another and that was it. The large bars were every bit as impressive as you might find at a computer convention in Silicone Valley: triple-deckers with two bars at each level, sexy lights, glossy pictures of vineyards, trade magazines, looped DVDs and giddy girls wearing nothing much more than a bottle-opener. But big didn't guarantee best. The giants may have been shifting thousands of bottles to a hundred destinations, but the demand on their product was as much to do with slick marketing as it was to do with classy wine. But it was an agreeable pause in the day's events to share a few alcoholic moments with them. After all everybody was looking to have a good crack at tasting this, spitting out that, rolling the glass here and sniffing elaborately over there. The presiding climate was one of goodwill.

The side shows were beguiling as well. There was a stand selling dining room tables with finely crafted marquetry depicting the great labels of the area. There were sack trolleys converted into mobile wine-racks, wonky wine coolers, opened trunks at least a metre and a half tall and inside a cooler, decanters, coasters and glasses.

At one corner of the hall there was a huge poster of a girl wearing a white dress standing behind a table. In front of her a v-shaped glass of dark-red wine was strategically placed at the top of her legs. The message was simple enough but hard to imagine being permitted at Earl's Court. There was another stand where a hundred bottles were balanced on top of one another in a pyramid. Others had big black plasma screens projecting acres of healthy vines heavy with fruit, old olive trees standing amongst lavender carpets and classic old farmhouses with the Provençal mountains in the background. It was every bit as good as advertising a land where everybody is happy and healthy.

These wine fairs are unique in that the more stands you visit the more questionable your report is likely to be. I know we are all meant to spit the wine out, but for junior players like myself this is quite hard to always remember, especially if the wine is good. It must be even harder when you're tasting something serious. When the corks have been pulled on the best there is, it's nigh on impossible not to swallow. A small contribution to the finesse of the occasion might be a quick mouthwash with some mineral water, but there isn't, I'm afraid, very much swirling and spitting.

It felt quite gratifying to have wangled my way into somewhere where I was not really meant to be, although it is not quite like passing the security guards at a political meeting for radicals, for example, or gaining a dubious backstage pass to a rock concert. (I remember a Led Zeppelin gig somewhere in the countryside about thirty years ago, where a giant multi-coloured snake crawled out of one of the band's speakers, slid in through my left ear and wound itself around my brain, then with a terrible tug it was ripped out and flung into the vinyl sky where it was quickly devoured by discarded plectrums and broken strings. It must have been the medicine I was taking.)

As I hustled along, checking out the Luberon wines on display, I heard my name called out. 'Hey, Alex?' I turned and saw a tall girl smiling and walking towards me.

'Hi, it's me, Georgie-Lou. Do you remember I brought an empty case to –'

'Georgie-Lou!' Of course I remembered. I was pleased to see her happy face again. 'How're you getting on? What brings you here?'

Her hair had grown since I had last seen her. She was wearing a dark-green velvet coat with a long white silk scarf around her neck. She looked different but the big smile still beat out of her like a late-afternoon sun. 'I've been sent by Tom to further my education and report back to him. Actually I'm a bit fazed by all these stalls and endless tasting sessions. I've had enough and was about to go,' she said.

'Is Tom here?' I asked.

'No, he's in the States. I'm pretty much running the place without him.'

'I was about to find the lunch tent, get in there early before the rush starts. Would you like to join me?'

'Why not?'

We set off, and Georgie-Lou rather sweetly linked her arm through mine. Suddenly the wine show had become a whole lot more fun.

The restaurant tent, 'Le Virage', was the size of a small

village. Everywhere you looked there were temporary restaurants, ephemeral cafés and, as if you hadn't had enough, wine bars. The selection was vast and the food on offer enough to reassure you that France could indeed do it better than most if not all.

A couple of hours later I said goodbye to Georgie-Lou and watched wistfully as she drove off in her white van.

That night I lay alone in the home I had rented whilst the builders wrestled with the one I had recently bought. It would be a neat little house and courtyard when it was finished but visiting the site only made me wonder if it would ever be completed and whether I even wanted to live in the place.

The light wind moved the white curtains to and fro, and in the shadows of a low moon I saw myself wandering aimlessly within a desolated building. All the broken doors were flung open and although I could see no one, some old friendly voices with familiar footsteps bade me welcome. Through tears I made for some golden barley-sheaves laid out on the floor, and, weighed with heaviness, fell onto the comfortable straw and slept. In my suspended consciousness I heard myself whisper to the ghost that I had come from a secret garden and wanted to be embalmed in the petals of the lotus blossom so that decisions of where to live could be put off for ever. But suddenly there were giants dressed in the French national flag bending over and prodding me: *'Vous n'êtes pas autorisé à quitter ce pays avant l' achèvement de votre mission.'*

Chapter Six

The next day was Wednesday and, in common with most junior schools around here, it was a non-schoolday. Theo was sitting in the car next to me half reading an Asterix book while pressing buttons that made his seat go back and forward, up and down, and flatten out. He was OK about Asterix but not committed. As we drove along I told him a bit about my strange dream of the night before without pushing too hard on the uncertainty of staying in France angle; that would have raised alarm bells. Besides, as long as he was in France and happy, then I had to suppose I would be, too. On the other hand, if a decision was made with Mum to return to England then that would swing my position. Talk about being indecisive. Yes, and there again no.

'I had a dream last night as well, Dad. There was this pink monster, with big lips shaped like violins and it had a carnivore's teeth that sawed across its mouth. It liked to eat humans. Particularly parents,' said the nearly eight-year-old Theo.

'Well, he must have run out of things to eat quite quickly if he only ate his parents; after all, there are only the two of them and there's not much to eat on Mum.'

'Yeah, maybe, but plenty on you! Anyway, it's not just his parents but any old parents and I think teachers as well.'

'What else does he do with those big musical lips? Does he kiss other monsters?'

'He's not a friendly monster, Dad. 'Tually he's made sleeping very difficult. I think I'll ask Mum if she'll sleep with me tonight just in case he comes back.'

'But it's not you he wants to eat, is it?' I said. 'But he might gobble Mum up if she's there.'

'Not good, I agree, but you see, if he's really hungry he might eat any old humans, including me. That's the worry.'

The little chap had never been a great sleeper but recently his mind had been invaded by monsters, creepy noises and moving lights. Everything was fine during the day, even flippant, but come bedtime a demon crept in under the door and plundered his peaceful thoughts.

People trying to be helpful offer psychobabble, such as: 'It's probably because you left him overnight at his grandma's for the first time last week. He subconsciously felt abandoned and now needs to keep as close as possible to his mum, especially at night. Of course, your separation won't be helping.'

Living in France while the rest of the family remains in the UK means that the child experiences none of the day-to-day 'dropping off' at grandma's or an aunt's that most children take for granted. Theo therefore came to his first separation rather late in his young life and it seemed to have destabilised him a bit. Not that he admits to it, of course.

Whatever way it was viewed, it meant that the nights were short on sleep, producing shortened tempers, low tolerance levels and a struggle to keep working during the day. Through the already unsettled weather of our marriage had come an inevitable little by-line.

But sleep and I struggle, too. We're good friends but rarely go to bed together. Occasionally we fall into each other's arms in the afternoon and although we've tried it at night, it always seems to collapse around four or five in the morning. Just when you have escaped into Slumberville I am hauled out of the pillow into the pre-dawn void. Sleeping pills don't make me sleep. They just drug the devil in the dark and leave you feeling heavy and slow at daybreak. Better, I find, is the soul-calming act of meditation, freeing the mind from mundane routine.

'What's a Gaul?' asked Theo, jerking me back from my wondering. He was blinking in the sunlight trying to finish Goscinny and Uderzo's latest adventure. He was too small to make use of the car's visor.

'French,' I said dislocatedly.

'A French person, do you mean? Is Asterix a Frenchman?'

'Certainly is, and a very old one at that. He's probably the most famous Gaul of them all after Vercingetorix.'

'Who's he?'

'The unfortunate hero who rallied the Gauls, or French, to stand up against the Romans fifty-two years before Jesus was born.'

'What about Obelisk?'

'Oh, he's famous too for being very strong.'

'What's that thing he carries around, manure or something?'

'A menhir. It's called a menhir.'

'What's it made of, Dad, is it stone?'

I could feel a Gaul Stone joke coming on but sidestepped it. 'Well, it's more like a rock. It's an effigy, a kind of rough statue. It's meant as a commemoration of the heroic, I think.'

One of the fringe benefits of having kids is that in attempting to answer their questions you learn more than you ever did at school. You can't just sit there guessing or blinding them with boring dates; they need hard facts. If you don't tell them the Internet will. Which is why we google.

Gaul (from the Latin Gallia) was the ancient name for an area roughly equivalent to modern France, Belgium, Luxembourg, and Germany west of the Rhine. The Celts, whom the Romans called Galli (Gauls) had by the fifth century BC established a fairly uniform culture typified by the art of La Tene (that's the Iron Age artefacts found at La Tene, on Lake Neuchâtel in Switzerland) and had begun to cross the Rhine into Gaul by 900BC.

In the first and second centuries AD, Gaul flourished through the export of food, pottery and wine. It just shows what a successful commodity wine was even then. In those days the art of wine-making was vastly inferior to what we take for granted today, yet it had the innate and sublime properties to attract the attention of just about everybody. In the third century Gaul suffered devastating barbarian raids and their ineffective defence led to the downfall of the short-lived Gaul kingdom. By the fourth century AD, Christianity predominated and weakened Celtic culture further by using Latin in worship.

The biggest threat to the marauding Caesar, however, came in AD52 when a coalition of tribes in central Gaul under Vercingetorix (chieftain of the Averni) rose against the Romans. After a heroic battle Caesar finally thumped Vercingetorix at Alesia. Vercingetorix was brought to Rome, exhibited in Caesar's triumphal march, and ceremoniously executed. Without their Che Guevara, any serious Gallic resistance had petered out.

Thanks to some good illustrations and gory infills Theo kept his concentration, although I knew that only 5 per cent would stay locked in whilst the remainder would flow out of the other ear as easily as oil. But at least he had had some of his questions answered.

Then, just as I was patting myself on the back, he threw another one at me: 'Where did France come from?'

With a bit of paraphrase it went like this:

Although Europe can't compete with the archaeological records of, say, Africa, where 4-million-year-old *hominoid* remains have been discovered, the ancestors of *Homo sapiens* were already to be found in France 2 million years ago. Evidence of *Homo erectus*, bless him, has also been found dating back to approximately half a million years ago. After that came the short, stocky Neanderthal with his large, rugged, deep-featured head in about 100,000BC. It wasn't until 40,000BC that *Homo sapiens* himself arrived, in whose more conventional bodies we recognise ourselves. He probably arrived in a thaw period, when travel was more practical.

Man's evolvement from there has been pinned down through the use of tools. Stone, metal and iron ages give distinct indication of lifestyles. Throughout these early periods France was subject to migratory movements. People would shift in search of food or the need for kinder climates. New people brought with them new cultural patterns and modes of behaviour, which could then be adopted. Nobody did it better, of course, than the Romans, who settled in France in the first century or so before Christ. They brought with them a relatively complex and sophisticated culture, including two hugely important and edifying benefits – writing and, as mentioned earlier, wine-making.

The two 'W's' as they must have been known, may have been imported but art was already up and hanging. Not portable art of course, but some highly entertaining cave work. Finger marks, stencils, rock engravings and paintings produced in charcoal and ochre. There is a cave 12km south-east of Marseille, the Cosquer Cave, which dates from what is recognised as the Magdalenian period about 17,000 years ago.

When you look at that ancient wall with its art and try to imagine 17,000 years into the future, will our Sony plasma screens be every bit as fascinating to the people of 19,005? Probably not because historical information will have been available at all levels for so long that the shock of discovery will be a concept impossible to imagine.

This ancient art was often done in caves that were highly inaccessible, frequently located in dark, secret places, far away from normal habitation and lit only by fat-burning lamps. In some cave sites paintings are over a mile from the cave entrance, through chambers that professional speleologists find challenging. In the caves at Lascaux some of the paintings are 15ft above the ground and must have involved some form of scaffolding. At Cosquer it is difficult to gain access because of the rise in sea level. Does this mean art might have been forbidden?

Experts have been trying to fathom out the story of these paintings ever since modern man discovered them. They probably had some ritual connotation as so many of the drawings were of animals; horses, bison and ibex seem to be the most common but there were also chamois, cats and even some seals.

Theo was looking, and I was feeling, exhausted by now, so we went to bed early. The next morning I was on my way to Beaujolais.

Chapter Seven

Driving down through the local country lanes to Beaujolais, my spirits were quickly floated by the massive swathes of wild flowers that had taken up their positions. The wheat fields infested with nodding poppies were edged with blue wild thyme, stealing the ground away from yellow euphorbias. White centranthus pushed ever further onto the banks. The hedgerows sagged with the weight of the flowering honeysuckle and common sage. A bonus of dark-blue iris, probably spread by the mud on tractor wheels, held fast. Long grasses waved cheerfully from around the base of olive trees awaiting the first cut of the season. Whatever was happening in our family, nature was doing its absolute best to counteract grey thoughts by wrapping them up in optimistic colours and sunshine.

Just as in London, it began to dawn on me that the problems I was having with living in France, or specifically Provence, were not so much the fault of France per se but much more to do with me. You can't blame the weather bank just because it's not handing out enough sunny days but you can, if you try, calm the expectations. If only I could think of life as a passage to paradise, each year offering something in its own right like the ageing bottle of wine, an evolving state to be enjoyed but ultimately left behind in favour of something more coherent. But I, Presbyterian by birth, am far too doubtful of eternal bliss. As one wag put it when asked if he believed in reincarnation: 'I didn't in my last life, I don't see why I should now.'

As I headed towards Beaujolais, I recalled a story that a chum of mind told me about a clergyman from that region, the Reverend Pierre De La Roy. He was a worried man, said my pal, because his congregation was shrinking. In 1995 when he took over the diocese there had already been a fairly paltry attendance reported by his predecessor. When he had arrived, he had created a fussy little surge of curiosity, which swelled the holy audience to perhaps half the village, or at least half the ones over the age of fifty. It had soon dwindled back to what it had been, some say even fewer. But worse for poor Pierre was the newly announced statistic that only 7 per cent of his parish attended church at all, ever. Not even a Christmas Eve special could excite them. Everybody knew this fact to be true because it had been posted up on the noticeboard in the vestry by Pierre's young assistant, Giles. No doubt the intention of the keen youngster had been to shame people into coming to service.

One Sunday Pierre was giving holy communion to Major Bastide, Monsieur Brun and Madame Aubert, who were the church's only supporters that day. Normally the wine for the chalice would be delivered by the lad from the local *vinicole*, but due to a particularly foamy cold he hadn't been able to carry out his duty at the last minute. Pierre had dug around in his not inconsiderable cave, and pulled out a bottle of St. Emilion '82 by mistake, thinking it was an indifferent Côte de Rhône, taken it round to the church without looking closely and pulled the cork half an hour before the service.

By the time the trio kneeled graciously down to receive the blood of Christ, the chalice was full of a noble and elegantly classical wine. It took the Major all of fifteen seconds to recognise this. Wanting to reassure himself of his accuracy, he humbly asked the Reverend if he would be so kind as to indulge him with another sip of the good Lord's offering. Slightly taken aback, Pierre passed the Major the gold cup and watched in astonishment as the retired old soldier took an almighty gulp. Monsieur Brun, nodding with an accomplice's encouragement, held out his hand, flexing his fingers. By the time it had been passed to Madame Aubert there was nothing left. She was slightly bewildered by the unusual break in form but did her best to sip at the empty instrument.

After the service, and in traditional manner, the vicar stood outside in order to shake hands and passed the time of holy day with his shrivelled congregation. As the trinity approached he was wondering what to say to them about the 'seconds' when the Major enthusiastically shook his hand in both of his, winked and said – or would have done if he had been English – 'Damned clever idea, vicar. A fine wine adds great poignancy to the Lord's sacrifice, what?' Already perplexed, the Reverend de la Roy was completely lost when Monsieur Brun suggested a little *foie gras* on the wafer for the following week.

If you are unfamiliar with the rolling hills of Beaujolais, especially on a warm clear evening in late May driving a car with a perfectly fettled chassis, you should add it to the wish list. Imagine Wales with vines growing all over it and powered by a mild Mediterranean climate. Change the warm pint of heavy bitter for a glass of light wine and the transformation is complete.

The Beaujolais destination had been programmed into the car's GPS so all I had had to do was get to the music and drive. Nothing, apart from the fleets of lurching, swaying caravans was going to get in my way. In fact, these drab forms of transport are mostly hired mobile-homes nowadays. Migrating down from the north, they flock into Provence like batty geese. And the names are terrible: Compass Cruiser, Atlas Tracker, World Shrinker, Globe Hopper. They must make small hotel owners depressed. They spend their money in supermarkets, park up in gaggles on the outskirts of beautiful medieval towns, bristling with TV aerials and gas bottles, simultaneously making road terrorists out of the rest of us. There you are driving along in a perfectly normal way on a pretty country lane, when suddenly you come face to face with an American Planet Squeezer. Complete with flight deck, command centre, navigation quarters, galley, lounge and bedrooms with en suite ballrooms they do their best to intimidate you out of a corner. They shouldn't even be on such roads but instead of being the slightest bit contrite they glare down from their superior position, blast you out with air horns and move obdurately towards you.

If you could just haul up anywhere and park in someone's field like a gigantic snail it might be all right, but it seems you have to find a spot that offers electrical sources, lavatory experiences and sixty other like-minded people. I am not a camper by nature. I have never much liked those rickety little beds about a centimetre off the ground, hurricane lamps that go out and tents that make you feel like you're a contestant on a game show. Opening tins, metal plates and whooping it up round a gas campfire? Not really. Even when I was backpacker age, I preferred to fly to California than head off to Guru-land on foot.

I did, however, once spend a night in the middle of the Masai Mara in Kenya. It was an expensive, chi-chi little camp called something like Camp Kenya or the Rangers Retreat. It had cute little tricks to make you feel like you were out there on the edge with the great white hunters. There was, for example, a night watchman who used to pile up hippo droppings outside the entrance to your tent just to make you feel involved, a roaring lion tape, and the hot shower that was rigged up to make it look as if it had come out of a sun-heated bucket with holes in it. In the morning stressed-out executives needing a break from dealing the world markets would float in on hot air balloons for an exotic breakfast. Certainly better than sleeping in a bivouac on a rain-drenched Suffolk coast but I still didn't really get it. Not like my friend who turned up late for breakfast one morning explaining his delay by telling me that a herd of elephants had surrounded his little tent and that he had had to crawl out between their legs. As a veteran Kenyan camper he didn't want to know about spending the sort of money that our camp was costing, and understandably so – it was absurd.

But where were his wife and young daughters? I asked.

'Oh they are still in the tent. I thought it best to leave them,' he said, tucking into his craftily split Guava sections. 'Where's Susanne?'

'She went off early to watch a kill,' I said. 'Should be back soon. More coffee?'

The exit from the *autoroute* into what I thought was southern Burgundy, not far north of Valence, was really still part of the Rhône valley but celebrated as 'Hermitage'. It was decorated on both sides by billows of yellow broom and tall parasol pines. Having collected a speeding ticket, it was a relief to plunge into a slower-moving rural countryside. Tucked into one side of the road, a couple in an open-sided van were selling baguette sandwiches filled to brimming.

Brie, *saucisson* and thick slices of ham, or salad and toma-toes with garlic dressing. There were also a few bottles of red and white wine open and ready by the glass. A pair of large, slightly torn umbrellas offered a bit of shade to sit under surrounded by baskets of locally grown fruit, vege-tables and various conserves. It was a typical little French vignette.

I pulled up and walked back to the stall, ordered a 'stick' of deliciousness, a glass of the well-known white, Chante-Alouette, and settled contentedly beneath the umbrellas with the scent of pine trees drifting on a mild breeze.

Opposite me an open-air pottery was placed strategical-ly close to the road. This was not so much a discreet little billet with charming handmade terracotta pots and urns but more a temple to unhinged vulgarity. Near-naked nymphets fought for space with grinning dolphins, lascivi-ous cherubs made eyes at Snow White's perverted little dis-ciples. Sexy mermaids with big bosoms had been glazed in burnt caramel or racy azure blue. There were windmills under which kissing young yokels sat unsteadily aboard a donkey-drawn cart. There were fat farmers in waistcoats squeezing fish so hard that water was spurting out of their mouths, their eyes popping like frogs, all watched over by eagles, parrots and Beethoven. That says something for his reputation. Metres of plastic trellis displayed an endless assortment of tragically decorated half-pots in forbidden colours. I wasn't going to cross the road for it.

'*Bonjour, monsieur.*' An elderly farmworker, painfully thin with a ruddy face topped by a cloth cap, limped over to join me in the shade. He too had a grand sandwich and a glass of wine, which spilled a little with each step he took. He ate slowly and smiled a lot. It wasn't easy to understand what he said, talking as he did with a full mouth and a heavy regional accent, but I did gather that the heap of rusty metal that he pointed to lying in the grass was his bicycle and that he thought it was now dead. He removed his oily cap, stroked his head a few times and then settled the thing back just so. He offered me a glass of wine but I was ready to go.

It was time to head for the town of Tain l'Hermitage, which is en route to the Domaine des Clermonts, another of Tom's suggestions.

Apart from being located right beside the river, Tain is an unpretentious and uneventful town. Although it has something of a reputation for making chocolate, it is mainly the sampling of the renowned Hermitage and Crozes Hermitage wines that attracts people to visit, and I was no exception.

I soon found an unexpected sort of a wine bar. The window displayed many possibilities and the list even more. Inside, amongst a dingy setting of gingham-covered tables, worn floorboards and fading pictures, I spun my finger, let it drop onto the card and then asked the nervous man behind the bar for a glass of my choice. He looked at me with a frightened eye and quickly disappeared only to return a few minutes later from behind the beaded curtain with a huge fellow wiping blood from his hands on his apron. I smiled; he didn't but raised his chin. I tried again explaining my selection of what I hoped would be a fine Hermitage.

'A glass, *monsieur?*' he said, his voice rising as if I had spoken of the devil.

'*Voilà et merci,*' I said gratefully.

The two men looked at each other as if caught out by something I was doing or saying. They hesitated and after a pause the big one blinked almost imperceptibly at the other. Its effect was as good as a mighty nod, for the shaky assistant smacked a glass down on the bar, slipped behind another curtain and quickly returned with an unopened bottle, the very one of my choice, the opening of which took an interminably long time. Without talking or taking his eyes off me, he poured a little into the glass. I hovered then took a sip, as my audience, which had now grown to four or five, watched me for reaction. It was fine, nothing to crow about but good enough, although I wasn't quite sure if this measure had been for me to taste prior to filling the glass properly or whether they were just a mean bunch of wine thugs. No more wine was forthcoming so under a terrible scrutiny I went to sit down and finish the rest, maintaining my composure. The stuff was getting stuck in my throat as I shrank into the corner. Still they gazed, still I couldn't think of much to say so I went for, 'It is very good, *monsieur*, I would like to take the bottle.'

This I thought to be an honourable way of extracting myself from the shop, which had become something of a hell hole. Besides I felt a bit guilty about the opened bottle about which they all seemed to harbour such deep and reverent thoughts. I drained the glass, stood up and pulled out some money, and looked at them expectantly. The gaze continued. I was beginning to think I had tripped onto the set of an episode of *The Cult*.

The frightened rabbit who had hidden behind the big man's body whispered, '*Ah non, monsieur, ce n'est pas possible.*'

'Oh,' I said, now lost in a hopeless confusion.

The room trembled with tension. '*Alors, merci pour le morceau*,' I managed, put down a few euros and smiled weakly. 'Right then,' I said. '*Je pars* – I'll be off. *Au revoir, messieurs*, bye-bye and *adieu*.' I legged it quicker than a hungry cheetah. At times like this I just speak any old stuff that comes to mind. What the hell had all that been about? There lurked a heavy suspicion that I had either behaved in a way unknown to them or else I had made some kind of faux pas. Either way it put me off trying any more tastings in Tain.

Tom had proposed the Domaine des Clermonts not far from Lyon not only as a good Beaujolais stop but also because Erik Borja, a member of the family that owned the *château*, had created a wonderful Japanese garden there. It is unusual for wine-making to be associated with oriental horticulture, but as soon as I arrived it was evident that a comfortable partnership existed.

The garden is open by appointment only, principally to ensure that not too many people arrive at once and crowd out the tranquillity. Mr Borja, a fine-looking man in his late sixties, extended me his hospitality unconditionally and led me to the *jardin de méditation*, gave a brief outline of the property and left me to walk it alone.

I stayed put for the first ten minutes, studying the perfectly raked gravel as the pattern wound around large stones and up to the edge of the carp pond. Isolated rocks, devoid of scale in their sea of chippings, moulded gracefully with the surrounding clipped ericas and heavily pruned lonicera, their amorphous shapes suggesting a landscape of soft round hills.

The very job of raking – the perfection of the systematic arrangement and design, the removal of any unwanted debris – has a meditative quality about it. It has a transitory perfection that is consistently broken by weather, clumsy feet or arguing cats and dogs.

'Every month has a story to tell,' Erik Borja had explained. 'The colours change, the leaves come and go, the light alters, the ground gets wetter or drier, all this makes for a shifting landscape to the observant eye. It is really only August when things seem to stand still in a state of exhaustion.'

The top pond is the start of a long series of water events, which descend from something not much bigger than a puddle via rills and streams, over collection basins down through natural cascades and on into a small lake far below. The stone steps, the grass, moss and *Ophiopogon nana* blend easily with the small gauge gravel that leads you along. Hostas and ferns, lamium with helleborus, ginkgo trees, purple acers and pines all share space. Elsewhere astrantia, clipped berberis, hypericum and euphorbia dance beside box hedges containing roses, poppies and campanulas, cornus, cotoneaster, and a massive selection of grasses dare the purple sage to get any bigger. The poodle clipping of the low cyprus and yews along with endless snipping of the ligustrum and lonicera produced a tight and controlled kind of gardening that implies discipline and concentration. Elsewhere blue and yellow water iris played round the edge of the ponds with dwarf bamboo.

At all points of the garden various forms of stone were used to give accents and relief. Cobble stone, callade (the art of making patterns with small smooth pebbles), bits of old buildings such as ancient friezes and cornices, stepping stones and sculpture. As I wandered, I caught glimpses of the house with its own warm ochre stone and ageing render set off by light-blue shutters.

After a calming and stabilising hour ambling and sitting, thinking and smelling, I ended up talking to Erik Borja in his sitting room. We drank a light infusion while he told me how a celebrated wine-maker became a celebrated garden-maker.

Starting the project of a Japanese garden thirty years ago, he came naturally to gardening having been trained in the cultivation of the vine. He felt it was an area of academic study that required a profound sense of awareness to the needs of plants, and that it was not therefore such a big leap to start a garden.

Drawn to the subtle and sophisticated understanding that the Japanese have of creating open spaces for meditation coupled to their ability to blend the highly cultivated almost seamlessly into the wild and savage landscape beyond, Erik found himself adopting the philosophical principles to his own estate which he now considers a metaphor of life. The result is perspicuously achieved.

I asked him if he found it difficult to recruit gardeners. I counted at least six of them on my tour. He replied that it was a 'family affair' with the backbone of gardeners staying faithfully within the fold. If someone left the more transitory support group, the apprentices, then the slack was soon taken up by one of the many young hopefuls whose name would be on a waiting list.

'We are a fully integrated set-up,' he said. 'The doors are always left open, no one is ever locked out but the gardeners must share the passion.'

As enthusiasm, rage and manic craziness are all part of gardening, it would be fair to say that no great garden can be created or maintained without passion.

A few hundred metres down the road, the family's smart production and sales room, built in 1972, was selling wine that celebrated the garden's thirty-year anniversary. After the Japanese landscape the room felt a little soulless, but Cuvé Zen stood proudly on display. It tasted pretty good, too, needing only the patience of time to raise its game. But gardeners have patience by the gallon.

The little inn in which I stayed was basic but serviceable. Nobody checked you in but they didn't bother to check you out either. It was very discreet and full of naughty travelling salesmen. The plump little puddings serving dinner in white shirts and black split mini-skirts did their job with friendly smiles and served a pretty sharp menu. One had an oversized ring through her nose which any bull would have been proud of.

I came close to eating frogs' legs that night, but when the waitress asked what I would like to eat I flunked it. Like fat grey snails I just can't get my head around eating these things, along with calves' brains, ox tongues and pigs' feet. Ashamedly I'll quaff *foie gras* but that, like bacon, has got nothing to do with animals, has it?

The next morning I lingered a while on the banks of the massive and magnificent Rhône. The fast-moving water transported long, thin tourist boats loaded with enthralled participants, while larger cargo vessels slipped seamlessly by, just clearing the bridges. Here was one of the great rivers of the world that had given its name to one of the most famous wines in the world: the Côte du Rhône. I was upstream now, quite a bit further north, but it was still mesmerising, like watching a bonfire flickering with an ever-changing story. Mountainous volumes of water passing by at high speed, ephemeral images brought from far away only to disappear before I could grab them.

The gentle countryside revealed row upon row of vines that covered the plains, climbed the hills and flowed towards the valley, relieved only by the occasional freshly rolled haystack closely inspected by crows. Periodically a *château* would pop up in the background, grand and noble with tall, pointed, almost Parisian slated roofs reaching up for the sky. And the birdsong, always the birdsong. I was happy as I headed off to see Georges Duboeuf.

Duboeuf is one of the very biggest and most commercially savvy wine entrepreneurs in the region if not in all the wine-growing regions of France. Next door to the old railway station in Romanèche Thorins, his enterprise has a huge shop that not only displays and sells most of the wines of Beaujolais but is backed up by wine merchandising at its most sophisticated, showing just what an enormous trade there is in Burgundian wine. His support acts include books, posters, cards, bottle-stoppers, wine glasses – big, fat, short and thin – battalions of decanters, piles of plates, egg cups, T-shirts, napkins, tablecloths, chefs' aprons, key rings, candles, chocolates, calendars, silver funnels, *tastevins*, letter-openers and crachoirs. There are gift sets available in sets of three, six or twelve, mixed or matched. In reference to the neighbouring old train station and yard that this bazaar occupies, there are dozens of books on the great railways of France, including miniatures and museum pieces. But it is the corkscrews of all denominations that win the best-of-show award. They come in silver, stainless steel, wood and simple metal, and show a hundred ideas of diversity from cabbages to kings, elves to elephants, and even risqué little numbers involving loose women and over-excited men. Some were even self opening.

There are smart check-out counters that could show Sainsbury's a thing or two, and point-of-sale goodies like brightly coloured bottles of wine in orange, blue and red glass with jolly graphics that say, 'Wine is fun! Wine is for young people, too!' Next door is an enormous bar, or bars, where the dozens of different varieties of wine are sold by the glass from several posts to happy punters. Loud music on videos (also for sale) hammers out across the floor.

I drove out of the converted rail yard, and turned left under the old station footbridge. It was just like a scene from *The Railway Children*, and I found it easy to imagine the three children leaning over the railing waving to the train as it passed underneath. On the narrow little road, separated from the railway line by a row of poplars, an old man driving his equally old tractor bobbed along with his ten-year-old grandson perched on one of the mudguards. The sun fought through the leaves and softened the focus of memory. If ever sadness can mix with happiness and produce tears of total melancholy it is surely with the recollections of youth.

The day was turning into a warm and turquoise evening, and I was late for my next appointment, which was at the Château de la Chaize in Odenas, reputedly the most important wine-estate in Beaujolais, located between Mâcon and Villefranche-sur-Saône about 40km north of Lyon.

When I arrived – at the stables, not the main house – there was a stiff but professional welcome from the woman whose job it was to receive people like me. I apologised for my delay to a frosty face wearing thick glasses. She stood with her arms crossed in a royal-blue suit and natty hair-do. With a minimal nod she moved into gear and whisked me off on a whirlwind tour of the cellars and vats, only pausing

once to draw my attention to some photographs of her
employer entertaining the Clintons and Chiracs. She then
spun me into a tasting room of the main cellar, bunged some
indifferent wine at me and then, before I could really get a
hold of anything, bundled me off with brochures and the
usual PR blurb. It was all over before it had started.

Anyway I thanked her for her time as graciously as I
could and asked if it was possible to now look round
the garden. This was pushing it but worth trying. The
headmistress looked horrified: 'Goodness, no, *monsieur*, not
this evening. The grounds are closed; they open again
tomorrow. Nine to six. I am sure you will find your way
around.'

And with that I was dismissed. No special treatment
then. Well, she had done her bit, albeit reluctantly. I didn't
blame her but asked permission to at least go up the drive
and walk round the edges to take a peep because it was
unlikely I would be able to return in the morning. With her
consent I crept the car up the winding driveway with its
mown edges and white corral fencing. A small group of
people – estate workers, no doubt – were out with their
children collecting wild flowers and feeding them to the
young horses. What a treat for the gentle creatures. Poppy
and clover salad with a little fresh rye grass on the side.

The *château* itself is also one of the most important
buildings in Beaujolais. It is vast. A robust four-storey central house with Palladian frontage, it is flanked by a pair of
20m, two-storey wings that terminate with immense
matching square turrets. The terraces run the full width of

the *château* with twin staircases descending regally onto the formal lawns below. Punctuated by clipped yews on either edge of the gravel paths, the grass extends on down to a colossal round pond. It was from above this circle of water that I stood taking it all in.

Over to the left, behind tall beech hedging but accessed via a walk though a pruned hornbeam chase, was the *potager*, an extravaganza of cuisine crops: lettuce and red cabbage with tulips down the middle, strawberries and peas, *aromatiques*, *sariette*, basil and thymes with fennel, bays and lemon and orange trees in giant pots – presumably so that they can go indoors in winter – artichokes and chives, rosemary with campanulas and delphiniums.

The whole garden was very grandly composed and elegantly set off by the uninterrupted, surrounding mounds of countryside, which rose and dipped behind the castle. Below and to the right in the lower field, the cows grazed in the calm heat of the evening sun, swishing their tails under the sycamores and limes. A soft breeze hardly disturbed the leaves. Swathes of field between the cows and the horses with foals had been mown into long walks that tempted you to follow. Mowing through rough or long grass with some premeditated plan is a cheap and rewarding way of dealing with large areas not being cultivated. It demands that you mark out your route first so that the effect of long curves and corners look comfortable to the eye; either that or you are instinctively good at driving a lawn tractor with precision. By setting the blades at varying heights grass can be cut in such a way that any number of patterns can emerge. High on maintenance, of course, but nothing compared to the man who 'paints' extraordinarily complicated designs on to the lawn by dragging the back of a rake carefully across selected areas of the grass in the early morning dew. This stunning effect is dried out and gone by mid-morning.

The Berze le Chatel, whilst having nothing to do with wine, was a local point of interest and promised a good garden, although visits are strictly by appointment. At least it was not difficult to find this massive eleventh-century castle that lords it from high up on a hill over miles and miles of rolling countryside. It is a heavy and threatening place, and although it tries to be welcoming, it can't seem to hide its general distaste towards approaching outsiders.

The car park was completely empty, not even a few buses or caravans, so with the car left under the shade of an old spreading oak, I started the climb up the last few hundred metres towards the gates.

The view down along the *allée* of lime trees towards the inner archway was plain and simple. Built on top of the arch were at least three storeys of ancient gatehouse. As I neared the inner sanctum, accompanied by two chicken outriders – Rhode Island Reds – a van rushed passed me at considerable speed, blanketing the view in every direction with swirling clouds of dust. As it disappeared I stood there, layered in a coat of pale-grey powder, looking, I fancied, like one of the castle ghosts. So did the chickens, only they shook it off more easily, evidently used to the game.

Had someone tried to kill me or just give me a diabolic fright? I wondered.

I passed under the arch and came upon an elderly lady, bespectacled and frail, who lifted her head and waited for me to explain what I wanted. I introduced myself, assured her that I had had my rendezvous confirmed and, well, here I was, grin grin.

'I don't know who you spoke to because I never confirmed anything, and I am the owner,' she said haughtily.

I kept smiling, apologised for the mix-up and turned to go.

'I do not have much time but I will show you quickly around,' she said then, having, it seemed, melted a bit.

But quick it was. There was something in the austerity of Berze le Chatel that made me think of the *château* in Lacoste, the village I had lived near for most of my time in Provence. I was just telling her about how Pierre Cardin had bought it and how he was about to restore it and had invited me to quote on redoing the garden terraces, when she decided to terminate the tour.

'It belonged to the Marquis de Sade,' I said bashing on, 'and now Monsieur Cardin is going to–'

'He's dead, isn't he?' she asked.

'No, he's old now but very active,' I said.

'The Marquis de Sade, you say? Hmm, I don't know the name for sure, but I think he may have died recently. Do you like the wisteria falling over the wall like that? I think it is perfect.'

So with little more than a glimpse of the endless

terracing, the box hedging and the tidy little paths, I bade my guide farewell and headed back down the drive.

Possibly the most interesting thing to notice was the incredible position of the tennis court. Perched within a terrace on the side of the lower battlements it would have been very unforgiving to over-enthusiastic ground shots.

The kindly old lady in whose nearby bed and breakfast *château* I had spent a sound night, or sound for me at any rate, bade me farewell with a broad grin and a shaking handkerchief. I would not have thought it possible the previous evening.

I had arrived to a gruff old dragon who seemed insulted that an oik like me had chosen her well-to-do abode as my crash palace for the night. Evidently there was no one else staying and as she looked me up and down – I was tired, unshaven and attired in rather tatty jeans – she deliberated about which room to give me.

I drew 'Les Bouquets des Fleurs', which I imagined was a euphemism for 'dank cellar' and headed off, key in hand.

'Dinner is from seven-thirty and the cook can't get here tonight,' she said with some satisfaction, as I departed. 'So you'll just have to make do with what we can manage.'

I assured her that was no problem, and went off to see the bouquet of flowers. In fact, she had awarded me a decent room with a huge bed. The bathroom was stuck in the fifties with a tiny bath and period fittings just waiting for an architectural salvage company to rip them out and recycle them back to the lifestyle junkies of Paris. There were only two electrical plugs and they had been designated for the bedside lamps. So reading was off the agenda if I wanted to charge up the phone, camera and computer batteries. Oh, these things are sent to try us.

Changed, shaved and with my hair nicely combed I went down to the dining room and ordered some whisky whilst I looked at the menu she had handed me.

I sat at a small table next to a pair of caged budgies – one caramel, the other mimosa yellow – who warbled and chirped happily enough in their confinement. Always uncomfortable with caged birds and animals, I watched in fascination as the older of the two seemed to flirt with the younger one. He hopped from one perch to the other, ruffled his feathers, rolled his eyes and finally nuzzled up. I supposed idly that if you are in love you don't mind being in a metal cage together. It's when that love wanes that it must be pretty grim – unable to get away from each other, locked into an environment you don't want, trapped by circumstance. God, I thought glumly, I'm sympathising with budgies these days.

Throughout dinner the old girl kept dropping in for some splintered conversation and after a bit of daft French from my side she finally smiled. It was an embracing experience. There was no stopping her after that. I think she would have liked to sit down and join in, probably a bit lonely, but as she was thrashing around in the kitchen it was not possible. The less remembered about what was for dinner the better other than it was perfectly congenial and after a little more local wine I bade her goodnight having considered kissing her on both cheeks. Next morning, after an adequate breakfast, I paid the bill, tipped generously and drove off. In the mirror I could see she was waving her hankie.

Next stop was the appealing little town of Givry. It was market day and Givry was bustling as it must have bustled for centuries. The town was dominated by the Round House, which had official offices upstairs and was showing work by local artists downstairs. I bought a little water-colour for Theo (which, when I gave it to him, he looked at as if it must have been found in somebody's dustbin). But the point of being there was to visit the beautiful eighteenth-century cellars of the Domaine de Thénard.

I found their shop tucked down a side street and thought it as good a place to start as any. No gardens, no *château*, just the small labelling workroom that looked and smelt Dickensian. When I announced myself to a small rat-like lady, who was scuttling about with handfuls of sticky labels, and asked to see the celebrated cellars, she looked as if I had just asked to see her naked. 'Certainly not, *monsieur*, it is not possible today. By appointment. Too busy.' She then ignored me completely, so just to annoy her I bought three bottles freshly off the labelling line and returned to the small streets of Givry to wander amongst the traders.

The smell of roasting chickens on the spit floated over the flowers, vegetables, cheeses, meats and a plethora of other everyday necessities. These small town markets have become so much a part of my existence now that I can't imagine life without them. They are a good honest part of French life. Ignoring the overdone efforts you find on the new waterside developments of London, for example, British markets seem to share the same camaraderie, the social interaction and the simple homegrown produce, but a certain Latin ingredient is missing. I'm not the only convert; most tourists in France head for the local markets and while away a happy morning.

I passed a bicycle shop as I ambled. In the window was a racing bike that cost 5,000 euros. It was an incredibly expensive bit of kit for such a small place. But with its beautifully welded frame, piston suspension, dozens of gears and tyres as thick as Einstein, it must have been in the dreams of the town's teenagers who yearn for the yellow shirt. In the café, cheerful shoppers and traders alike, caps in place, were knocking back pastis or coffee, playing Rapido and Lotto, exchanging news and views. Outside the traffic had ground to a perfectly acceptable halt. Cars and vans were not so much parked as abandoned, sometimes even with their doors or boots wide open. Coveys of old men leant against their bicycles, swapping stories of *boules* victories, and comfortably spread ladies tattled and laughed. Children and dogs ran free, darting in and out of boxes and baskets. It was easy to forget that there might be anything troubling anybody, including me.

Traffic roundabouts are a great art in France. Extravagantly commissioned by the *mairie* and installed by the local gardeners, they try their best to outdo each other. Usually they attempt to reflect the character of the commune. Prizes are given and drunks drive all over them. Leaving Givry, I negotiated one that had mini-rows of vine, box hedge cut into cubes, cypress arches and blocks of burgundy stone. The scenario changes as you continue round the circle.

After lunch in Nuits St George it was time to pay homage to the legendary 'golden slope' of Romanée-Conti. Here is real estate that makes Madison Avenue or Mayfair look cheap. This *domaine* of the Côte-d'Or doesn't produce very much wine but it is the very best.

Leaning on a stone wall looking up the slopes, I wondered why Tom MacArthur hadn't included a bottle of this on his list. The answer became glaring obvious a little later when I went to a smart wine merchant in the centre of Beaune.

It was a beautifully laid-out shop with all the wines of the region parked neatly and conveniently on shelves that sparkled with promise. Added to which were a handful of malt whiskeys, some rums, Calvados and a variety of fruit-based head-bangers. The more expensive wines were displayed in open wooden cases supported by all the fringe equipment needed to be a professional wine-head. It was clean and comfortable. At the back, however, was another room cut off from the average shopper by a red rope slung between a pair of golden stands and acting as well as any lock and key. Here was the serious stuff, the *vieux millésimes*, the aristo-wines with price tags unsuitable for a family newspaper. I asked the efficient young woman in charge if I may go in as I was looking for a bottle or two of Romanée-Conti that was ready for drinking.

'*Bien sûr*,' she replied, and let me pass to the inner sanctum, handing me as I went a list. This included not just the boss wine itself but the other Vosne-Romanée favourites: La Tache, Richebourg and Romanée-St Vivant, aided and abetted by the hardly inferior Echézeaux. One of the things about getting older is people tend to take you seriously. Trying to keep a normal face, as the sales lady talked me through the list, I asked if the price of 13,720 euros for a case of the '78 could be discounted at all.

'Each,' she said. 'They are 13,720 euros each.'

That's about £9,500 a bottle, or £114,000 a case. Not that you would ever find a full case. You can still buy a house for less than that. There were also a couple of 1986 double magnums very reasonably offered at 21,400 euros each (£14,250).

I knew now why Tom hadn't suggested this. After the shock of the Conti, a 2000 Echézeaux at 360 euros seemed like a gift. 'It will be ready in about fifteen years but best left for twenty,' said the woman. 'I have a few bottles left if you're interested.' She opened a temperature-controlled drawer that held the entire stock of four bottles. She also opened the magnum drawer and there, lying quietly on their sides, were a selection of bottles worth around a couple of hundred thousand pounds. I couldn't stop thinking about breaking in and stealing them all. What a hoot! Keep them for a few more years and back they could go onto the market, sold at auction for a huge profit. Of course, you would have to drink at least two of them.

As I stared at the most expensive bottle of wine I had ever held I was desperately trying to imagine what it would taste like. I mean, good or even excellent wine can only reach a certain level, can't it? Maybe the superstar taste-masters of the universe can discern a higher level than lesser punters but to you and me it must flatten out way before it gets to £2,000 a glass. How do you move bottles that cost that much? Can you insure against breakage? What happens if it doesn't taste so damned good when you get to it? Should you leave it open for a while before drinking? Should you decant it? Should you share it with someone you love or drink it all yourself? Have you got any empty bottles I could have to leave lying around the place?

I checked into my sleeping quarters for the night – another upmarket B&B *château*. It was owned by a chap who produced a perfectly good wine but was happy to supplement his income by having paying guests. It was far from a full house and I had a choice of bedrooms. Being well over 6ft a double without an end is best, if at all possible. I sleep particularly badly in single beds. My room was on the fourth floor and was reached by climbing a well-worn stone staircase that seemed to wind round and up for ever. I had a bath and then went back into Beaune that evening to find something to eat.

Lunch on your own is one thing but going out to dinner with yourself is quite different. At lunch it's just doing what you have to do, but in the evening it becomes something of an occasion, a treat or a surprise. You dress up a bit, make an effort, drink without worrying about working a couple of hours later, relax and generally have a good time. Booking a table for one, on the other hand, is a bit sad. You sit there either gazing at everybody else having a great night out or you try to read a book, maybe a magazine (a bit big on a small table), or write notes as I do.

I found myself in a regular little restaurant in the centre of town. It was buzzy and I felt perfectly comfortable with my potent dish of *oeufs en meurette* made with poached eggs and a rich sauce of bacon, vegetables, fresh herbs, good red Burgundy and a dash of brandy. I was just finishing some cheese when a short fellow of about seventy years old but in fair shape wearing spotless dark-grey trousers and a crisp-fronted white shirt came up to my table.

'You are English, no?' he said with such geniality I was neither surprised nor put off by his entry.

'Nearly. Scottish.' I smiled back at him.

'Ah, *l'Ecosse*. I hope I am not disturbing you,' he said smoothly, 'but I heard you speaking French to the waiter with an English accent and because I lived in England for some years after the war I can never resist saying hello.'

'Hello,' I said, and was about to ask him if he wanted to sit down but he was ahead of me. 'I hoped perhaps you might like to join us for a digestive as you are on your own?' He smiled and held out his hand. 'My name is Maurice Bonnard.'

Maurice turned out to be an exceptionally well-preserved seventy-eight. Before the war and as a young man, he had worked on his uncle's small vineyard in the Côte d'Or but as the Occupation took hold he had been recruited into the Resistance and later found himself in London placed under the exiled de Gaulle. Billeted at the Rembrandt Hotel in Knightsbridge he had worked closely with his future president and obviously did his bit successfully. When peace was settled he had stayed on in London and taken up a position with a smart wine merchant in the West End as their man from Burgundy.

He explained he was having dinner with his wife, son and daughter-in-law and that it would be a pleasure to introduce them to me. I accepted and quickly met his kind, smiling and relaxed family. Maurice filled my glass with some fine, velvety Vosne-Romanée and proposed my health. I told them my name and why I was in Burgundy. There were questions about my work and how it came to pass that I was practising in the south of France. I dutifully explained a bit about my landscaping and how I mostly worked for the *'maison secondaires'*, the second-homers from the States, Australia and South Africa as well as the mostly northern European countries – 'Just about every nationality except the French! Not surprisingly, they prefer to work with a Frenchman.' They understood this naturally enough but flattered me none the less on a talent that they didn't really know I had or not. As Maurice filled my glass, I mentioned how, earlier in the day, I had been looking at bottles of wine that cost the same price as a decent family car.

'Ah *oui*, the Romanée-Conti.'

'How can it cost so much and who drinks it at those kind of prices?' I asked him, still incredulous that one might buy a bottle of such expensive red wine.

'It is a mixture of many facts. The '78 you refer to is of course ready to drink and it was a good year without many bottles. That immediately makes it more expensive. Also, it is a legendary vineyard and produces very small amounts. It is, therefore, very much in demand and this too must affect the cost. But finally, and most importantly, the *terroir* on the "Golden Slope", as it is referred to, is simply the best there is. Who buys it? I don't know. Kings and presidents, restaurants and clubs, Americans and Japanese. And you know, people purchase it as a commodity. They buy the wine young and hold onto it for many years, then sell it again without having ever opened a bottle. It gets passed from cellar to cellar gaining in reputation and value.'

The trouble with having only one bottle of a really good wine is who do you share it with? You could, of course, drink it all on your own but that is a little sad. You might share it with a friend but do you blather to him or her about its wonderfulness or do you keep quiet and just die a thousand deaths if it is chucked back without comment? One hopes that if it is so damned good they will spot it, but really it is in the choosing.

I put the question to Maurice, but he was starting to look a little tired, and his wife quietly suggested that perhaps it was time to go home.

'It is,' he agreed, 'but before we go I want to tell our Scottish friend a story.' The waiter brought some more coffee with chocolates. The room was wine-warm and the chairs comfortable.

'Once when I was much younger a close friend of mine asked me to go round to his house for lunch one day because he had acquired a bottle of *premier cru* Romanée-Conti. I can't remember how old it was exactly but it was at its upper level. Nor do I remember how he had acquired it. What mattered was that he wanted to share it with me. There were no more bottles available anywhere as far as he knew and he wanted to keep it very quiet that he had it. I bought some *foie gras* and went to where he lived – just off the main square. I took my old collie dog, Fleurie, with me.

'My friend was very excited and told me how he had been thinking about this wine for a long time, when and where to drink it and with whom. "But of course I knew all along it had to be you, *mon ami*!" he declared, preparing some toast and polishing the glasses until they sparkled like new crystal. He had a low table set between two sofas on which he arranged the plates and knives, the glasses and the almost mythical bottle of celestial nectar. He found a pair of starched white linen napkins and pulled the cork, which he smelt and sighed deeply, kissed the top of the bottle, poured it out and went into the kitchen for the toast.

'The wine was a deep brown-red and breathed such promise that I couldn't sit still, I had to go and help him make the toast. As I got up to join him Fleurie also jumped up, thinking, I suppose, that we were leaving. As she excitedly moved round the low table, her big bushy tail knocked the bottle over, which crashed into the glasses, smashing them. The bottle rolled to the edge of the table, pouring its contents everywhere, including onto the carpet. We turned as one and gazed dumbfounded. We couldn't move. Wine was everywhere, except in our mouths and bodies. Fleurie was unaware of her faux pas and stood in front of me wagging furiously and lightly panting.'

Maurice paused, partly for effect and partly to nibble his toast.

'What a terrible story,' I said. 'What happened next? What did your friend do?'

The old man took off his glasses, picked up a corner of the tablecloth and started to polish them. 'Well, you know, Serge was always a very dignified man and at this moment he excelled himself. He put his arm around me and said quietly, "Maurice, *mon ami*, let us eat that *foie gras* before Fleurie does." With that we turned our back on the scene of broken dreams, ate the *foie gras* in the kitchen and even managed to laugh. Just.'

I got back to my B&B *château* well after midnight, all the richer for having spent half the evening with Maurice and his brood.

Another town, another *château* with its tiled roof and turrets. The architecture of the region that only a few days earlier had been so different and particular was now becoming the norm, and doing everything alone was turning out to be a double-edged sword. On one side I was more open to adventure paced to suit myself, on the other was a lingering loneliness at not having anybody with whom I could share these experiences.

In the middle of the night I was awoken by the sound of an old steam train puffing its way across the countryside. The rhythm that it made was unmistakable. I could hear it coming from miles away, then it rattled through the station without stopping and trailed off into the distance. The same noise woke me again a few hours later.

The next morning, as I was waiting in the library for my boiled egg to be laid, I asked my host where the railway station was.

'Station?' he said. 'There's no station, I'm afraid. Where do you want to go?'

'Oh, nowhere,' I said. 'Nowhere at all. It's just that the trains woke me in the night. They sounded very close so I thought . . . '

'There has never been a railway station here,' said my host. He didn't look at me but it seemed to be the end of the conversation.

The egg was the best I had had for a long time but I wasn't going to stick around for another. One night was enough.

Chapter Eight

Getting back to the office pulled me up short. No more excuses for wine-tasting, no rambles round pretty gardens, just a pile of work to sort out and a self-inflicted warning to start behaving like the gardener I say I am. It's fine once I've begun, it's just getting to it that takes discipline.

I am surprisingly methodical when applying myself to my client's landscaping programme, and even quite quick. But at the end of this working day, instead of leaving the office and nipping home to all the things I loved – my little boy, my garden, the security of home life, the location of the farmhouse, its peace and tranquillity – I was joining the traffic and heading over to my rented *gîte* near Orgon, a one-celled city of broken hearts. They say we get quickly institutionalised, adapt to our surroundings however grim, and start to make the most of the situation, but as I arrived each evening at this second-division set of self-catering apartments, my already heavy heart put on weight. I was there for nearly four months and don't remember laughing once.

Two phone calls at the office the next day raised my spirits considerably. The first was from a client. She is a senior stock adviser for a multi-national investment group; her husband is an international lawyer. Between them they have so much fun with their spending power that you can't help but applaud their performance. The phone call was good on two accounts. One, they were pleased with the work so far, and two, they were transferring my payment direct to my account.

The second call was from my South African client and chum, Edward Austin. He had done as he said he would and had arranged for us to stay on the de Rothschild estate in Seriousville, Bordeaux.

Frantic project planning, internal meetings, and the cajoling of my workforce meant that I was ready for more Vintage Gardening by mid-June. (I did, of course, promise them a bottle or two of something special.) I even texted a message to a chum in London to make him jealous, but being slow and new at texting I sent it to the wrong person. Got to be careful with that kind of thing.

'You can come with us,' said Edward. 'I've hired a car with plenty of room.'

'Does it have satellite navigation?'

'Of course.'

'Just as well or we would be lost within minutes,' I said.

The thought of reading a map and randomly asking people in the street where you are or how you got there leaves me cold nowadays. People argue that the Global Positioning System takes the adventure out of travelling. Not so. It helps you avoid taking the wrong turning off the *autoroute* and ending up in the centre of, say, Lyon, where the pleasure of travel is distinctly absent. It gets you as close to your destination as you want then you can turn it off. Then get lost. You can even turn the lady's voice off if she's getting on your nerves and just have the maps. It's easy and nigh-on mandatory if you're travelling a lot, I say.

Anyway when we finally did get going to Bordeaux, guess whose car we were in? My Benz, with GPS. The Hearse – as Madame Austin called my elegant black autoroute cruiser – was packed and ready to run.

One of the wines on Tom MacArthur's list was, of course, a Bordeaux, or more specifically the Haut-Medoc. It was inconceivable to leave out the most famous wine-growing region of France if not the world, and he was not going to muck about with anything less than one of the elite red wines. He had, he said, deliberated long and hard and had decided that a bit of proper money needed to be spent. It was, as he put it, 'unavoidable' and in the end had gone for Château Lafite-Rothschild: 'Besides, if they don't have a good garden then who the hell would?'

This was a fortuitous choice because, as Ed Austin and I had tasted and tripped our way around the Rupert-Rothschild Fredericksburg estate in Stellenbosch, we had resolved to meet again in Bordeaux and behave in a similar fashion. It had seemed far away and far off at the time, but here we were about to extend our knowledge and introduce ourselves to the timeless tradition of superior wine-making on one of the most celebrated vineyards in the universe.

There is something approaching the royal about the de Rothschild family. They are so well stitched together with such enormous security that one feels even their soul has some kind of insurance against depletion. We all know that money can't buy love, but we also recognise that it eases the passage of progress. So to have amassed such a formidable fortune from banking and wine-making, not to mention all the support acts, is inspiring in its combination. Banking would be unbearably dull without a bottle of exquisite wine, and wine growing would not last long without some serious backing from a bank. *Voilà*!

Some time ago I had worked for one of the de Rothschilds in London on a project that ran for a little over a year. It should have been a couple of months but his wife enjoyed changing her mind, as was her right, about what she wanted. This is something we all do a bit, but with such clout behind her she could afford to wait until the garden was finished and then say, 'I'm off Italianate. Let's try William and Mary. What do you think?'

She was referring, of course, to William of Orange and

Mary II, who held the royal court for thirteen years between 1689 and 1702. The seventeenth-century English garden was very formal and derivative of continental fashion of the time. There were, admittedly, some over-excited flurries into the symmetries, proportions and compositions of the Chinese garden, but little else. It wasn't until the eighteenth century that garden design was really stirred up, when the English broke away from the stilted forms of their European neighbours and introduced a considerably more informal and looser style. Out went poodle topiary and all such excesses of artificiality and in came what some referred to as 'wilderness gardening'. Park lands, lakes with bridges, swooping, bending driveways, domed temples and surprise vistas were all the rage.

We would, we hoped, be providing the de Rothschilds with a successfully stylised version of William and Mary's Anglo-Dutch hybrid landscaping techniques. Then we would be thrown a line about the late Islamic period or Euro-American beginnings, and on it went until we were finally sacked – richer for the acquaintance but poorer for the diluted result.

After a long drive up from the Luberon we arrived at one of the de Rothschilds' homes: Château Clarke just outside Listrac-Medoc.

Ed and Suzanne Austin had been easy companions and by the time we were near Bordeaux, Suzanne had managed to mimic the voice of the lady on the GPS to such a degree that it was impossible to know which was the real thing

and which wasn't. The net result was that we finally managed to get really lost. Increasingly embarrassing phone calls
were made to the de Rothschild offices where minions
were working overtime trying to guide us in.

'I can't call again, I really can't,' said Ed. 'You do it.'

The GPS couldn't be expected to find the *château*, so it
was turned off. After a turn here, a u-turn there and a bit of
reversing, we found ourselves still lost in a courtyard the
size of Victoria station. One more sheepish call was made
and the slightly off-colour voice explained that we had
arrived. We were in the *château*'s grape delivery bay.

'Go round the corner past the bus that has some,' slight
cough, 'workers sitting in it, patiently waiting to go home,
and you really can't miss the lady standing on the corner.'

'He doesn't sound as if he has much of a sense of
humour,' said Ed.

In fact, both the man – a young and charming fellow
called Jean-Claude – and the lady – Anne-Marie, who was
a little more mature and wearing a floral-patterned cotton
dress and a sweet, intelligent smile – could not have been
more genial. They welcomed us as long-lost friends, as well
they might after the screwed-up map-reading and the epic
telephone conversations that had recently taken place.
Without any hint of impatience they explained that while
Jean-Claude took people home on the family bus she
would take us down to the guesthouse. The Baron
Benjamin and his wife, Arianna, were not, regrettably, able
to 'host' us as had been the plan as they had had to stay
unexpectedly in Paris, but instructions had been made that

we were to be given full regimental honours in their absence and treated as VIPs.

The guesthouse was part of a developed area of the *château*. It had probably provided living quarters for upper management originally, but today, restored to within a centimetre of its old self, it stood proud in its smart new suit and was as comfortable as a ten-star hotel. Arranged on three floors it could sleep twelve with ease and a few more if they were children. The ground floor offered a fine *salon* that had two completely separate sitting areas with deep sofas and armchairs. The antiques were perfectly chosen, balanced and original, fitting in gently with the tapestries and rugs. The huge oil paintings, mostly by seventeenth-century artists, were themed to the Bacchanalian delights and joys of louche little satyrs getting off on the pleasures of fine wine and women. The dining-room table was laid by two or three members of staff. With a quiet graciousness they served from silver tureens into hand-painted porcelain, carved gossamer-thin slices of partridge, which they proposed with just-setting cream potatoes cooked in fresh tarragon. The heavy candlesticks, not strictly necessary, flickered on the summer's evening air and the decanted wine flowed unhurriedly into the glasses, turning them a deep tawny red. Outside the sun dipped over the lake.

The origins of the Château Clarke estate date back to the twelfth century when the Cistercian monks of the Vertheuil Abbey planted the first vines. Much later, in 1818, Lord Tobie Clarke, an Irishman and Catholic escapee

from the religious wars, joined up with the other Irish
expats in Bordeaux such as Lynch (Lynch-Bages) and
Barton, and started making his own wine. He loved
Château Clarke with a passion and, apart from his evident
understanding of viniculture, he created a wonderful property with swooping gardens, lakes and grand vistas. But all
the time the core of the estate was, and still is, a tribute to
the mighty grape. His son built on its fledgling reputation,
and subsequent generations kept the business going with
varying degrees of success. However, by 1973, it had
become run down and out of sorts, and was finally sold in
1973 to the Baron Edmond de Rothschild, part-owner of
the legendary Château Lafite. The neglected vineyard was
replanned, replanted and completely recreated between
1974 and 1978, attaining a wine-producing area of 54
hectares. Today, the vines are planted on clay-limestone
hilltops that enable the Merlot grape to express itself at its
best. The wine has been steadily improving ever since. The
ancient buildings have been restored and the techniques
and equipment used in the wine-making process have been
brought up to date. Since September 2001, the hand-
picked and carefully transported harvest has been received
in beautiful oak vats. The grapes have been meticulously
sorted in the wine store and vatted through simple gravity.
The wine is then placed in new barrels and left to mature
for between fourteen and eighteen months.

It is strictly forbidden to water vine plants, apart from
the first or possibly second year after planting, just enough
to establish their roots. After that it is a dry old do. The

terroir at Clarke has lumps of chalk in the fields on top of a limestone plateau. This allows for a bit of 'sponging' or water retention, which it then releases slowly into the soil of its own accord in a kind of inbuilt irrigation system.

'Clarke,' Jean-Claude told us, 'is good to drink after two or three years but has great potential for ageing.' Lucky thing. There is no classification at Château Clarke as such, but Jean-Claude who knows a thing or two about all this, assured us convincingly that it is every bit as good as a 'third-growth' Lafite.

Château Lafite-Rothschild on the edge of Paulliac in Bordeaux is, of course, one of the best-known clarets in the world, along with its cousin Mouton-Rothschild and the legendary Latour. All from the same region, they are all categorised under the evocative title of 'first growths'. This is a sub-division of the sixty-one 'best' red Bordeaux wines grouped in the famed 1855 Classification, which came about through the efforts of Louis Napoleon, nephew of Napoleon Bonaparte, who was in charge of promoting France to the rest of the world. To do so he brought about the National Exhibitions, a clever idea which attracted the best of produce from around the country and which was a forerunner to London's Great Exhibition at Crystal Palace. However, the best Bordeaux wine-makers were reluctant to exhibit their fine wines lest they were lost amongst a sea of lesser vintages so a deal was struck. A list of the very best of Bordeaux's wines, the 'first growths', was compiled under the heading of 'the 1855 Bordeaux Classification'. In all the subsequent years only one more wine has managed to elevate itself into the Classification's hallowed hall of fame. Guess what it was? Exactly, a Rothschild – Mouton-Rothschild, to be precise, in 1973.

After Edmond de Rothschild's death, his son, Benjamin, took over the reins with his wife Arianna. Now both in their forties, they seem to care deeply for the *château* and are dedicated to continuing the revamping of the property and the development of their wine. Benjamin's mother, the Baroness Nadine, is a formidable character well known to the French people through her regular television appearances. A veritable TV star, she does much to promote the business in general and the de Rothschild vineyards in particular.

As Tom had said, if the de Rothschilds didn't have an impressive garden then who would? In fact, there are essentially two gardens at Château Clarke. The Old Garden was created around the *château* by Edmond in the 1970s, and the New Garden around the restored outbuildings, guest-houses and conference centre by Arianna during the last five or six years. They are both extremely well thought out and brilliantly describe the different takes on garden design that successive generations inevitably produce. The old is informal, warm and relaxing. It has a favourite old pipe sense of comfort, and while much of it is cultivated parkland, it retains a family-friendly intimacy. The new garden guesthouse is altogether more modern.

On the upper plain the swimming pool of the Old Garden is reached by passing under a long rose covered pergola. Simple and restrained it makes a strong dynamic with its rural surroundings. On the other side of the pool and opposite the pergola, a tiled-roof, open-sided little summerhouse is swamped with wisteria and more roses. The table and upholstered chairs seem to ache for use. The composition is wonderfully balanced and traditional. On the lower reach of the garden, before it becomes vineyard, a gentle curving lake lies in the hollow. Fringed by pines and cypress trees mixed in with willows and poplars, it provides an ideal spot to pause. An ornately carved stone seat beckons for you to sit and contemplate. Nothing seems hurried here. Lying casually over a huge rock in the dappled shade of an oak tree a naked figure reclines with one arm trailing in the water and his head resting on the other. Not immediately obvious, the impact is all the more impressive when you catch sight of him. No doubt another member of the Bacchanalian boys' club easing up after a hard night.

The Old Garden is charmingly unceremonious with lots of grass and random island beds cut into the undulating lawn. Shrub borders of acers, skimmias and delicate hydrangeas abound. Others have hostas, lamium, ferns and cornus interplanted with tall waving lilies to catch the eye. Elegant well-shaped rocks are strategically planted next to the trunks of the tall, spindly pines, protecting the high-reaching acanthus flowers. Elsewhere a huge dark-green viburnum makes a stark contrast to the white marble statue of a scantily clad maiden with a basket on her shoulder. Full of bosom and thigh she is caught in the movement of bending slightly towards the fruit bush, frozen but liquid all at the same time. Further around is another life-size statue. Cast in lead, it shows a young girl picking grapes, assisted by four chubby little children.

Most of the herbaceous borders are edged with a 20cm-deep basketwork retaining strip. The small interweaved branches make a lovely natural barrier, establishing a clean break between flowers and grass. Watched over by mighty magnolia grandifloras with their big waxy white flowers, the garden seems to have relaxed into an easy well-kept space that ties in with the unpretentious house it surrounds.

When the current owners decided to renovate the out-buildings, which lie about half a kilometre from the main house, it was also planned that a new garden should be installed. A vast flat area stretched between the guest wing and the conference or reception rooms. It needed to be tackled carefully as each guesthouse required an integrated terrace of its own. The brief was simple: keep it simple. That meant unfussy planting, minimal construction and perfect balance. It has been achieved with stunning effect.

Heroic expanses of remarkably weed-free lawns are dissected by wide straight gravel paths, timber-edged to keep them exactly on line. From the far side you look out across the neatly mown space, the eye following a long path straight into the impeccably pruned hedges of vine, the modesty enhanced by the well-positioned sycamores which frame the middle distance. The early morning sun was making shadows on the west side and the whole concept was just so pleasing, polished to perfection by the fabulously high standard of maintenance.

The disused quarry has been converted into a lake that supplies plenty of water to irrigate the whole layout. The edges have been softened by easy banks and spectacular tree planting. A foot bridge reaches over the centre waist of the lake, decorated by a pretty metal railing incorporating a bullrush design, and reflects in the calm water. Beneath, the real thing grows happily along with wild aquatic plants and thriving weeping willows.

Outside each guesthouse a tree has been under planted with clipped hedging, square and tight with a *boule* at each corner. In between the balls something more frothy softens the blow. My favourite was the purple cotinus underplanted with clipped rosemary, box balls and foamy erigeron. Another success was a bay tree surrounded by clipped silver artemisia and yew balls. Other combo's included olives with euonymus and santolina with teucrium *en boule*, kumquat with eleagnus, viburnum tinus spheres and red sage.

In the middle of the great lawn was a well, presumably once the main source of water; now in retirement it has become a feature and focal point. It is reached by randomly placed, irregular-sized stepping stones set deeply into the pile of the lawn.

The new garden is already a success but considering it is only six years old the full potential is still to be realised. The use of design accents without any hint of cliché says a lot for the prowess of the lady of the house.

The next morning, after a glass or two of freshly squeezed oranges so sharp they nearly caused Ed's head to implode, and a few other continental extravagances, it was time to get serious and head over to Lafite where we were expected.

Checking into the offices you are confronted by an army of ladies hard at work on the business of keeping Lafite running smoothly. From backstage emerged Marcel, a young, thin man who spoke fairly good English but with such a strong French accent he sounded as if he were sending it all up.

'It is the land at Lafite, the *terroir*,' he said, 'which makes the property quite unique. Nature, they say, performed a miracle when it created the perfect combination of soil, subsoil, exposure, plus that certain *je ne sais quoi* which makes the wines of Lafite incomparable.'

I'm sure he was right but he sounded scripted. We were not the first people to step inside these hallowed cellars.

Already recognised as outstanding in the London markets of the sixteenth century, Lafite received recognition at the court of Louis XV when Alexandre de Segur, well known as the *'Prince des Vignes'* – who also incidentally owned Latour, Calon and Phelan (all brain-meltingly good) – introduced the wines to the King and his favourite mistress, Madame de Pompadour. In the 1855 Classification Lafite was listed as *'Premier des Premiers'*.

The Lafite vineyard covers 100 hectares or 250 acres, and is divided into three separate areas: the hilly ground close to the *château*, the Plateau des Carruades and a small amount of Saint Estephe. I'll bang on a bit here if I may because, de facto, we are talking about the real thing.

This is as good as it gets. Even fourth-rate Mexican

off-licences selling cactus juice and mescaline know about Lafite-Rothschild, along with Latour, Margaux, Haute Brion and Mouton-Rothschild, the 'first growths'. The soil is gravelly, which means it is well drained, and is planted with three classical grapes: mostly Cabernet Sauvignon, a little Cabernet Franc and some Merlot. Petit Verdot edges its way in with a paltry 2 per cent. The vine plants reach up to eighty years of age, but of course by that time the harvest yield is low. The grapes are, naturally, picked by hand to avoid bruising. I would love to go back when it is harvesting time (*vendage*) and steal a few grapes just to lick, to roll round the mouth, tease the teeth and then pierce with greedy molars. I don't suppose they would taste much different from a Luberon grape but I like the thought of that million-dollar berry exploding inside my head.

The thing here is this: because the famous five first growths are so in demand and consequently so expensive, the profits are huge. This means that Lafite and its cohorts have much more money to spend on ground and plant maintenance and on the cutting-edge technology with its sophisticated instruments. Lesser producers will never manage to keep up with, let alone overtake, the grand masters. Lafite even has its own cooperage. On top of this the big players can afford the legendary oenologists, such as, for example, Michel Rolland, the *maître de chaise*, one of the superstars of his *métier*, who is as much in demand for his extraordinary palate and understanding of wine-making, as the stratospheric wines he creates.

We wandered around amongst the machines for

de-stalking (Marcel made it sound like deer-stalking) and grape-sorting; we climbed up and down perfectly constructed oak staircases across platforms with hand-carved banisters; we tapped the maceration and fermentation vats, and generally ooh-ed and ah-ed at the splendidness of it all. The tour, as always, wound up in one of the big, dark cellars for a tasting. In this magnificent round room, deep in the chest of the estate, carefully temperature- and light-controlled, immaculately laid-out barrels were arranged on top of one another, two or three deep and fanned out around a central clearing. It was here that a small stage had been built to accommodate musicians for any of the musical activities that are presented from time to time. The grand cellars are available for receptions, weddings and conferences. 'Not rock 'n' roll raves though, it might upset the wine,' added our guide as he drew us up in front of an ancient barrel on which a fine linen cloth had been settled. A few shiny wine glasses and an opened bottle of the current vintage stood to attention awaiting our appraisal, the prize for having survived the journey. A spittoon lurked in the half-light, ready to receive the waste from the gurgled and gargled but unswallowed wine. It is at this moment that the usual inane questions are asked so I threw in, 'What's the oldest wine you have here that could be drunk?'

'The 1797,' said Marcel automatically. 'There are six bottles left and every twenty-five years the corks are changed and the bottles topped up with either the same year if there is enough or the nearest they have to it.'

'What, you mean somebody has been surreptitiously skimming a little off every now and then?'

He looked quite shocked. 'Goodness no. That could never happen. No, it is the natural evanescence.'

Ed remarked, 'So technically, the bottle from 1797 has only some of the original wine in it?'

That seemed to stump Marcel for a moment as his head attempted some mental arithmetic.

'How long do you recommend keeping a bottle of Lafite before drinking it?' I asked to put him out of his misery.

'Ideally fifteen to twenty years, or more. It has a long life.' He then poured out a little 2002 for us to try. This is where I lose the plot. If he was saying that the wine needed to rest up for a couple of decades before it could be really enjoyed, why was he giving us something that was hardly out of nappies? He must have known that we had only a layman's experience and were hardly in a position to spot the future gallantry of his offering. Of course he wasn't going to produce a bottle of '82 just for a bunch of hopefuls to swill and swallow, but as the stuff he had poured was no better than a hundred other wines I had tasted, what was the point?

'Good on the nose but a little disappointing on the palate,' I offered not wanting to seem ungrateful or disappointed.

'Elegant, open and charming with great promise,' he countered.

I'll be dead by the time this is ready, I thought. 'What would you suggest I should buy a case of today that I'll be able to drink within my lifetime?'

Marcel looked at me carefully, weighing up my life expectancy, and said, 'The '99 will start in about ten years but you cannot of course buy it here at the *château*, as we do not sell directly to the public.' I knew that already, and told him so. He was beginning to treat me like an unripe grape.

'Can you give me a guide as to price for the '99?'

'I think if you can find it here in Pauillac it will be around 500 euros a bottle.'

I did find it in a wine merchant's shop on the sea front at 460 euros. I bought a bottle on Tom's account and packed it carefully into the back of the car.

We Brits should have started buying up Lafite, Latour et al in the Middle Ages when Bordeaux belonged to us for two hundred years.

Unfortunately, as the de Rothschilds were not there, we couldn't see the gardens of the Lafite *château*, as they are not open to the public and I hadn't thought to make an appointment. I discreetly looked through the cast-iron railings, however, and saw pretty much what I expected: formal hedging, swathes of well-attended lawn, magnificent trees with low, swooping branches, and neatly combed paths. A formal place for formal occasions, it lacked the warmth and welcome of the gardens at Château Clarke.

From Pauillac to the Atlantic coast takes about an hour or so. Before heading back to the Luberon, we had decided to visit a small hotel with a growing reputation on the peninsula that is known as Cap Ferret. Not to be confused with

Cap Ferrat on the Côte d'Azure, Ferret is an altogether different Cap.

Born out of a family seaside resort, it loped along for years supported by oyster farming, sea fishing and a little bit of local tourism. But a few years ago things changed, or at least they did in one small corner near to the edge of the sea and close to the biggest of the oyster farms. A small wood-clad house morphed itself into a shabby-chic little hotel known as La Maison du Bassin, got written up as one of France's hippest hotels, fired the Parisian achiever's imagination and came out of its corner wearing pretty bedrooms, timber balconies and verandas. The decked terraces were covered in bright climbing plants and were screened from the tatty old road by an oleander and pittosporum hedge. Here was the New Orleans of the eighteenth-century meeting its twenty-first-century French cousin.

Inside a surpassingly large and well laid-out dining room clad in limed wooden panelling, a dozen tables were laid for dinner, with another half-dozen overflowing onto the terrace. In the half-light of a late midsummer's evening, the puddles of low-burning candles glimmered romance over the dwelling like a soft fog. The stiff linen tablecloths, rattan chairs, champagne ice buckets and solid eating tools were enough to convince you to sit down and get stuck into a bottle of white Bordeaux and accompanying lobster without further ado.

The rooms – cutely known as *les chambres d'amour* – were only six in number, but more were being added, the receptionist hastened to inform us. Mine, being a single with a short double-ended bed, had bugger all to do with *amour*. The restaurant, *le Restaurant des Passions*, did seem a reasonable enough place to be passionate, but when I went to get a drink from the '*le Bar des Rêves*' I was going off the boil a bit. *La Terrasse du Soleil* and *le Chemin du Bonheur* finished me off completely.

The tourists outside of the hotel, such as they were, came from the surrounding region and the houses were simple affairs of little architectural interest. As this was not a wealthy commune the low rates reflected the up-keep of the little seaside town.

The Atlantic is a cruel sea. It comes up from the pole delivering strong currents and cold water. It carries no certainty that swimming will be fun before deep summer, but it does toss up waves that are substantial enough to attract keen rubber-suited surfers. Hawaii it isn't, but to learn the art of surfing it offers just the right amount of challenge. It also has ridiculously beautiful white sand beaches that stretch in both directions for as far as the eyes can manage. In mid-June the sun was up and the few people that were around lazed on a warm sand. One or two braved the water in their swimsuits, but you would have to be horribly hot to want to frolic for long.

Chapter Nine

I got back to the office late that Thursday and was told by Lélia, my P.A. and ultimate link between our two countries, that two *gendarmes* had passed by that afternoon looking for me. 'Something to do with renting a car,' she said.

I have never needed to rent a car in France during the last nine years, having always had my own, so I was confused, and pushed her to tell me more, being forever wary of anything to do with the police.

'Well,' she said, 'two *gendarmes* arrived at the office, they were very aggressive and impatient and demanded to speak to you. When we told them that you were away they insisted that you report to Bonnieux police station as soon as you returned. They would give no more information other than that it was to do with a car rental.'

The next day Lélia and I arrived at the gate of the *gendarmerie* and pushed the bell. We announced ourselves through the entryphone and the gate opened. It's quite bizarre this feeling of immense virtuousness that comes over me every time I go to a police station voluntarily. I savour the sense of innocence, get off on the fact that I am there to complain, report or advise on something, and not there to be charged. Not that I am a well-worn criminal or anything like that, but I have had enough tussles with the law on minor misdemeanours over the years to know how tedious it can be.

A fresh-faced young subaltern approached the desk and asked what we wanted. We explained what had brought us to the station. Lélia, who had only been working in the office for a few months, was not entirely sure what she was doing in a police station with her boss, about whom she really knew very little, but being a trusting sort and giving her employer the benefit of the doubt, she battled on with the rookie. 'One of your policemen came to our office and told us to report in here, something to do with a rented car.'

'Are you sure it wasn't Gordes that came?'

'Absolutely certain,' replied Lélia. 'He said Bonnieux.'

'Did he give you a bit of paper?'

'No.'

'Would you recognise him if you saw him again?'

'Oh, yes, I am sure I could.'

'Right,' he said, after thumbing through some kind of day book, 'I will see if we can establish which officer it was because we have no record of this. None at all.'

I was glad Lélia was with me because anything to do with policemen and *avocats* requires full attention. She was an insurance against any misunderstandings that might lead to difficulties.

'Henri!' our young officer called out. 'Can you come here, please?'

Henri appeared in the reception lobby of the station. He was a tall man in his late forties with a bristly moustache.

'Is this him?'

'No,' said Lélia, 'definitely not.'

'Laurent?'

'*Oui?*' A much shorter man who looked over-worked plodded in.

'*Non*,' said Lélia without doubt.

The three gendarmes stood impatiently in a row looking like they were going to arrest us just for the hell of it at any moment.

'Pierre?' Our keeper of the peace gave a plaintive and final shout.

An elderly and relaxed gentleman joined us, making up the full contingent of the Bonnieux *gendarmerie*, who were lined up – standing straight and to attention – as if for an identity spectacle. It was quite mad, but they seemed reasonably good-natured about it.

Little Lélia, who is not much taller than an olive jar, walked up and down the rank and file and announced, '*Non, il n'est pas là.*'

We left with promises to return if anything turned up.

A few months later we were to discover that one of my company employees had been driving a rented lorry needed for moving a big olive tree and had been stopped for not wearing a seatbelt. I went alone to the station to explain, and after the formalities had been completed, Henri said, 'An olive tree? Why my brother sells olive trees, I will give you his card. What about lavender and rosemary? He sells those, too.'

We have been buying from the brother ever since. Never on the black though, God forbid!

Exactly where and when the grape vine first emerged is open to conjecture, although it is recognised as the oldest, most cultivated plant known to man. In its wild form, *Vitis vinifera sylvestris* was probably twining itself around the scrublands of Persia some seven thousand years ago, albeit producing a fairly humble fruit, and archaeologists have found cultivated grape pips dating back nearly eight thousand years at the sites of ancient settlements at the eastern end of the Black Sea in what is now the Anatolian part of Turkey and Georgia.

The original geographical distribution of wine production has a chequered history with wine regions coming and going, the result of both natural and social shifting. Of the two, probably environment has been the dominant factor for change, as vines produce grapes suitable for making wine only in certain climates of the world.

The drifts of changing climatic conditions will have stripped certain regions of their capabilities whilst enhancing others. Socially, from the earliest of times, wine has been closely tied in to religious ritual whereby the drinking of it has been considered a means of attaining a level of spirituality that brought people closer to their gods. Significantly, by using wine in the Eucharist representing the blood of Christ and life itself, it integrated itself into the Christian ritual as deeply as any other profound statement of faith.

In its early manifestations wine was held by the Persians to be not only spiritually supportive but a medical imperative. (Incidentally, did you know that if an argument broke out at a Persian dinner party the host would pass a basket full of kittens to the ill-tempered guests who, after touching and stroking the little furry things, became much calmed and pacified?)

The Sumerians, who seemed to have had the earliest form of writing that we know of – consisting of stylised pictures called pictograms, drawn using a stylus on a moist clay tablet, produced the oldest known medical handbook. A Sumerian pharmacopoeia written in approximately 2200BC, and excavated at Nippur in 1910, recommended the use of wine as a treatment for various ailments.

The Chinese witches had a brew or two up their big sleeves, and they usually combined animals and wine to sort out a range of illnesses. Examples of prescriptions include one where a lizard's liver and the skin of the cicada locust were mixed in wine to procure an abortion. For another remedy the flesh of a pit viper was prepared by placing the snake in a gallon of wine then burying the sealed jar under a horse's stall for a year. The resultant liquid was a multi-talented drug for curing apoplexy, fistula, stomach pains, heartache, colic, haemorrhoids, worms, flatulence and bowel bleeding. The ancient Alcoholics Anonymous suggested donkey's placenta mixed in a little wine, one dose a day one day at a time, while the liver of a black cat stirred into a claret forerunner was a cracker for malaria. Oh, and try treating your cold with an old-time Night-Nurse: smother an owl to death, pluck it and boil it. Then, when the bones are charred, add some red wine and drink.

Wine can't be much older than the Neolithic period, a time when humans stopped wandering, settled down and began to farm animals as well as hunt them. They started to cultivate crops for subsistence in addition to collecting the berries and fruit, including grapes, that grew wild amongst them. Perhaps it was because they ate too many fermented grapes that it became difficult to get up and go hunting. The incurred laziness probably convinced them that building a hut for protection, initiating homegrown food and overseeing animal breeding was preferable to wandering the land with no particular place to go.

Wine has been called both a gift of God and the work of Satan; certainly it has always brought out the best and worst in people. But it was a man who was born in the Roman Empire in what is now Saudi Arabia that had the most devastating effect on the joys of wine drinking. Even if Arabian vintages were a little sandy, the more fertile regions of Syria, Iraq and the Yemmen produced a wine good enough to be a part of the daily life in sixth-century Mecca. Mohammed changed everything.

Mohammed did not write. When Gabriel spoke to him he repeated what he had been told to his disciples, who later wrote it all down. From these revelations we learn that the prohibition of wine in the Koran was the result of a change of heart. It had not always been so. Indeed wine had been seen as one of the joys of paradise to be indulged along with gambling. The single verse on which the prohibition of wine is based was dictated, we are told, as a result of an incident in Medina when his disciples were drinking together after dinner. One of his Meccan followers began to recite an uncomplimentary poem about the tribe of Medina, whereupon one of the Medinite followers picked up the meat bone from the table and hit the ribald Meccan on the head. It was only a flesh wound but Mohammed was distressed enough to ask the Almighty how to keep his disciples in order. The answer was unequivocal: 'Believers, wine and games of chance, idols and divining arrows, are abominations devised by Satan. Avoid them that you may prosper. Satan seeks to stir up enmity and hatred amongst you by means of wine and gambling, and to keep you from the remembrance of Allah and from your prayers. Will you not abstain from these?' The believers' answer was an emphatic yes and all the wine in Medina was poured promptly into the streets. Within ten years of his death in AD632 it was totally banned not only from Arabia but from every country that listened to his words. This included Egypt, Libya, Palestine, Syria, Mesopotamia and Armenia besides the whole of Arabia. Within another hundred years this was to spread to North Africa, Spain and Portugal, Sicily, Corsica, Sardinia and Crete, and western Asia as far as Samakand. That's a lot of lost sales for the early producers. With eighty lashes if you were caught disobeying, any Bacchanalian behaviour was soon tempered.

Four thousand years separates the known origins of wine developed in the fertile lands of the west and the establishment of an elite wine culture in Egypt. There is little known about viniculture before it reached the land of the pyramids. However, with the dry plains prone to flooding because of the bank-busting floods of the Nile, wine was never going to be easy to make. The problems of quality and conservation were not really conquered until 2500BC when the commercial and cultural links between Egypt and Crete were established and trade began in earnest.

The vine plant, being a climber, of course, was originally trained up trees, and still is in parts of Portugal. It saves on space, but with the difficulty of harvesting in this fashion, straight lines attached to trellises or wires are soon to become the norm. Probably originally grown within a package of various crops, the growing and harvesting of grapes had, however, become a fully fledged commercial enterprise, certainly in Greece, by the end of BC. It was possible to pack 25 to 30 litres into amphoras, those ungainly-looking but oddly attractive objects made from earthenware, with pointed bases and bodies that broaden at the shoulders, and often have two handles to ease the transport. They were exported to here, there and everywhere usually by sea.

Rome was being busy, too. The Etruscan wine industry was feeding, or drinking, the rapidly expanding populace of Rome who had grown to over a million inhabitants by the beginning of the Christian era. In AD79 with the eruption of Vesuvius, the important wine-shipping port of Pompeii was buried under a hundred feet of ash, annihilating the vine-rich hinterland. The subsequent shortage of wine and the inevitable higher prices encouraged far too many people to start growing vine. It became a big race to replace those vineyards that had been lost and to cash in generally. Net result was that a few years later there was a glut of the stuff. A wine lake.

The Roman statesmen started controlling how much land was given over to the grape, setting market practices and pushing the export up into the parts of Europe that they dominated. Although it was the Greeks who introduced wine to Marseille, it was the Romans who really peddled it to the Gauls. From Marseille it spread quickly within Provence and onto Languedoc. It was there that it extended into Bordeaux in the first century and by the third it had arrived in Burgundy. It dispersed itself like pollen on the wind. All the time people were fine-tuning the art of viniculture, and the blessed liquid was not only constantly evolving but becoming readily available to an ever-expanding audience, as we know it ultimately spread as far north as Alsace and even Britain. It was indecently popular because it tasted good, raised your spirits and gave you confidence; further, if treated with respect, it left you alone to carry on the next day. It was a drug, legal and minimally damaging if controlled. Same as today.

I should tell you though that Plato, whilst condemning drunkenness because it produced an anti-rational state, did suggest that it might be beneficial for older people. Drunkenness, he argued, was a means by which the old could recapture their youthful spontaneity. With relaxed inhibitions they would dance and sing. He didn't say at exactly what point he considered people 'older' but going to a football match the other night I imagine he meant anyone over fourteen.

But wine was also attributed therapeutic and health-giving properties. Hippocrates, he of the oath, commented widely on the relationship of various types of wine and digestion. He urged to go with the soft wines as they encourage the whole digestive system to perform better, whereas the harsher wines, being more dry and hot, have something purgative about them.

One summer's morning an invitation for dinner arrived at the office from my chums at the Château Vignelaure in Pertuis. Mr and Mrs David O'Brien were hosting a 'Black Tie' soirée for the *Confrérie des Echansons du Roi René* or the Brotherhood of King René's Cupbearers.

I accepted their kind invitation and a few weeks later dug out my much underused white tux and readied myself for the hooley. There is the usual moment of trepidation as you check in to see if the old jacket fits quite as well as it used to. You know it won't, of course, it's purely a measure to see if you can actually get away with wearing it at all. I reckoned I could if I didn't do up the middle button and kept my shirt sleeves short.

I have had a happy friendship with Vignelaure for several years, ever since the O'Briens invited me to sort out and reinstate the gardens there. Having resigned from a successful horse-training career in Ireland, David O'Brien and his delightful Mrs bought the *château* as a just-going concern some ten years ago and through hard work, wily nous and commendable chancing have brought it back to everything it ever was, plus some.

Driving through the Coombe, the winding road that transports hundreds of people every day through the Luberon hills, the sun was beating off the towering cliff-face and igniting the silver underbelly of the poplars' foliage, highlighting the green oaks and casting deep shadows into the inner crevices of the valley. Emerging on the far side, the broken white fields of wheat were as textured as an expensive carpet.

It was a dreamy drive and, taken slowly, the meditative conditions laid waste to most of my negative thoughts about losing creative inspiration, being dulled by aloneness or even doubting where to live. Like most people I adore a good bout of self-pity from time to time, but recently it wasn't washing so well. It was high time, I thought, to stop blaming France, mucked-up marriages, other people, myself and anything else I could think of, and start rebuilding the blocks. By the time I had arrived in Pertuis I had posed three questions that needed to be answered.

Do you want to continue living in Provence?

The answer was, I thought, yes.

Do you want to continue working as a gardener in the South of France?

That one was a more definite yes.

Do you want to get married again?

I drew a blank on that one.

At the *château* porters directed the car to a parking space and, as I climbed out, I noticed the man next to me putting on a turquoise embroidered jacket over dark-blue trousers. He had attached an army of medals, which pulled down one side of his bizarre garment, and had slipped on a pair of white gloves. His wife wasn't giggling so I had to suppose he was serious. I felt underdressed already. I hadn't got any medals other than the ones my grandfather had left me, and I was never quite confident enough of what he had won them for to dare show them off in public.

There must have been 150 people gathered in the garden (which was looking very good indeed, I'm happy to report). It was full of V.I.D.s (Very Important Dignitaries), but with all that ermine and black velvet, cloaks, robes and funny medieval headgear it was hard to tell. We looked like a meeting between druids and extras from a Robin Hood movie.

In fact, the Roi René the invitation had referred to was originally known as Good King René. Born in Angers in 1409, he went down in history as the Wine-grower King, son of Louis II, King of Scillily and Duke of Anjou. He also held a remarkable collection of other titles: Duke of

Lorraine, King of Naples and even the King of Jerusalem. A true scholar, he wrote romances, poems and treatises of moral philosophy; and built up a circle of writers and artists. Also an enthusiast with a real passion for wine-growing and wine, he introduced Provençal vineyards into most of Europe's royal courts, thus contributing to the increase of the wine's popularity. He founded a brother-hood and gave its Grand Masters the title of Knight and the right to carry a sword. His statue, dressed in all his finery and holding a bunch of grapes in his hand, dominates the Cours Mirabeau in Aix, where he died in 1480, and also stands on the Boulevard du Roi René in Angers. He was quite a king.

The brotherhood I was meeting that night was revived in the twentieth century with a view to promoting Coteaux d'Aix-en-Provence wines, the art of good living in the surrounding countryside, the quality of its products and the inhabitants' joy of life, in addition to the literary, artis-tic and scientific spirit of the beautiful city of Aix-en-Provence, which, for centuries, was the capital of the province and the seat of its parliament.

The brotherhood of King René's cupbearers currently boasts 600 members from all walks of life and its main activities include organising two 'chapters' each year: a summer chapter on a wine-making estate (Vignelaure, that evening), and a winter chapter in the city. Fifty of the brotherhood's members are entitled to wear robes that are an exact copy of those worn during the Middle Ages.

Cast amongst a concourse of weird wine masons, I made

a line for Mrs O'B for reassurance that I hadn't let myself in for anything too kinky. If it was clothes off at midnight and sacrificing wine maidens on altars made from old barrels to the pounding beat of a Duran Duran hit, it was beyond my parameters.

However, the ceremony, it turned out, was partly for the initiation of fifteen candidates into the brotherhood and partly for the title of cupbearer. They have to be presented by two patrons and are subject to the approval of the Great Council. One or two honorary cupbearers are invited along as guests during these chapters, and are held in high esteem. The chosen few had to be considered reputable and worthy of inclusion into this special wine fraternity.

Fortunately for the organisers, the *château* at Vignelaure lends itself splendidly to such an occasion. It has a double-sided swooping staircase which rises proudly up onto a terrace outside the long windows of the first floor. For dramatic purposes, it couldn't be topped. We, the audience, sat nobly on our white plastic stacking chairs below, looking up adoringly at the team above. Two trumpeters, dolled up in long robes and funny hats with bits that looked like warmers for long-eared rabbits, pointed their long horns into the evening sky and blew their heraldic hearts out. As the puffy notes died, a strong young subaltern with more strange headgear and lugs, covered in a robe that Michael Heseltine would have adored, stepped formally forward and announced the next aspirant.

First up, I was reliably informed, was the head of the French Air Force. Dressed in mufti, he regimented up the steps and then, standing as straight as a white line, was introduced to us by the druid standing next to him. Then, from behind the swishing skirts of the men in robes, came a girl who was dressed the same only looking marginally less silly. Her job was to pass a pen to the person of the moment so that he or she could sign the register. This managed, she awarded the knight his scroll and then melted back into a silky obscurity.

Without a wasted second, another wine mason announced himself to us. He was a big man with a huge moustache and held a shallow chalice which he passed slowly and deliberately to the recipient, who raised it to his lips and sipped. And sipped. And sipped. Finally he finished and a gong was hung round his neck. With tangible pride he was soon heading down the steps, a bigger man than when he went up.

Next to ascend was one little Chinese lady, who struggled bravely to finish the bowl of wine, then was nearly brought to her knees by the great medal round her neck.

The ceremony dragged on. Deeply gratifying for the newly appointed serfs, it became something of a trial for the spectators as name after name was called out. Then, out of the soporific continuance came the call to arms for what must have been the daughter of bull-breeding parents. Stockily built with an open smile, she swung up the stairs with a gamely gait, knocked back the swill with one enormous glug, held the chalice aloft and heartily shook the well-furred official's hand. The cheers went up and, provoked by a kind of cathartic relief to the essential boredom of the occasion, everyone went momentarily quite over the top.

The presentations went on and on, and I watched the recipients being humbled and overjoyed by their reward, their sense of achievement sharpened to new heights. How dreadful to be waiting in the wings hoping you would be included, only to discover you hadn't made it.

Exactly what all these people had done to deserve being gonged was unclear to me. Some seemed to be wine producers, others merchants and entrepreneurs, and still more probably blenders and general oenologists. But if we had had the head of the F.A.F, then who else might there be? Disguised spies, French Open winners, bottle-jugglers or possibly Inland Revenue officers? The last 'gong' went to Mrs Catherine O'Brien, and a popular call it was, too.

Dinner was served in several marquees set up outside in the vast courtyard. In the fading light it looked as romantic as a scene from *A Midsummer Night's Dream*. Music fell softly on the night air and the thousands of candles guided everybody towards their tables. But first we were taken on a well-orchestrated walk through the cellars and vats on our way from the terrace to the tents.

One surprise of Vignelaure is the small but significant art collection hung in the centre of the cellars. In amongst the caves of wine, where bottles neatly lie down, comes this unexpected bonus. There is a painting by Welch Roger which shows a man and woman playing chess with the Riviera in the background – simple enough until you realise it is painted onto the side of an ancient water bottle – a

charming figurative work by Bernard Buffet of a little girl
getting dressed behind her father as he reads a letter, and a
kind of collage by Miralda Antoni, which had a weird sort
of eroticism about it in a pop art kind of a way. I would
happily have taken the whole collection home with me.
There were also some succinctly delightful photographs by
Henri Cartier Bresson, none more suitable than the shot of
an old boy in his Sunday best, the worse for wear and tear,
sitting at a table glass in hand, gazing at a half-full magnum
and watched over by a painting of a disapproving grandma
on the mantelpiece. It works because it doesn't seem
staged at all, just a captured moment of gentle inebriation
on a Sunday afternoon.

An excellent, professionally catered dinner was cajoled
along by the Mayor of Aix, sniffing, tasting and pouring the
best reds that Vignelaure could offer. He was, of course,
enormously experienced in this particular corner of his
ambitions and I thought about how his nose must have
sniffed round the edges of more barrels than a brewery
worker.

I was just tasting the '99 Vignelaure with a wedge of
cheese when there was a bit of a commotion coming
from the corner of the marquee set aside for dancing. Bob
and the Zimmer Men were tuning up. One little old man,
who should have been in a cage he was such a pet, was
opening a case bigger than himself. From it he extracted an
enormous tenor sax, and with commendable dexterity
manoeuvred himself onto a chair with the instrument half
resting on the floor and half against his diminutive body.

The others hobbled about, twisting the taps on their guitars and running a slow trace over the snare. Then quite suddenly, and totally unexpectedly, they blew as one. The jazz simply flew across the tent, rhythms and riffs arresting one and all as it passed by. It was seventy years of showmanship flying off the walls of syncopated glory. There wasn't a still foot in the house, and before you could say Jungle Book nearly everybody was up and dancing.

This wasn't a drunken, reckless gathering like you might imagine a dinner celebrating the myths and mysteries of grape crushing to be. In fact, it had been rather surprising to notice during dinner how nobody had seemed to really get stuck into the competing 2003 and 2004 rosés during the first course or the 1997 and 1999 reds thereafter. Instead we had a congregation of tame sippers and swillers. These obnoxious little habits that wine-heads have are bad enough if it is only one or two people practising, but a room full of sommeliers is worse than being at a brass band practice. Never mind. I watched as the swing took the movers and shakers to heady heights of abandonment on the dance floor, leaping and skipping about playfully. It's good to dance. It took a moment or two for the less daring members of the fraternity to overcome their rusty steps and shake off any self-conscious gaucheness, but as they picked up the beat their spirits soared, jackets were removed and their rosy faces were flushed with a rekindled spirit.

It wasn't the Stones but I was still having a whale of a time chair-dancing. As I had gone to the party on my own, I didn't quite know who to approach for a quick boogie. It certainly wasn't going to be the Mayor's wife, I hadn't had enough of the '99 to manage that, so I just sat out at the table for a while. I was soon joined by a charming Frenchman who confessed he would rather deliver himself naked to the fiery gates of hell than romp around with his peppery old wife. We fell into discussing rugby and *'le foot'* instead and as our respective countries were now both out of the UEFA cup it was easy to get on and knock all the other competing countries.

However, with the prospect of a longish drive home and feeling exhausted from solemnising, I bade my new best friend *bon nuit* and left the warmth of the summer tent with its music and candles, frolicking dignitaries and full-bodied wines, and headed home, happy to have been included in this particular area of viniculture. I was beginning to feel like a bit of an authority, which bit of which authority had yet to be defined but in the shadow of that summer's full moon I reckoned that Vignelaure's wine was good and their garden even better. Maybe I should carry on.

A telephone call a few days later confirmed that I had been commissioned to design a garden in the south of Portugal. This was good news, not just because I liked the challenge of the site, but it meant a change of scenery, it was away from home and I would gain work experience in a country I had only visited on holiday.

The house was built about twenty-five years ago when going down to the deserted sea-shore for my clients meant a fifteen-minute walk through the serenely quiet pine

woods, where the only tracks were made by locals and the
chance of getting anything to eat depended on the catch of
the day. It has now become crowded with grandiose villas.
Wide-lapelled developers knock up ever more august con-
structions dripping with classical references including pal-
adin garages ready for their starry clientele. Places that hold
a quartet of principal motor cars and regularly include
Porsches, Bentleys, Range Rovers and clutches of Mini-
Cooper Cabriolets for the new kids on the block. Even the
main avenue is named after Ayrton Senna, so if you're not
into golf, football or cars, you might as well forget it. The
plots of land get ever smaller and the buildings upon them
ever bigger. The gardens are all the same coming from the
limited repertoire of a rationalised landscaper who under-
stands that to use more than a dozen varieties of indigenous
plants would be uneconomic. He favours the block-buying
of easily available plant stock and plugs it in between strategically placed rocks with insufficient root space for growth
(there's more money to be had in replacements). For a few
years the overblown display seeks and finds attention then,
exhausted, begs for some loving understanding.

Fearing the implacable encroachment of the developer's
machinery and the terrible subsequent loss of privacy, my
clients did the only sensible thing left for them to do; they
started buying up the land, or lots, that surrounded them.
At least on their own compound they could feel distanced
from the golden sportsmen, the delegating drug dealers and
zombied lottery winners. That is where I came in. Having
bought the costly real estate, they needed to reconcile it

with their existing garden. To make a continuity of space and a logical progression in terms of their cultivated grounds, letting it bleed out into a controlled wildness. To keep a calm naturalness whilst achieving a relatively easy-to-maintain link with the house.

Whilst nothing was going to be done until after the holiday season, the property was after all a summer holiday home for the family, and the family was extensive, it was a good job to have for the winter months.

The same day a meeting had been arranged with a young *maçon* who wanted to show me his work. He had rung and convinced us that we needed him, and that his portfolio was certainly worth looking at. Having been working in the Luberon for seven years it was not unusual to be approached by local tradesmen. They had heard that a Brit was garden busy and that most of the contracts required stone masons, electricians and plumbers, and it was and is my pleasure to meet them. We might be useful to each other.

But Alfred was something else. He arrived covered from head to foot in smile. He was a small, square fellow emanating friendliness and an irresistible bonhomie. We shook hands and without delay he started to make fun of first the Brits, then gardeners, people of my age (the music that was on in the background prompted that one) and inevitably my use of his beloved language. He was little more than thirty and the only lines on his face were around his eyes, betraying a hopeless inability not to smile or laugh at life. He was as good an example of the French likely lad as I had ever seen.

He explained that he had worked for his father for seven years and now, well trained, he had ideas of setting up on his own. He opened his plastic folder, which was well stacked with digital printouts of various walls, steps, pillars and piers. Mostly it was predictable stuff but well executed. Then he proudly opened a double-page-spread that showed a huge circular garden that rose gently towards the centre where an inner circle of retaining walls and converging pathways met a highly disciplined pond. The stonework was intricately detailed and the wall containing the rising ground had been meticulously graded using ever-decreasing sizes of stone. The grass and planting were maturing well and the overall effect deserved the double page he had given it.

'I like that,' I said, 'it is very well constructed. Did it take you a long time to build?'

Alfred managed to smile his way through some kind of explanation, shrugging and poofing, *alor*-ing and *donc*-ing and then started to turn the page, ready to burst forward with another fine project.

I put my hand on the page and held the double-spread open. 'Tell me, Alfred, did you design this project or just build it?'

'Oh no, I just built it,' he said, trying to move on.

It was my turn to beam. I looked at him and said, 'You see, I designed this a couple of years ago for Monsieur and Madame Apport, and it was constructed under my supervision by a *maçon* called Gene and his assistant Julian. It is near Bonnieux. Would you like to see the drawings?'

To his credit Alfred held his ground and, looking me straight in the eye, asked, 'Would you like to see some other things that I haven't done?'

Now three years further down the line Alfred and his working partner, David, and I have done a considerable amount of work together, some of it pretty advanced requiring highly developed technical skills. His constant good humour may well mask a tormented soul for all I know, but he is a constant lift to the spirit to all who surround him on any site. His humour is often at my expense as he plays to the gallery of his co-workers who wonder at his ability to wind up the boss (Brit or not) and get away with it. His cheeky chappiness is indulged although occasionally he has the most appalling things said to him in English by me that he cannot begin to comprehend. In fact I hone and practise my English workman's vocabulary of abuse on our Alfred, the Billingsgate slang landing lightly on the comedian who shows neither trace of insult nor outrage.

'If you don't get my house finished by the end of July I'm fucked,' I said down the phone-line to the contractor of my new home. It was now so overdue that I had nowhere to live. I couldn't stay at the rented *gîte* any more, as the lease had run out. I couldn't crash in my office in Lacoste any more, because a gap-year student was working there along with one of my assistants. The man had promised that the house would be ready for full occupation by the end of May, then the end of June and now it was nearly the end of July. I suspected the end of August wasn't going to do it either. I had no proper room for my child to hang out in when he came to stay with me and a final divorce hearing in Avignon at the beginning of September. I was grown up pissed off with the guy. It was so damned difficult to work quite apart from to live. I didn't know where to put my computer, drawing board or secretary. I lost my sense of humour, my ability to be friendly and, worst of all, the confidence to assure clients that all was well. I knew it was temporary and that it would soon pass, but in the sweaty moments of doubt I felt like a very fat man wading through his own body.

I headed off to a bar in St Saturnin, laptop under my arm and a few sheets of reference notes, ordered a *demi-pression* and settled down to work. As the sacrosanct hour of midday approached I asked for a cheese sandwich only to be told that they were not doing sandwiches that day. 'Best go down to the swimming pool,' the waiter informed me. 'They do them there.'

It was hot outside, probably 35 degrees, and nigh on shadeless. I virtually ran from the bar across the road and down the hill to the municipal bathing pool. I went in to the area where a cement shed had lifted its wooden flap to reveal not only cheese sandwiches but ice creams with additives, soft drinks with too much sugar and microwaved hamburgers. Heaven!

I stole a little shade from a small family and watched the proceedings. It was an uplifting and humbling experience. Here in a massive curved pool targeted by a merciless sun, the people of St Saturnin swam, plunged, jumped and dived. The children, instead of swimming in the protection of their own private pool with perhaps one or two friends, were out in force. Instant teams for water games: tag, polo, diving for discs, bombing and racing. This was proper fun. This was much much better than a personal pool if you were anywhere between six and sixteen. It was a social gathering, a shake down of personalities and a surf party all rolled into one. As the afternoon wore on, the pool emptied a bit and fathers without jobs sat helping. The cry for work may have been prevalent but it was far removed from the terrible sadness of an English pub on a wet afternoon with its extended opening hours. No hollow-eyed desperadoes sitting at the bar waiting for time to pass while others sleep in the corner surrounded by torn-up betting slips. A hot summer's day in a Mediterranean climate is different. Sunshine doesn't make the bogeyman disappear or the horses win but it makes him a whole lot easier to deal with. Fact.

Tom MacArthur rang and asked me to dinner. 'Just me, Jiminie and Georgie-Lou and perhaps Gertrude, my neighbour. She never confirms until she knows what's on the menu,' he said in his usual blithe way.

I happily accepted and at eight o'clock delivered myself into his kitchen. Gertrude had evidently decided that not only was the food on offer agreeable but it was worth taking photographs of. Loaded with big heavy cameras, digital and non-digital, lenses that slid in and out and knobs that pulled focus, she set about snapping the proceedings like the whole thing was a shoot for a major magazine. Which is exactly what it turned out to be.

Gertrude, it transpired, worked freelance for various glossies, had long since established herself as something of a food photographer, and had decided that the simple fare of a Provençal summer's night supper in the heart of a vine-yard merited at least a couple of rolls. 'Could tie it in with a feature on Americans living the second home dream,' she said. At seventy-three Gertrude was in a commanding position. Her work was well known and her fees were as big as her personality. Tom had produced huge bowlfuls of colourful salads, plates burgeoning with slices of fowl and an array of cheeses enough to make a restaurant trolley blush. Homegrown bottles of wine, uncorked and ready to go, fresh bread from the afternoon's bake, sauces, dips and dressings. The big kitchen table waited patiently to be attacked. Gertrude was already clicking away. In the background Miles Davis edged in on the proceedings a little too early to be smooth. I wasn't sure if I had just dropped by to see a friend or had won a competition to be part of a *New Yorker* article.

Jiminie sat in the corner watching TV saying very little while Tom burst around the room like a Delia Smith dumpling. Then Georgie-Lou came in. The first thing I always noticed about her was her enormous smile. It wrapped around you like a comfort blanket, making you welcome her as a long-time friend. Dressed in an old leather jacket, jeans and T-shirt she suggested that nobody

had ever worn anything like it before. Her hair fitted loosely around her head, her earrings glistened, and her soft, big
mouth was painted with deep-red lipstick. She cut one hell
of a figure. I had a feeling I had been on my own for too
long already.

Conversation covered food and wine, discussing the
mysteries of *botrytis* or Noble Rot, that peculiar fungus that
with the help of morning mists in autumn is encouraged to
hit upon the vine. Then, after a sticky dialogue about the
French foreign minister, Gertrude was onto Formula One.
She was, it seemed, a keen fan of motor racing in general
and of Michael Schumacher in particular. Georgie-Lou
muttered about the thrill of being driven very fast and
Jiminie said he wished he was a jockey.

We drank enough Château Tom to feel lousy the next
day, talked about tasting some of the wine that my French
leave would produce and looked at the photographs on the
laptop that Gertrude had taken. They were slightly odd, as
is her style, but undoubtedly interesting. Her next book she
announced was going to be called *Diets for Deserted
Duncans*, this being slang for overweight husbands or part-
ners that had been cleaned out, evicted or abandoned by
their much younger spouse. Or at least it was in Gertrude's
circle of cronies in Manhattan. (I didn't dare tell her that it
was my second name.) The idea of the book was that a balance of sensible eating and come-on photographs would
encourage the wounded soldier to get back into shape,
make another fortune and score with smart girls again. 'Ah
the illusion of hope, the aspiration of achievement and the

denial of failure,' I said. 'It sounds like an advertisement to me.'

'I loathe advertising photography,' she said. 'Over-paid, over-Photoshopped and over-done. Anyway, I'm well past any market targeting. Ain't nobody gonna try and seduce me with their product so why should I waste time with it?' She wasn't looking for an answer.

I went for a walk under the starry sky with Georgie-Lou and Jiminie MacArthur. I asked Georgie-Lou if she would be kind enough to turn me into a Duncan and she said she might at that. Jiminie promised he would if all else failed.

Chapter Ten

It was mid-July in London and a brisk wind was blowing up from the south. The English were being cheated of their summer again. Amongst the morning commuters spewing out of the Sloane Square underground were girls bravely wearing light cotton dresses, which the wind huffed tightly against their bodies, and men who were stoically directing their briefcases. The cafés, ever-optimistic, dressed their outdoor tables as if it were another beautiful day of sunshine and shimmering heat. Everywhere people rushed hither and thither in denial that summer had tossed in another broken promise.

Earlier I had bumped into a French friend on the King's Road; we had headed for the Bluebird Café for sustenance.

As it wasn't actually raining, an outside table it was. Some sort of French breakfast was ordered, our collars pulled up, and I listened to her talk about how she used to smoke thousands of cigarettes a day. However, it had been a late night, she said, and with strong coffee in the air, not to have a cigarette was tough. But it passed and we were soon chatting about who was doing what to whom and why it worked. Mid-sentence the sky cracked and a fang of lightning split the air. Seconds later came a rumble of menace and on its heels a downpour. When an *orage* hits in the South of France, everybody retreats indoors, grabbing any cushions that may be lying around. But here in the leafy suburbs of Chelsea people carried on. Afforded minimal protection by a small canopy the conversation hardly dipped. The watered-down cappuccinos and soggy croissants were gallantly consumed with British flair.

I was in the UK for two reasons. Firstly I had read about how the English wine-growers were gaining a reputation for producing a product that could hold its own against the big boys and wanted to check it out. Secondly I wanted to visit the Chelsea Physic Garden. Over the last few months I had been hanging out in some of the richest, most elegant wine-growing regions of France with the promise of even more to come. I had found myself spending afternoons dipped in classical and oriental gardens, fruit orchards, lavender fields and cultivated lakes. I was in need of some British balance. As the Chelsea Flower Show had come and gone, I was keen to catch the Physic Garden doing its summer thing.

This unique horticultural gem was founded in 1673 as the Apothecaries' Garden, with the purpose of training apprentices in identifying plants. The location was chosen as the proximity to the river created a warmer microclimate allowing the survival of many non-native plants – such as the largest outdoor fruiting olive tree in Britain – with the added bonus of attracting a diverse roll-call of birds. The fact that the garden is close to the Thames, the practice of leaving seed heads to develop, the provision of bird boxes and feeders and the minimal use of chemicals actively encourages bird life. There have even been a few rare migrant visitors: kingfisher, willow warbler and the spotted flycatcher amongst others. And the odd pigeon, of course.

Having lived in or around Chelsea for most of my London life I miss not only the Physic Garden, but also the small private gardens that open under the National Gardens Scheme, the bijou garden shops and of course the Chelsea Flower Show itself. Every May acres of canvas marquees are erected with military precision so that the best growers, designers, manufacturers and experts can gather together for a few magnificent days to proudly celebrate their undying passion for gardening. No other gardening show comes close and nobody cares if it rains – that's normal.

I had planned my tasting trip round my adopted country to culminate in Champagne in September, so I felt I should at least take a sniff and sip of the best of British in July. After all, much of southern England had been planted with vines by the Romans, and the geological structure of the terrain was similar to the successful vineyard areas of northern France, including Alsace and Champagne. If Germany could do it then surely Blighty couldn't be far behind. Additionally it would be interesting to see how much space and commitment an English vineyard might give to its surrounding garden. Much more, I thought, than the French.

The wind made it difficult to read a paper at the bus stop. Wrestling with the flapping pages of the *Daily Sport*, I gave up waiting for the bus and made a dash for it. I had a car booked with Hertz in Victoria, which would normally be a pleasant enough walk through Chelsea and Pimlico, taking in the antique shops and small art galleries, the shoe shops and markets.

There were going to be three of us and my two chums were not skinny. Constructed around solid frames, we all had a little extra padding in case of world starvation and the breaking down of the western world's economy. However, the back door of the Hertz would not close, so they upgraded me to a sparkling new silver Mercedes convertible. I wasn't sure who was going to cram in the back but as it wasn't me I showed little interest. I thought there would be precious little opportunity to flip the lid, but the renter was emphatic. 'Suits you, sir,' he said. 'Imagine the fun you'll have on the roads with this little pearl. You'll feel twenty years younger even if you don't look it.'

I sat inside and asked the attendant to demonstrate how to drop the roof should I need to. He pointed to a button, I pressed, it didn't do anything.

Half an hour later, three Hertz men were kicking, tugging and pushing as I screamed that I just wanted to leave this hell-hole multi-storey car park. Next they rolled in a Mercedes 4x4 with blacked-out windows and bling wheels. Robust and menacing, I figured it would do for the M25. Trouble was, they had to change all the rental papers.

Two hours later I left, incapable of politeness.

I had forgotten how elevated one was in an SUV, how superior. Suddenly I was eye to eye with about 85 per cent of the other drivers in London. It was early mid-morning and all the other drivers were young women. Most were wearing dark glasses behind dark glass but at least they felt safe enough to look at you, even smile, darkly, sometimes. If only ephemerally, I had joined that off-the-wall, off-the-road 4x4 executive club sponsored by Range Rovers, BMWs and even Porsche.

Having bullied and caressed my way through the central London traffic in equal parts, I drove boldly up onto the pavement, or half onto it, got out to give the lads a call, then turned round to get back in the car only to find that an absurdly over-uniformed Nigerian had pinned a £50 ticket on my screen. He seemed to have materialised out of the exhaust fume ether like an avenging angel.

'You can't have given me a ticket already?' I said.

'Well, it's not exactly *given*, sir,' he said. 'More like sold, if you see what I mean.'

My instant anger was absorbed by an understanding nod and a gentle, compassionate smile. 'I know sir,' he said, 'it's very frustrating. But you must understand that just because we are on commission for every car we book doesn't mean we hate you, the driver.'

I bundled the boys into the wagon and we were off.

We were going to the largest privately owned vineyard in Europe and it was just outside Dorking.

The dark rolling grey sky continued to spread out over the English landscape and the rain threatened to strike before the afternoon. It didn't take long to discover Denbies vineyard, which nestles in the Mole Valley on Surrey's North Downs.

We were met by Christopher White, the genial general manager and son of the owner. A highly focused young businessman, he knows exactly how to make money out of a vineyard and it wasn't all to do with grapes. In fact, he struggled to answer some of the more specific questions that were put to him about wine-making, but he was the main man and held a high general knowledge of Denbies as a £4 million turnover growing concern. To achieve such a figure it is necessary to diversify. I had seen it up to a point in Burgundy with Georges Duboeuf but here, in a catchment area of prosperous retirement, Denbies had made sure that when you dropped in to buy a bottle of the home-grown you uncorked a whole new world.

The *château*, for want of a better word, used to be somewhat less romantically a pig and cattle fattening farm until 1984 when Adrian White purchased the estate. Now there are 265 acres under vine. By comparison the average size of the other 400 English holdings is 6 acres. They produce about 350,000 bottles each vintage and grow over a dozen different varieties of grape. A bit of French – Chardonnay and Pinot Noir – and lots of German, such as Reichensteiner and Dornfelder. Their techniques are whizzingly up to the minute with tools like Eco-friendly sprayers, which recycle up to 70 per cent of all spray thanks to covering the vines in protective curtains, 800 diesel heaters battle the huge losses that late frosts can cause as well as clever vine guards that deter deer, rabbits and birds from damaging the shoots. At any one time there can be up to fourteen wines in the range through all three colours.

Mr White junior explained that three of the major supermarket chains stocked their wines but this was really just a PR exercise as there was little profit selling at that level. The main income came from what they refer to as the Visitor Centre, a well-designed, flint-clad building with handmade roof tiles and pretty coloured bricks designed by a firm of local architects. It manages to cater for just about any occasion, including garden parties and wedding receptions, provides a conference hall and lecture rooms, a performing arts library, a picture gallery showing local talent – or lack of it – and, of course, several restaurants. It is all interconnected by a glass box lift that slips seamlessly up and down one of the interior walls, proving popular with bored grandchildren – and me.

The courtyard was by far the most successful part of the landscaping works. With a cloistered surround, the area in the middle was planted up with neatly pruned rows of vine at about 2m high growing out of a well-mown lawn. It was simple and effective. Outside, at the entrance the gardening was predictable. Shrub beds with all the usual crew: hypericum, lavender, conifers, viburnum, senecio *et al.* From the eaves of the roof, hanging baskets brimmed with petunias and geraniums. About the only unusual planting were the Bohemian olives, *Elaeagnus angustifolia*, otherwise it was all out of the rationalised landscape book for unimaginative gardeners. Minimum choice, maximum return.

There is also a gift super-shop. Just how many things you can stretch into having an association with wine is staggering, and all these possibilities are on show in the emporium. About the only thing missing was a zimmer frame with a glass-holder and wine-cooler attachment. But before we were let loose on the wine-tasting, we were taken down to the indoor station to experience 'A Voyage of Discovery'. This was an internal tour lasting about forty-five minutes that kicks off with an impressive 360-degree cinema showing a vineyard in England. Then it was onto 'the People Mover' train, a sort of docile big-dipper that hurtled along at one mile an hour taking us through every stage of a working winery, where modern technology meets the ancient art of wine-making. All the time a comforting Radio 4 voice talked to us through the little carriage's loudspeaker, explaining in a kindly, almost soporific way just how wonderful it all was. Then like a ghost train, we suddenly veered to the left, shot down a slope, skidded dangerously round a corner and found ourselves whipping along past twelve posters showing the state of a vine bush during each month of the year. Next it whipped out through a curtain to be met by a cadaverous lady offering us a chance to taste the wine. Or at least three of the white wines.

First she poured out an offering of Surrey Gold, a perfectly drinkable medium-dry white wine with good aromas and a hint of spice. This was followed by the drier Flint Valley, another German cousin, which was quite delicately oaked with hints of vanilla. After these last few months I have become quite familiar with the custom of looking and sniffing, sucking and swilling and then unglamorously spitting the whole thing out into the spittoon. I hardly think about it any more but when I did it here in Dorking it was just behind an elderly lady's back. I don't think she had realised that the spittoon was just behind her, or indeed would have known what it was for, because when I loudly spat out my load, she twirled round and looked at me as if I was a delinquent throwing up after a bingeing night down the pub. She dug her husband in the ribs, which knocked him off balance and just as he was about to polish off his measure it spilt all over his waistcoat.

'Oh come on,' cried another, 'it's not that bad!'

'Do you need a doctor, dear?' asked a kindly old girl, steadying herself on her stick. 'I'm sure there must be one in the house.'

I felt like explaining that what with the speed of the train, the hot sun outside and perhaps just a little too much fine English wine I was feeling a little off-colour but I didn't. Instead I asked for some water, washed out my palate to even more ripples of shock and horror, and held my glass out for the next tipple. Further down the cellar a group of suits were studying a series of large, oval, English oak barrels (oval allows more contact with the wood, you see). Resting on their heavy stands, each barrel was complete with hand carvings that would have pleased Grinling Gibbons and in turn depicting Pruning, Training, Harvesting, Pressing, Maturation, Bottling, Tasting. In other words the seven stages of wine-making.

When we emerged back into the fray of reception our genial host asked, 'Would you like to take the Vineyard Train? It is specially for disabled, infirm and elderly visitors.' He looked at me and the boys with a resigned understanding. 'It will take you to visit some of the most spectacular spots in the vineyard. The round trip takes about half an hour with two short stops to let you enjoy the panoramic views.'

Without looking at one another, we free kings legged it to the mega merchandising outlet where a bar in the corner encouraged you to try their 'champagne' and some of the reds. Bluntly, not a good idea.

The sparkling wine attacked with huge aggressive bubbles, blowing you up like a helium balloon, and the reds, poor darlings, grieved their lack of sun. Admittedly young, they needed at least fifteen years to come round and were meanwhile just sad. The curiously named Yew Tree Pinot Noir 2002 was described by the girl behind the bar as a sumptuous and elegant red wine with a lavish blackcurrant bouquet and velvety richness. Well, she had clearly never tried it. At a pocket-bending £14 a bottle it was a shambles of unconnected ruderies. Ruinously dissonant, totally lacking in good manners, devoid of music and pompous for its age. Spotting the grimacing faces, the young lady conceded that it didn't drink well when it was so young. One of the chaps bought a couple of bottles in the spirit of the occasion to take back to London, but reported later that it didn't travel well.

When I told Tom I was visiting an English vineyard for the sake of comparison, I even told him that the standard of England's wine, especially the white, was on the up.

'Up to what?' he retorted. 'The only good thing about English wine is that it reminds you how good everybody else's is.'

I still bought him a bottle. Incredibly they sell a million bottles of their wines a year from this visitor centre alone. But if you study the average visitor you can see why. It makes for a day out, it's sociable and geared towards the superannuated. The shop offers a stupendous choice of 'gifts', including cleverly bottled grape juice for recovering alcoholics and children alike. Moreover, it has a gentle adventure built in. It is clever marketing of an ambiguous product, but as far as a vineyard goes it hovers at the perimeter of the game. Its existence owes much to the loyalty of locals and the support by regional supermarkets. It has a novelty value amongst tourists, and has managed to carve some kind of a niche, but it is a marginal player on the pitch of wine-making. It is impossible to imagine the French loading up their Renault Espaces with Dorking's best, and bending their axles as they rush for the ferry home. The whites might survive on the home market but the lack of heat from continuing sunshine should make their reds blush. There is no warmth in the English Pinot Noir.

We found lunch in a nearby pub and thought it honourable to order a bottle of something from Denbies but tellingly the house didn't stock it. 'No call for it,' said the barman. 'None at all. What about a Chilean red?'

The moon was up there somewhere, but on the night that I arrived back, my first ever in the new house, it was hiding. The clouds were heavy with undelivered rain and the welcoming smile of a deep summer's evening was absent.

I climbed out of the car with trepidation. I hadn't been on site for a couple of weeks and was not sure what to expect. There were no gates to the courtyard but the front door was locked. The shutters banged on their hinges and the key didn't fit. Well, it did, in fact, but in my anxious state my hand was insisting on using the wrong one. Gingerly I eased my way in and turned on a bare lightbulb. There was a smell of paint, which was encouraging, along with dust sheets, a cement-mixer, a thick blanket of dust and piles of unpacked boxes. I remembered how to find the kitchen, which was about half fitted, and turned on a tap. Hallelujah and praise the angels of displaced gardeners, it came through hot and wet.

Then the alarm went off. It had been cleverly set to allow enough time for a burglar to get in, rifle through the boxes and escape with whatever he fancied. If I had been stressed before I was now on heart attack alert. It was deafening my brain and I didn't know the code. Then the phone rang. Scrambling over half-lit furniture I edged towards the ringing, picked it up, yelled yes into the mouthpiece and was greeted by the burglar alarm company checking to see how the burglary was going.

In the event, sleep was easy. I was so tired by the time I had figured out where to find a mattress that I could have slept on the bare floor. Waking up was even easier, however. At eight sharp, a full battalion of builders, electricians, plumbers and decorators swung into action. The house was crawling with busy people. Why hadn't it always been like this? I wondered. It could have been finished months ago. Then it struck me. In a week's time it would be August and every French person known to man drops tools and goes on holiday. However, the mass attack on my house was not so much to do with getting it finished quickly for poor old Alex who is having to live amongst the debris, but with getting paid before they packed up for the summer.

It is depressing trying to get dressed when the decorator keeps dripping paint on your clothes, disconcerting trying to make a cup of coffee when the electrician keeps turning the power off, but downright constipating trying to go to the loo only to find a fat hairy plumber already using it and making a few phone calls at the same time.

I needn't have fretted about the difficult conditions affecting my son and heir. He arrived and, having made instant friends with the professional house cleaners, set about establishing his quarters. He thought the whole escapade 'awesome'.

By the time the August exodus was under way I was

happy to see the back of the building boys, even if the house still had a way to go. It was now clean, the courtyard, which wouldn't be turned into a garden for some time, was cleared of rubbish, a temporary wooden wall had been erected to keep strangers out and a veneer of tranquillity slowly descended. Like it or not, I was now in residence.

The sea of calm was soon broken by a phone call on the following Monday morning from Mr Dugard, the man responsible for the smooth running of a house renovation near Mousanne. Against my better judgement, I had agreed with the client to start the garden before the contractors had finished in order to try and speed things up. It is under-standable, of course; the more done at the same time, the less hassle for the owners when they move in. But it seldom works out. We had nearly completed the earthworks, shaped banks and changed levels, even sown a certain amount of grass seed. What shrub and tree planting there was had been kept away from the house, but delivery lorries, diggers and workmen's vehicles were parked randomly and carelessly.

To keep everything alive and let the grass seed germi-nate, irrigation was mandatory. In the height of the summer no water meant quick death so an automatic system had been expensively established. All things being equal it would tick away during the holiday break and we would return in September to find happy plants, long grass and big bruising weeds. But as usual, things weren't equal. Dugard told me that his digger driver must have accidentally ripped up the main irrigation pipe before the weekend and not noticed. It was completely severed, had been leaking mains water all over the place for two or three days, and would I get it fixed quickly.

'You broke it, you fix it,' I said.

'Not possible. All my men are on holiday and so am I. You are lucky I passed the site to make sure the gates were locked,' he said.

'I'm lucky? Did you say *I'm* lucky?' If I hadn't been working here for seven years I would not have believed it.

'*Oui, monsieur, très chanceux. Au revoir.*' And he was gone. He had probably locked the gates and I didn't have a key. Maybe I'll go back to work in Scotland, I thought. You don't have many garden irrigation problems there.

Despite the obstacles, by the evening it was all sorted out. But it had cost a lottery. Bribes and promises, applause and rewards were given by the skipload and the client never knew. At least, not before the water bill came in.

A few days after that the postman brought an invitation that read:

Jean-Claude Gaudin, Maire de Marseille, Vice-Président de Sénat, et Han Zheng, Maire de Shanghai, ont le plaisir de vous inviter à l'Inauguration du Jardin Traditionnel Chinois.

Thiebaud de Bechard, a delightful Frenchman, had obtained his degree in physics and marine biology in France and later capped it with a Masters from the University of South Carolina. This gave him a big lead over most people in our region when it came to creating lakes, ponds and cascades. Not a natural addition in the Luberon, you might say, but thanks to well-organised water collections and the canals of Provence and Les Alpilles, such augmentations to the landscape were now a real possibility, providing of course they were of the rubber-lined and re-circulating variety. Now running his own company 'T'bow' and I had, despite a twenty-year age gap, not only struck an alliance in work but had also become friends. Slightly encouraged by the fact that we were both imminently to be divorcees with young sons of about the same age, and aided by his command of English, or American, we had formed an easy relationship. Thiebaud had talked about a project he had been working on in Marseille that involved the Chinese government, but he had been vague and limited in his information. Then, at his discretion, I had received this invitation from the mayors of both Marseille and Shanghai to join them at the opening of a traditional Chinese garden, celebrating the close ties that both countries enjoyed with each other and their respective cultures, particularly gardening.

The ceremony was due to kick off at midday and, as the hour approached, we stood patiently outside the gates in the Parc Borély waiting for the main men to arrive. It was already hotter than a rude afternoon and people, dropping their dignity, hustled one another to gain shade from the big oaks and chestnuts. At last the cavalcade came swinging into view. About eight motorcycle outriders guarded the fast-moving snake of blacked-out limousines. With dazzling efficiency and army-like precision, the dark-suited, sunglass-wearing bodyguards importantly leaped out of the cars before they had completely stopped, made a show of adjusting their gun belts while scanning the crowd for would-be assassins, then opened the rear doors for the Very Important Mayors and the Very Important Mayors' Wives. These dignitaries were ceremonially met by what could have been either the Head Park-Keeper or the Deputy Chief Officer of the Foreign Affairs Bureau for all I knew. The V.I.M.s made their way into the closed-off area followed by lots of other important people, including T'bow and me. I wasn't sure if a few of them hadn't been at the Brotherhood of King René's Cupbearers garden gig at Vignelaure the other day or not, but there was a familiarity to some of the faces I'm sure.

The area designated for the Chinese Garden wasn't very big, not much more than one of the larger sites at the Royal Horticultural Shows. It was dominated by a large red and gold pavilion with the orthodox steep dipping roof that curls up at the corners. This in turn was connected to a smaller satellite pavilionette that stood up to its knees in water. It held a quintet of young musicians ready to play and sing some well-loved Chinese folk songs. The surrounding little pond was stocked up to the gills with oversized Koi carp that T'bow had installed just to make sure Mr Han Zheng felt secure. With all the to-be-expected little bridges, the ordinary use of planting and the predictable oriental accents, it was startlingly unoriginal and dull. To be reasonable, the invitation had said a traditional Chinese garden, but it would be a fine thing if the business dynamics of the commercially emerging country could have moved us away from the clichés and introduced us to some of their more evolved ideas.

Drinks were on offer but as the massive line-up of bottles was only beaten by the even bigger line-up of thirsty Franco-Chinese delegates we called it a day and slipped off to the old port of Marseille to find a quicker route through to a glass of beer and look at boats for a while.

It was the Phoenicians, over 2,600 years ago, who first set up residence on the shores near to Massalia, the settlement that is known today as Marseille. They cleared the coast and planted fruit and olive-trees and made the area a point of intense civilisation.

Then at around 600BC the Greeks took over and turned it into the most successful trading port in the west Mediterranean. While near the mouth of the Rhône, it was far enough away to avoid the common diseases associated with the swampy deltas of that region but sufficiently well located to develop the eastern trading routes. Three neighbouring cities were founded, Antibes, Nice and Monte Carlo, all in the eastern edge of France, and became important stops along the route to the east.

Marseille also traded heavily with the west but with the ceaseless harassment of her shipping from Carthage, especially when the cargo-laden ships passed the narrow straits between Sicily and Carthage, it was a salty struggle. Piracy was a government-supported way of life. It was no coincidence that when Hannibal marched across the Alps, he wisely avoided Massalia, entering the Alps further to the north.

When the Greeks introduced the grape to the area, they stimulated an extraordinary and radical change upon the inhabitants of the province, kick starting what is today some of the most famous vineyards known to man or beast.

By the eighteenth century Massalia, or Marseille, had become a truly international port enjoying worldly success. The culture of the vineyard and the olive tree continued to expand throughout the region, luxurious manors were built in Aix-en-Provence and long-distance trade developed through the harbour, which enjoyed untaxed exchanges with the Middle East and southern seas. Then, quite suddenly, it was struck by a catastrophe. The Great Plague. Quarantine was not sufficient, the plague swept through the town and, in May 1720, Marseille was cut off from the rest of Provence. The parliament in Aix forbade any communication with Marseille upon pain of death but it didn't stop and soon the whole country was touched by it. The city lost half its population and went into decline but you can't keep a good metropolis down and, apart from a dust-up with the Germans in August 1944, there has been calm and expansion in the capital of the south ever since.

Now that my house was up and trotting, the pressure to get the offices moved was mounting by the day. And this was meant to be holiday time.

We had no news from France Telecom about when they were coming to install lines or indeed what our new numbers were to be. We still waited for what seemed like an arbitrary decision by some engineer or planner as to whether we were going to be allowed to keep our old numbers and the mobile looked increasingly like being the only link between us and Planet Provence until people came back from the seaside.

Beyond this the business was busy turning itself into a S.A.R.L. (pretty much the French equivalent of a British limited company). To establish this more sophisticated form of trading it required depositing a prearranged sum of money with the bank, which had to guarantee paying the government should any business misdemeanour occur such as bankruptcy or tax evasion, for example. In the usual fashion of extreme bureaucracy the paperwork was stultifying. It involved government departments, banks, accountants, medicals, secretaries and total patience. Waiting for the induction into the society and the subsequent awarded company numbers, testimonials and certificates was just another test of extravagant fortitude. All this meant we couldn't get our new writing paper, invoice sheets or even change of address cards finished.

To further aggravate the molecules, recent French legislation demanded that all swimming pools must have either a 1.3m-high fence or a hard cover. This particular method necessarily requires a motorised unfolding system similar to the metal blinds that protect shop windows, or as a third possibility an alarm system could be installed that rings when a child breaks the circuit. As this is equally easily disturbed by dogs and drunks it is not much in demand. The hard covers are expensive and even more so if an existing pool has to be adapted so the 'enclosure' is the most popular alternative. In the panic of impending summer holidays we were spending more time erecting these rigs than anything else. And we were meant to be on holiday. They don't have many private swimming pools in Scotland.

The office had been packed into boxes and moved to the new house, except computer equipment, which had been moved to a more secure resting place, other containers were still in the old office, and some had even managed to migrate to the garage where all the planting equipment is kept. Our efficiency sank. It seemed whatever bit of paper, drawing or reference book was needed it was always in the other place. With four or five projects running it was becoming sloppy. A change within the workforce exacerbated the confusion, add in the chaos of the impending divorce-court scenario and you could see why it was time to go and collect another bottle from Tom MacArthur's list and get inspired by some well-established gardens. I wanted to meet some people who were not builders or office technicians.

With a bit of dodging and weaving, delegation and list-making, phone calls to clients and employees' understanding, I could commence the plans for heading north to one of France's most beautiful regions, the Loire Valley, to collect a bottle of Sancerre, which Tom had suggested. Not a holiday, you understand, strictly business.

A few days later, on a fading August afternoon, Tom rang the office. He sounded very up and asked how the mighty search for the great wines and gardens of France was progressing. I felt rather bad that I hadn't reported in but had thought it would be better to complete the trip, conclude the story and then get together with him to celebrate. I told him as much and suggested the best way would be to knock off a couple of bottles of 1979 Romanée-Conti just as soon as I had finished.

He laughed deeply and said something about how he had very determinedly left Romanée-Conti and the Golden Slope off the list. 'Nice try, Alex,' he said. 'But hell, you have a bottle of Lafite, I think. Maybe we can stitch that little number onto our wine-tasting badge?'

I agreed and assured him that the little treasure was waiting in the wings to be let loose. Lafite was not the only good wine on his list – which had after all been made up by a fellow who knew his grapes – but it was the only really expensive bottle that he had selected. I told him a bit about the adventure so far and that it was working well as a project to augment my feelings that France was where I wanted to be. 'I just wish I could mainline the language into my brain more fluently,' I said.

Tom answered obliquely about it probably being just as well I couldn't and then said, 'Do you know anything about the Garden Festival at Chaumont?'

'Sure I do,' I replied. ' I am planning to tie it in with my trip to the Loire Valley next week. I am off to find your bottle of Sancerre, look at the region and hopefully take in the Garden Show at the same time. Why do you ask?'

'Well, I was thinking we might come with you on this next leg of the adventure. Join the party and see the exhibition. We could use a break and it is summertime.'

I thought momentarily that perhaps I should have asked

him before if he had wanted to join me on any of the sojourns. I had been rather tied up in my own world with all its implosions and had forgotten that other families and couples might like a break. Besides, I had been looking forward to getting on and cracking it at my leisure. But I said, 'Great idea, why not? Who's "we"?'

'Me, Jiminie and Georgie-Lou. Jiminie came home the other evening with the International Garden Festival brochure and it looked quite fun, then I thought of you chasing the Sancerre dragon, which is why I'm talking to you now.'

'OK, let's do it,' I said. 'I'm booked out of the office as from next Tuesday for three nights, and as you know, the schedule that takes in the *châteaux* at Ladoucette, Chaumont and Muscadet. I'll ask Lélia to see if she can organise some more hotel rooms.'

'Great, excellent and right on,' cheered the old Californian, 'it's a party. Can we go in your car?'

I thought he might say that.

In fact, MacArthur and crew did not come to the Loire Valley after all. Tom was feeling poorly. 'A sort of bronchitis, I think,' he had said. 'It makes breathing a bit difficult and I'm feeling bushed. I'll catch you on the next one.'

I was rather disappointed.

So it came to pass that on an early morning in late July I set off, as originally intended, on my own in search of some classy white wine, a garden festival and one of the best-kept secrets of France – the Loire Valley.

Chapter Eleven

From as early as AD380, vines were grown in the Loire Valley. According to records of the time, Saint Martin had vines planted on the hillsides of Vouvray. Later, in 582, Bishop Gregory of Tours wrote about the flourishing vineyards of Sancerre. By the twelfth century, the vineyards of the central region had been widely developed, largely thanks to the efforts of the monastic establishments of the region. In fact, before the English acquired neighbouring Bordeaux, the Loire was France's main wine-producing region.

During the sixteenth and seventeenth centuries, the Dutch played a major role in the development of the Loire wine industry. They were largely responsible for the canalisation of the tributaries of the River Loire. It was also the Dutch who introduced white grapes into this formerly red grape-dominated region. Van vine.

Disaster struck during the exceptionally severe winter of 1709 when virtually all the vineyards of the Loire were destroyed. But with incomes depending on it, the vineyards were quickly restocked with vines brought from Burgundy by the monks who were eager to re-establish a lucrative wine industry. They introduced the Melon vine and this grape is still used to produce the famous Muscadet wine of Nantes.

The largest vineyard area of France lies scattered about the course the River Loire has carved for itself through the centuries, from Languedoc to Brittany. There are dozens of wines, of the most diverse aspects, adorning the length of the river, offering a great variety of bouquets and styles. The celebrated water flows through the Great Loire Valley, known as 'Le Jardin de la France', from its source to the estuary, majestically passing *châteaux* and stately homes. Stretching from the centre of France to the Atlantic Ocean, it is where the north meets the south and traditional links with modernity.

The history of the Loire Valley is closely connected to the history of France. Though the first vines on the Atlantic coast were planted by the Romans, those of the Loire owe their development to the princes of ancient times. There are texts showing the existence of vineyards in Sauvignon, Berry and Niverne even before Roman times. They planted Cabernet Franc vines, which have stuck around for almost a thousand years. By the eleventh century, the Loire wine districts were already renowned. Vineyards continued to develop, thanks in particular to monastic viticulture, trade with England, and the fashion for the French Royal Court to set up their grand country retreats along the banks of the 'royal river'.

The first signs to Sancerre gave me the same tingle that I had on seeing Lafite or Latour in Bordeaux or Romanée-Conti in Burgundy. Legendary words in the vocabulary of French wines that had hitherto been nothing more than a drawing on a wine label. Suddenly here was the great river, wide, flat and gentle. In St Satur, a few kilometres from the town of Sancerre, children were bucketing and spading on the massive pebbly beaches, fathers skimming stones with eternal little jumps and hops. In the middle a few canoeists paddled against the lazy current like lazy ducks half-heartedly looking for a reed to nibble. Small forests of mature bohemian olives rode the shoreline, their leaves trembling in the breeze coming up the river.

Tom MacArthur had listed Château de Ladoucette as my port of call for the mandatory bottles of Pouilly Fumé and Sancerre. ('You have to collect a bottle of each but we'll list it as one!' he had said.) Tom had chosen them not because they were necessarily the best of the region, but because the *château* that produces the wine is quite won-drous to behold, set in a beautiful garden and surrounded by a parkland.

Approaching the castle through the vineyards, you

would be hard pressed to find a weed anywhere. The neat and tidy, uniformly pruned vine-fields are edged with tightly clipped hedges of pyracantha and privet set back from a road flanked by freshly mown lawns. They run in all directions for as far as the eye can see, hugging the contours of the soft rolling countryside.

The largest and most famous Pouilly Fumé vineyard has been in the hands of the Compte LaFond and Ladoucette families since the 1790s. The present Baron Patrick has perpetuated the traditions of high quality, and thanks to tenacious work on the Sauvignon Blanc, has become a specialist of this variety of grape, maintaining the name's formidable position and reputation. The Baron later extended his know-how to the vineyards of Sancerre and now makes two special white wines that are celebrated throughout the wine-drinking world.

Driving up to the offices and *dégustation*, you see just how beautiful the *château* is. It really is quite exquisite. Built on five or six levels, it has a mass of cartoon turrets, their roofs stretched like witches' hats. Beneath the highly architecturally detailed windows that let themselves into the roof line, balconies run round the extremity of the white stone buildings and then, like a fantasy fire escape, they start to descend, the steps unwinding like a giant climbing vine clinging to the body of the building as it lowers itself grandly down to ground level.

The sloping gardens are dominated by the serene trees of giant oaks, chestnuts, planes, copper beeches and limes that open out to a lake in the flat land below. As befits and is expected the immediate garden around the *château* is formal with the ubiquitous box hedging and roses. It is traditional and balances well with the stature of the building it decorates.

Just outside the offices, a part of the old stableyard, the encroaching vines were not vines at all but *cassis*, blackcurrants. What a simple but effective idea. Buy your dry white wine and squeeze in some newly picked currants and *voilà*! You have your *kir*.

The antique, partially open-sided outbuildings with their steep tiled roofs protect a gaggle of white spidery tractors. Vehicles unseen anywhere else but on a vineyard, the lightweight machines dance along perched on spindly legs above the precious vines, pruning and spraying as they go.

Tasting took place in a charming, low-beamed room with a round mahogany table in the centre. I was assisted by a pretty girl, who, with her shapely bottom, low-cut dress and comfortable bosom cradled in a frilly bra, looked more and more like a Tudor wench with each glass of wine she poured. She told the tale of the *château*, the vintage and the promise of 2003 being a fine year. I asked her how she thought her wines compared with the same grape grown in other countries.

'Sancerre,' she explained, 'is less intensely herbaceous than New Zealand, more assertive than South Africa, more concentrated than Bordeaux, racier than the Italian and very food friendly.' She sighed and smiled knowingly, then moved onto the red. She didn't look particularly surprised that I didn't like it very much; it was probably an acquired taste and I was behaving predictably with my rejection of it. The Pouilly Fumé and Sancerres were, on the other hand, a delight. 'Why *fumé*, why smoked?' I asked. 'They say,' she said, 'it is because when the grape is harvested it is surrounded by a fine grey film, looking like it has been taken out of the ashes of a fireplace.'

As the evening sun filtered in through the mullioned windows the polished furniture reflected the bright, clear wine glistening in the glass. In the distance the chugging of a returning tractor added to the slightly charged tranquillity. Perfection hung around me for a moment or two only to be damaged by the noise of my own swilling and spitting. I placed an order and while the fragrantly bucolic lady bent over her desk to computerise my wish-list, I tore away to go and get the car. I had, not for the first time on this adventure, exceeded Tom's suggestion of one or two lonely bottles and had taken advantage of the situation, stocking up beyond the original quota. I was certain that had he been in the same situation he would have done the same. I was not, of course, expecting him to pay for my excesses but I was looking forward to sharing them with him, and Georgie-Lou and Jiminie for that matter, as they had so nearly come on this trip. That evening I rang to see how Tom was. Georgie-Lou had said he was better but was going to see a doctor the next day for a quick check-up.

So utterly grim, depressing and uncompromisingly out of date was the two-star Hotel Panoramic in Sancerre with its purple neon nameplates, brown fabrics and plastic everything that I was thrilled to be out and on my way again. The room would have reduced me to tears had it not been for the panoramic views as promised by the hotel's name. Looking out over the yawing countryside, I realised that my room was about level with the horizon of the huge mass below. Eye to eye with the ridges of the hills on the other side of the valley looking towards Chavignol. In between lay a rich tapestry of small farm-holdings, vineyards and cultivated swathes of arable pasture. Over to the right the hills banked round in a semi-circle giving the whole community the security of resting in the folded arms of natural superbowl.

The previous evening had been warm and clear as I set out to discover the town. Climbing up through the narrow streets with their tall, thin buildings, highly decorated balconies and shops, one emerges out onto a large market square bustling with shopkeepers selling hard and restaurants preparing for the night's trade. At the far end was the Café des Arts, a lively but understaffed joint swollen with locals and tourists alike, all enjoying the evening air with a drink or two, a cigarette or ten and some genial conversation. I joined the throng, found a table featuring full ashtrays, dirty glasses and a nearly broken chair, ordered a cold glass of wine and mixed people-watching with reading *Deco Sud*.

One feature in my newspaper ironically showed a hopelessly over-art-directed shot of a French café in the golden evening light where a couple must have popped off to the loo. The flawless cotton tablecloth cascaded perfectly onto the *Topdeq* chair, upon which a *Le Bon Marché* carrier bag brimming with silk had been momentarily abandoned. On the table a candle flickered beside an exceptional red rose whose stem, dipped in Evian water, was held by a slither of elegant glass. Two brightly coloured mugs and a Philip Starck cafetière nudged a copy of *Le Figaro*. The scene set a polished story about a slick cosmopolitan duo whose babies don't need nappies and whose dogs never make mistakes, without actually introducing them to us. No matter that the cloth was held in place with glue, the rose went up in flames and the bag was full of rubbish. It is just the little conspiracy between stylist and photographer in a well practised game that has put lifestyle magazines into advertising land. A place where everything is perfect, flawless and pretend. How we keep on succumbing to the message is at best worrying and at worst, Kafkaesque. It is the evil of fervent hope, the dream. We are beaten into submission and told that everybody who's anybody out there has white teeth, slim figures, tons of money and a stress-free life.

A friend was shooting a car advert in the States and it involved an external shot of a period truck from the 1950s. It was only in frame for about four seconds but the stylist had not only hired the truck and driver but had gone to inordinate lengths to ensure that the newspaper lying on the seat was in period, along with a pack of cigarettes, a passport and driving licence hidden in the glove compartment. None of it was needed, none of it was seen and when asked by the producer why she had run up such a big and unnecessary bill she replied, 'The deeper the authenticity the more weight to the product.' The average budget for a thirty-second car commercial could settle a Third World country's national deficit; what difference does a little hidden authenticity make?

With a distinct lack of enthusiasm I headed back to the minus-two-star hotel, wondering whether to risk eating in its restaurant. Convenience and compromise won through and I was soon living it up at the Hotel Paranoiac. Now one thing you can virtually count on, one thing that is fabulously French, and that is, no matter how uninspired the decor, how cheap the furniture, how resistible the dining room might be with its hideous overhead lighting, when the food is trolleyed out it is always good. Of course, we all know this is a cliché, but if I had doubted the culinary talents of such a dreary hostel, the concoctions and creations spawned by a low-profile chef in a minor dining room was enough to make you want to send postcards. I know now that having lived in this country of contrariness for many years you should expect the unexpected especially when it comes to food, but dinner that night was a surprise.

First was a plate of *fruits de mer*. The Atlantic and the Loire are perfect sources for a wide range of fresh shellfish. A plate arrived onto the table displaying crab, langoustine, prawns, shrimps, clams and *moules*, all aided and abetted by large wedges of lemon and wide glasses of chilled Muscadet. Afterwards I ordered some goat's cheese, Crottin de Chavignol and Tomme de Chevre, with salad. Coffee and some local chocolates came with *l'addition* (they weren't risking putting dinner on the hotel bill: they probably knew the room was bad enough to excite a mid-night runner). Then it was up to the bedroom balcony for a last look over the valley. The crescent moon had risen steadily over the tame, sloping hills below, and the sparkling stars were up working the dusk-to-dawn shift.

With a dogged look at the bed with its nylon sheets and single sausage bolster, and a quick wish that a mini-bar might appear, I was yours Sancerrely, out like a light.

The 30km road between Sancerre and Bourgueil invites you to belt it. It is long, straight, well surfaced and presum-ably Roman. That morning it was early and trafficless, and there was no real reason not to bend the rules and pile on the power.

The lines of chestnuts, grass verges and secretive wood-lands zipped past, occasionally revealing huge wheat fields, pale biscuit with the rising sun glinting off the stubble of the newly harvested fields. One such field had a rectangle of sunflowers growing in the centre of it, an unusual and welcome bit of farmer planning. It will be crop circles next in a multitude of tints.

This was another country from Provence and it remind-ed me that I hadn't moved to France but to the South of France. It is completely different. As the speedometer climbed up towards 200kph, the blur of colour was not Mediterranean but more like England. The shades of green were lusher than the Luberon at this time of year and the landscape considerably less parched. It was beautiful, no question, but for myself I doubted the point of uprooting

from the UK just to be somewhere that spoke a foreign language and was, I felt, no more seductive than the Vale of
Evesham. I was really looking forward to unwrapping the
Loire Valley, discovering the river life and playing castles
but I was just visiting, nothing more. I braked hard, pulled
up on the grass verge and got out for a quick walk round
the car. Was I feeling homesick? Was this bucolic frolic getting to me? Homesick for what though? I asked myself.
Britain or Provence?

After about half an hour's motoring, the idea of breakfast manifestly took root. I used to think that a couple of
fried eggs, a few rashers of bacon backed up by a tomato or
two was the way to go. Moreover, I felt that France, despite
its wonderful food and inspirational menus, needed to take
a look at the way the Brits did breakfast and get a grip. Now
I think that a croissant with *confiture*, a *pain au chocolat*
dipped in milky coffee and a bit of passive Gauloise smok-
ing is where it's at. Sometimes on Sunday mornings I will
sit with my best pal in the world, in the universe, and
indulge the both of us with a scrambled egg, but generally
speaking I am off that type of food. It's not to do with
waist-watching so much as to do with balance. Trying to
create a rhythm to the day's eating, peaking with lunch and
bowing out with a light dinner unless invited.

The International Garden Festival at Château Chaumont in
the Loire Valley has been a regular annual event for the last
twelve years. Created through the initiative of the Région
Centre and the support of the Ministry of Culture and the

Conseil Général de Loire-et-Cher, it began as a festival to demonstrate the renewed creativity in the discipline of garden and landscape design. Without doubt a success, it has also been developing partnerships with other gardens and parks to share its ideologies, particularly with Hestercombe in England, that quintessential English garden in Somerset designed by Sir Edwin Lutyens and planted by Gertrude Jekyll in 1904, and Les Jardins de Métis in Quebec, one of the premier gardens in North America that hosts its own international garden festival.

Chaumont's success has encouraged the organisers to invite an ever-wider field of designers and contributors of all ages to come to the party and participate. Apart from the show gardens themselves, there are workshops, lectures and training programmes.

I had heard a lot about it but never managed to get up to the region to witness at first hand what is loosely called France's answer to the Chelsea Flower Show. First things first. It is not anything like Chelsea, either in terms of plant growers, the first and foremost *raison d'être* of the Royal Horticultural Society's annual show, or in terms of diversity of exhibitors. Moreover, the French festival is open for a full four months as opposed to a full five days, it attracts some 150,000 people over its entire run whereas Chelsea does that each day, it is located some distance south of Paris whilst Chelsea is in the heart of London. What Chaumont does do, however, is to provide a spectacular backdrop for the installation of some thirty different gardens, all completely original but working under one cajoling theme. This year it was 'Chaos, Order and Disorder: Mess, Confusion, Jumble and Turmoil'. Sounded scarily appropriate.

Each 'site' taken by a contemporary designer or team of designers comes oven-ready with a surrounding beech hedge. This eliminates the expensive requirement of erecting a screen between you and your fellow exhibitor, leaving more finance for the garden itself. It also gives a harmony to the show ground. The people who exhibit and interpret the annual theme are from a suitably wide background of different participating countries. Besides the actual show gardens, a starter for ten is given by the *château* itself.

Chaumont has always dominated a strategic point on the river ever since the tenth century when Eudes, Count of Blois, established a fortress to protect Blois from the constant attacks waged by his neighbour Foulques Nerra, Count of Anjou. It was then rebuilt by the Amboise family in the fifteenth century after Louis XI had had it razed to the ground as some kind of kingly puffing-out-of-chest to show who was boss. After a succession of proprietors and guardians that included Catherine de Médicis, it was handed over to the State by the ruined Princess Charlotte Say in 1938. Today it remains a classically turreted Loire *château*, albeit a little heavy in its proportions by comparison to some of the others, standing proud as a venue for the International Garden Festival.

The grounds were re-landscaped at the end of the nineteenth century by Henry Duchene in the style of the grand English garden which was so popular in France between 1850 and 1870. It incorporated the characteristic gently undulating land, lawns bordered by sweeping paths, trees in isolation or grouped in copses with cedars, sequoias and local species, gaps between the trees and copses being left to direct the gaze towards the outstanding features of the site: the forest, the valley, and above all, the *château* itself.

However, it is the smaller section of garden beyond the stables known as the Goualoup, that is more variable in level and lends itself to the festival. You enter via a picturesque cement bridge that is Duchene's little masterpiece. In true folly style it has two levels linked by a spiral staircase, housed in the trunk of a mock oak tree. Deep below is the Misty Valley. A former ice pit, it is now a wild gully, which can be traversed by another bridge, this time a suspended wooden structure. Beneath tumbles a 20m cascade of water, fighting its way through a manmade hissing, steaming valley of tree ferns, irises, maples, peonies and herbaceous plants. But the French being the French, an insurgent group blossomed and demanded that the English influence be kicked out in favour of something more French, naturally. Thereafter the French style, such as it was in the nineteenth century, took over.

Nevertheless, the wit and charm of this designated area wins through and helps the designers, botanists and horticulturists come up with ticklish ideas year after year. A few that caught my attention were the binding together of pollarded willow trees to make a distinctive face, or the daring Madame Arpel who used plastic grass (naughty) or Shun-Boa Du, Bin Hu Zhang and Hai Qian Zen (promise) who gave the Chinese garden a good intellectual toss with

'Archipelago'. The Mayor of Shanghai should have whistled up their talents for the Chinese garden in Marseille. Japan was ready for the shoot-out with 'Palestine' by Shodo Suzuki where a miniature garden made from dry stones mystically replicated the Bedouin stone workers of Bethlehem. My favourite was the 3m cypress trees planted in a series of rocking planters. Children, sometimes joined by their self-conscious parents, were invited to stand at the base of the tree and make the container rock. To see some thirty conifers all waggling around in different directions seemed to suggest a sublime chaos.

Other ideas were above my head, abstract to the point of removal, such as a garden that seemed little more than an incomprehensible jumble of burnt-out tree trunks. The explanatory plaque read: 'Anamorphosis is a rebus, a monster, a prodigy . . . an escape that implies, however, a necessary return. First comes the destruction of the figure, then the true representation. The image engulfed by a torrent or in a confused whirlpool emerges, as a clear picture, in an oblique vision or mirror.'

Another, this time from our own adopted American architect Charles Jencks, whose Scottish garden based on twentieth-century physics has received much publicity and applause. Here he was up to his old tricks again challenging with 'Can war be a garden theme?' I suppose so, if you base it on *La Malédiction d'Agamemnon*, incorporate irrigation guns, catapults, blood-red canals and a water wheel with an off-centre paddle, and some giant rhubarb in different stages of development. Even without gripping the inner meanings or implications, the set was a lot more pleasing than its title might suggest.

The sun was hot and without a hat my head needed to cool down. I wandered off the track and into the woods where the shade was as good as a drink. I sat down, leaned against the trunk of a sycamore, lazily looked around the small clearing, and there they were. A pair of enormous bosoms nearly the size of single-decker bus. I couldn't believe I hadn't noticed them before. I must have been half-baked. Cleverly carved from pink foam rubber with nipples the size of dustbins, they seemed like a far better place to rest my head than against my tree. Albeit self-consciously, I settled myself into the mammary warmth to read the brochures and catalogues.

Back on the track I was ready for the next brain-jerker. It was offered by Anna Costa and Carlo Contesso. Their explanation read: 'In the tradition of the initiatory gardens of the Italian Renaissance, our garden takes inspiration from Fibonacci numbers, a simple sequence of numbers with no apparent logic, but which mathematically explains numer-ous natural phenomena, such as how shell spirals are formed, how leaves are arranged on a plant, the number of petals on a flower . . . and the pattern of the heart of a sun-flower. From the entrance of the garden to the exit, a rib-bon endlessly repeats the same poetic phrase in twenty-one languages (a Fibonacci number). The garden is like a carpet of flowers arranged according to this famous series of num-bers. Two colours dominate: yellow, the colour of madness, and violet, colour of knowledge and human genius. These colours blend, showing once again how fragile the barrier is between order and chaos, genius and madness.'

Just shows you the deeper you dig the harder it is to garden. Here we are being carried to the origins of the world, to that instant before creation, where anything is possible, where liberty and latitude is all we know and Dan Brown beckons.

I wandered round a couple more stands that included giant pick-up-sticks, a human beehive and some degenerating weeds, then it was time for a stuffed aubergine sandwich, a glass of orange and carrot juice, additive-free ice cream and decaf coffee.

On the edge of the restaurant was a droll sculpture – a long glass table was laid with a dozen plates all brimming with living plants, *aromatiques*, herbs, vegetables and fruit. Beside each plate was a tall, curved tube dripping water onto the 'foods'. Beneath each plate and under the table was a conical stainless steel container from which the plants sprouted. The twelve seats were actually Perspex stools and the absence of anybody actually eating the dishes made me suspicious that they might have been consumed by giant slugs or snails.

Leaving Chaumont's garden festival I reckoned it was much more akin to the garden design exhibition staged at Westonbirt Arboretum in Gloucestershire. That too had been staged for several months, had designers from around the world and was in the grounds of a fine old house about a hundred miles from London. In fact I think I recognised one or two of the contributors at Chaumont that I had seen at Westonbirt.

Whether either were truly inspirational in terms of creating anything that people would actually want in their garden was debatable. One of my ongoing gripes about landscape architecture, particularly in the private sector, is that people are very shy of commissioning cutting-edge or radical design. They might have completely off the wall house architecture and interior decoration but when it comes to the garden they would invariably err in favour of tradition. It was best therefore to think of these exhibitions as galleries rather than shops. Like fashion, not many people actually buy on commission, but thank God that McQueen and Co dare to thrill with extravagant one-offs.

Travelling around France these last few months in search of grapes and gardens, biodynamics had been a word that regularly cropped up in wine-speak. It was considered the only way forward in some vineyards and techno gobbledygook in others. Nothing short of a cataclysmic burnout is going to stop the world evolving, even in questionable and controversial ways. Genetic engineering is coming at us, like it or not, and man's insatiable curiosity ensures that the frontiers of medicine and anthropological research will break through barriers, regardless. That it may be dislocating the soul and altering the settled state is neither here nor there. If science develops at even half the speed that it has done in the last hundred years we will certainly know fifty times as much as we do now about the human condition by 2100.

Awareness of what should and should not be sprayed on

crops is growing with each generation, and wine is no different. So what is the Biodynamic Method created by Rudolf Steiner in the early 1900s? For the uninitiated, Loire wine-maker Nicholas Joly probably explains it as well as anyone: 'Biodynamics is essentially an extension of organic viticulture – but it is no small extension. Biodynamics is much more than simple organic viticulture. Biodynamics recognises that wine is made in the vineyard, not the cellar, and that a vigneron must understand his soil before he can make great wine. Some of the core ideals of biodynamics involve enriching the vineyard and treating vineyard pests using methods that are in harmony with the vineyard.'

Those that practise biodynamics tell us that the application of intensive agricultural methods to a vineyard plot results in the death of soil micro-organisms. These micro-organisms keep the soil alive, and may have an important influence on the final wine. Followers therefore eschew herbicides, pesticides and fertilisers, although the use of the 'Bordeaux Mixture' that includes sulphur is permitted. In addition, the soil may be enriched with manure. This may even be added in homeopathic quantities, having been diluted down many times. Nicholas Joly keeps a herd of rare Nantaise cattle for this very purpose.

Biodynamic vineyards are just as prone to pests such as red spider-mite and other bugs, snails, parasites and so on, as any other vineyard. As pesticides are excluded, a popular choice of treatment is a plant infusion sprayed on the vines.

Typical infusions used include nettle, camomile and

dandelion, to name just a few. Other pests require more bizarre treatments. Joly's response to an infestation of rabbits was to burn a rabbit skin each year, the time of the burning determined by the alignment of the planets. The rabbits never returned; they obviously knew what was bad for them. This treatment reveals one of the more unusual aspects of biodynamics – the importance of astrology.

Joly again: 'Astrology is of great importance to those that practise biodynamic viticulture. As the sun passes through the various signs of the zodiac it is believed that it has a strong influence on plant growth and health. Water signs (Pisces, for instance) are favourable to vegetative growth, fire signs (Sagittarius et al) are favourable to growth of fruit, earth signs (such as Capricorn) favour root growth – obviously – and air signs (Gemini, etc) favour flowers. Consequently the timing of routine vineyard and nursery practices such as planting out, pruning, weeding and so on are tailored to suit. The moon also has an influence on vineyard and cellar practices.'

One of the uphill struggles anybody at the frontiers of alternative or supplementary medicine has to face, whether it is for humans, fauna or flora, is that as the uninitiated listens to the passions and beliefs of the intrepid practitioner they start to lose the plot, and begin to wonder if the guy is a bit of a loony. Working the vineyard 'in harmony with nature' is one thing. But some of Joly's beliefs are a little too much for even the most ardent follower of biodynamic principles. Nicholas Joly believes that the shape of the barrel is a strong influence on the developing wine – after all, it does strongly resemble the shape of an egg. His belief in the adverse effects of electrical pollution is another step too far for many.

However, if biodynamics is so strange, then why does it appeal to so many great wine-makers? It would seem that the reason is, whatever the mechanisms, biodynamics works. Most producers move over in steps, committing only a small vineyard plot initially. Impressed by the results – judged by the quality of the final wine – producers move over entirely often within a few years.

When I first came to Provence I was struck by how our neighbour undertook his farming practices based on the movements of the moon but to him it was completely normal.

I went to Domaine Huet, located between Sancerre and Anjou and one of the best-known biodynamic producers. I bought half a dozen bottles of very good white wine. Albeit a little more expensive, it appealed enormously to my rather jaded sense of cosmic compatibility. Listening and reading about biodynamics reawakened a take I had had on gardening when I was younger. I had at one point skirted around the radionic treatment of garden ailments, and although it demanded more time than was possible to give, it nevertheless jogged the faculty of thinking. The lady I spoke to could determine the ley-lines of an agricultural or horticultural site by dowsing with her pendulum. With this knowledge she was able to direct the farmer or gardener into the most productive areas of his estate. To comprehend the magnetic ley-lines is to understand that biology arranges its molecular centres into fractal symmetry to allow non-destructive charge distribution – which is the very definition of life. Therefore seeds sown within the boundaries of the ley-line are going to perform better than those outside it. As the man said, 'Some fell on stony ground.' Nothing is new, it may appear to be cosmically hip, but it is simply way ahead and behind us.

It was only a hop or two over to the beautiful, moated Château Villandry, the last of the great Renaissance châteaux to be built on the banks of the Loire. Like most castles, Villandry has a history of mixed ownership each with huge egos demanding that the building be pulled down and rebuilt on a scale so grand that it challenges belief. From its feudal simplicity of 1532 through the highly decorative adornments of the seventeenth century it moved into more modern times when in 1906 the *château* was bought by a Spanish doctor, Joachim Carvallo. He, like his forebears, declared that the castle was to be demolished. This high-ranking scientist, grandfather of the present owner, abandoned his brilliant career to devote his time to rebuilding and restoring it, as it was in the sixteenth century. Significantly this included recomposing the gardens in keeping with the Renaissance architecture of other French castles. (The original layout had been destroyed in the nineteenth century to create an English-style park around the grounds, not something that was destined to last for long, needless to say.)

This combined two styles: the gothic tradition on one

hand, floral with medicinal plants, kitchen gardens and flower beds, the finest examples of which were to be found in the monasteries, and, on the other hand, Italianate. This was more architectural and made known to the French during the Italian campaigns. Whether Gothic or Italian, these gardens exceeded the utilitarian or decorative production of fruit and veg to rise to giddy heights inspiring poetry or indeed the philosophy of practising an elaborate symbolism of the quest for love, earthly or mystical.

The ornamental garden, made of high, cut box hedging is divided into four *'salons'*, representing tragic love, inconstant love, tender love, and the madness of love. If you're not told which is which you could get yourself into a right paddy. The kitchen garden, not to be outdone, is divided into nine squares. The geometrical effects of the shapes and colours of more than twenty types of plants, all of which would have been cultivated in the early sixteenth century, that is around the time the *château* was built, form the basis of the design. They include the lovely red bowl lettuce, purple and white aubergines, white peacock kale, yellow and green peppers, begonias, silver cineraria, blue salvias, the Tokyo white cabbage, kohlrabi, Toga spring onions, cardoons and totem tomatoes, to name a handful. Every year there are two plantings: one in spring which lasts from March to June, and one in summer, from June to November. About forty species of vegetable belonging to eight botanical genera are used each year. (No potatoes, incidentally, as they hadn't been discovered in sixteenth-century France.) The plants are always laid out differently at each planting and are watered by an underground irrigation system. The third Renaissance garden combines simple herbs, *aromatique* and medicinal plants. Next, on a yet higher level, a water garden surrounded by a cloister of vegetation is connected by gravity to the moat. Swans must like it because there was a kindergarten of cygnets paddling along behind mum and dad, busy trying to keep up while checking things out at the same time.

The newest addition is a hedgerow maze recently opened along with a children's garden grown to absorb bored little people while their parents cruise the grounds.

The scale is breathtaking, the maintenance mind- and pocket-wrenching and the effect overwhelming. It is the most conceited garden I have ever seen but a little narcissistic indulgence was always part of the game and Villandry provides an astonishing showcase of vainglorious days. Part of the pleasure is to stall for a while, sit on a bank and watch other people taking it all in. Children under five roll down the banks squealing with joy, while the over-fives run around in a gleeful state of amazement that a garden can reveal so many hiding places. Amateur photographers, cameras on tripods, line up the swans and the fountain spray with the mighty hedges and click away eagerly, elderly people shoofty around knowing all the answers and the young stand aghast that such opulence might have belonged to one family. I wondered if the gardens that I humbly make could be around in four hundred years' time. I guess some of the private estates I currently work on might be considered important enough to preserve and open to the public by 2405. Others might become the equivalent of a yellowing CD, unable to find a machine old enough to display its contents. Unless, of course, it has all gone up in globally warmed smoke, melting ice and suicidal terrorism.

Nowhere else in the world to my knowledge can boast such a phenomenal amount of heavy rural real estate as the Loire Valley, which was once the centre of French power. When Paris had surrendered to the Anglo-Burgundians, Charles VII, the dauphin, moved his fragile power and the royal administration to the Loire. Travelling endlessly from one town and *château* to the other, the King felt at home from Gien to Chinon, from Saumur to Angers. Thus, from one end of the Loire Valley to the other, his presence was everywhere. Princes of royal blood, great lords and ministers, under his reign or that of his successors, bought and built, creating an exceptional wealth of historical castles.

Now that I was in the thick of it I thought I might as well see at least one more pile on my way to La Chatonnière, my day's destination and a small *château* with an allegedly wonderful, relatively new garden. Two major *châteaux* had been put forward by a man I spoke to at Villandry. It was an arbitrary choice but he reckoned that Chambord was the most magnificent – absolutely enormous and ornate but with no garden at all. The antithesis of Villandry, it was simply acres of mown lawns that ran away from the house bleeding into parkland and heavy woods. The grandeur knew no limits and its design by

Louis XII's son-in-law and his team of architects realised a dream that few men could pull off. Next the barfly thought I might like Château Chenonçeau, built as it was across the river, a kind of hybrid between an outrageous bridge and a palace. Nothing in Venice touches it, but again it was surrounded by extremely formal gardens and I had done that, worn the cap, held the spade, clipped the box. I would have loved to have seen 'The Three Graces' by Carl Van Loon in all their modest nakedness which they have in one of the anterooms but the effort outweighed the motivation. So it was that I found myself heading for La Chatonnière with no intention of any diversification.

Then up came the story of 'Sleeping Beauty'. Whether this has been depicted by the finest Pre-Raphaelite artists showing a brave a young hero battling his way through a recalcitrant briar rose to find and save his childhood sweetheart, or has been revealed as a simple tale of a boy winning through against Disney's adversity, it remains a great yarn.

The majestic white outline of Château Ussé lies at the edge of the dark and mysterious forest of Chinon overlooking the valley. It was here that Charles Perrault, the celebrated French children's story writer, discovered the fantastic towers and gables of the castle and was inspired to write his famous fairy tale about the princess who suffered the chilling prick of death that plunged her into a medical nightmare of horror and violation that was to last a hundred years until she was finally awoken from her suspended animation by one hell of a kiss from a great-looking young prince.

A few minutes after driving through the village of Azay-le-Rideau, the quintessential symbol of the medieval fairy-tale castle, mainly inhabited by brave lords, beautiful ladies and romantic poets, comes colossally into view. Capitalising shamelessly on the good fortune of the castle's notoriety, Madame Tussaud, or one of her colleagues, has once again waved her magic wand. As you climb towers and turrets you are able to see tableaux of the Sleeping Beauty about to be woken by her hero (is that a whip in his hand? It is a little hard to see through the grimy glass), and although this is the high point of the story the castle's proprietors who commissioned the wax works did not stop there. There are playrooms with children fettling their wind-up railways, a strange jump of date but it doesn't matter, then in another room there's a lady-in-waiting to another, presumably older, princess, and as you climb the stairs you may well meet an attractive woman descending gracefully, dressed in a long white silk dress with a tightly waisted, embroidered three-quarter-length velvet jacket. And was that a maid I spotted replacing the cut flowers on the landing?

In 1664 the Marquis de Valintnay commissioned the legendary landscape architect André Le Nôtre, who had made his name at Versailles, to design the formal gardens which surround the *château*. Nothing much to report really, especially as one was now becoming seriously blasé about the fancy-dressed gardens that surround the *châteaux* of the Loire Valley.

That night was spent at the Hotel de France (memorable for its 3m banana tree) in the elegant town of Chinon, built on the Loire river that seemed to remain as calm as a waiting bath despite its tremendous size. I remember that Chinon had some beautiful narrow streets with old stone houses and corner turrets, built on brick-filled timber frames much favoured during the Middle Ages. It also had perfectly acceptable municipal planting that included verbena, gaura, pale yellow marigolds, geranium and variegated hydrangeas.

Earlier in the evening I had leant over a big stone retaining wall to look at the clear water below and the majestic trees on the opposite bank, which were dipping their dark green branches into the water. I could see fish darting in and out of the dilapidated old wooden punts. Behind stood a statue of Chinon's great literary contribution: François Rabelais. He looked quite pleased with himself and had probably recently finished *Gargantua and Pantagruel*. 'A book for those who love bawdy and bathroom humour,' a teacher had told me at school, so we all rushed off and bought it. The text parodies everyone from eminent classical authors and schoolmen to Rabelais's own acquaintances, and is smart with its use of sexual and execratory satire. Literary slapstick at its best. Chinon is clearly very proud of their man. On the Rue Voltaire is the 'Crèperie Rabelaise', around the corner a *vinothèque* called 'A La Pause Rabelaisienne', and close by 'Le Café Rabelais' squeezed in between a music shop selling fantastic accordions decorated with folksy artwork and a bar where I sat

outside watching Chinon go about its life. The tranquillity
was broken every so often by the noise of a horrid little fake
train.

It is fair enough that tourists should want to take a tour
of the town they are briefly visiting, to see the sights and
get a quick flavour of the architecture and local culture, but
why they have to be made to do it in a little lorry dressed
up as a steam engine dragging a set of open-sided carriages
is beyond me. It is so embarrassingly Noddyish. It wasn't as
if the thing was full of kids, they would have been avoiding
it at any cost, I imagine; it just had a bunch of ordinary
people doing their best not to look like extras on a TV
series. Old people were occupied watching young people
wearing phones and conspiratorial smirks.

Soon I found myself drawn into conversation with the
man sipping his wine at the next table. He too was people-
watching, only I was the people he had been watching.

'English?'

I turned. He had no legs but there was something of the
cavalier about him. One of his trouser legs was coquettish-
ly tossed over the other in a drawing room sort of a way. He
had a pair of shoes thoughtfully sewn onto the turn-ups,
was bald with a Douglas Fairbanks moustache, and must
have been in his fifties.

'*Ecossais*,' I said with a friendly smile.

He raised his glass and said jovially, '*Santé*!'

We bought a round or two for one another and talked of
what had brought us to Chinon on a summer's evening in
2004.

Emmanuel Gubert, it turned out, had been born and brought up on the banks of the Loire right here in this town. He had finished university, gained his degree and taken it to London where he started work as a sub-auctioneer for Christaby's. Enjoying the game, and the company, he quickly moved up through the ranks and was soon on his way to work for their offices in Paris. Later, he splintered and set up on his own relying on his considerable reputation as not only a fine wine auctioneer, but a celebrated (locally at least) expert. It was during these days he had learnt to speak English. It was only when I told him about my Gardens and Grapes tour that he let me into a more intimate side of his character. 'I am a crook, you see,' he said. This was a bit tricky for me for although he spoke English well, he had quite a strong accent and I was not at all sure he had said crook or cook, so I waited for him to go on.

'One day a wine auction was scheduled and I was to be the man with the gavel. I had had plenty of warning and knew about a month before the sale that some very special old wine would be under the hammer. Now, you must understand that all my grown-up life I have been an alcoholic.' He took a good-sized slug of his beverage. I caught the waiter's eye and ordered another round. 'Not an alcoholic who will drink spirits, never, nor an alcoholic who throttled bottles of cheap wine, beer or cider. No, no I was an alcoholic who has to have fine wine, the very best, the most poetic.' He went on:

On either side the river lie
Long fields of barley and rye,
That clothe the wold and meet the sky;
And thro' the field the road runs by
To many-towered Camelot;
And up and down the people go,
Gazing where the lilies blow
Round an island there below,
The island of Shalott.

'Lovely,' I said, a little embarrassed.

With a slightly restrained cough he cleared his heart-chocking throat and said, 'Tennyson, Lady of Shalott, Part One.' He too was a little embarrassed because he didn't know whether to tell me in case I knew, but on the other hand didn't want to take credit for it or indeed let me miss out on one of his private readings. It was all good stuff.

'C'mon, Emmanuel, you were saying?'

'Oh yes, the wine auction. My salary as an auctioneer, successful as I was, did not cover my, shall we say, requirements, and over the years I had often thought about some way in which I could, in public, fix and accept my own bid. It meant it had to be a phone bid. It meant I had to rig the reserve and it meant I had to have somebody to make the dummy bid for me. I worked on it feverishly.'

The scam, of course, had gone spectacularly wrong. He had been exposed and dropped overnight. He had lost his wife and children's respect and had slunk off back to Chinon under the protection of his innocent parents.

Predictably enough Emmanuel was soon drunk as a punk and had a car accident.

'I lost everything, my family, my job, my money, my legs.' He paused, then said, 'I am content now.' And he was.

Another day, another castle, another garden and another bottle of wine. How much can a chap manage? Plenty is the short answer.

Each morning brought fresh assurance that I was on the road to redemption. I was becoming less of a stranger to France, familiarising myself with a diverse heritage and indulging myself in wine and roses. As an outsider it was not possible for me to discern any regional behaviour differences and even accents, it was not obvious without research whether I was amongst Catholics or Protestants, or what bias the politically troubled years of war and peace had instilled and what discontents bubbled beneath the surface of apparent social rest. My overall impression so far had been superficial if not glossy. I hadn't been caught up in a strike or witnessed stampeding youth bent on destruction, there hadn't been a national catastrophe or even a local disaster. Life had just been trucking on under the summer sun glowing on the French countryside. But I kept feeling positive and smiling at people. I had taught myself a shorthand of appreciation when it came to villages and towns, quickly identifying the regional architecture, spotting what plants thrived and noticing how the surrounding countryside affected the market produce. I was a gardener on a wine trip looking to inspire my soul, and it was working.

It would soon be time to leave the Loire Valley but not before seeing La Chatonnière. From all accounts the gardens were much less formal, which would be a relief and definitely worth the trip. So bags packed, bills paid, and topped with petrol, the Dingwall-Main show was back on the road yet again.

La Chatonnière, between Bourgueil and Tours, and about 25km from either, was, by the standards of the last few mega-dwellings on the list, really quite small. Again Renaissance, it boasted a paltry seven towers and one courtyard, and all the better it was for that. It was easier to identify with. Quite manageable really.

The 7 hectares that surround La Chatonnière are occupied by various different areas known as the gardens of: Abundance – laid out like a giant leaf with the arteries being separate beds containing herbs, aromatiques, vegetables and fruit, Intelligence – entered by noble steps through mauve-coloured roses scrambling over pergolas leading to four quarters of intense herbaceous planting, followed by Romance, Silence, Elegance and Senses. Next up was the garden of Science growing plants such as méline, mint, marjoram and certain grasses that have all been used in experiments. Add in the Magic, Wild and Exuberant gardens and you can see that things are far from ordinary here.

Beautifully planned and laid out, it is a delight to experience. After having been round the entire site, they suggest you choose your favourite and tarry awhile. For me it was the Garden of Silence but unexpectedly it was guarded by four ferocious, seemingly underfed, battle-ready

Dobermans whose growling, barking and gnashing of teeth undermined the concept. So next on the list was the Garden of Senses where I found the laidback Ahmed up to his neck dead-heading some standard white roses. Actually all the gardens are linked by a devotion to roses (2,000) and lilies (3,000). In spring, 6 hectares of poppies and bleuets and marguerites decorate the ground while around August there are over a thousand dahlias showing off their plumage.

The whole site was clustered around the bottom of the meeting vales in central Touraine and had vast views of the River Indre and the forest of Chinon. I just loved it there. The happiness and calm joy of the place seeped into my being and lifted the sprits higher than they had been for months. Finally here was a private garden bursting with originality, sensitively aware to its global environment and quietly cosmic all at the same time. For all the fun and games at Chaumont, for all the classical indulgences of Villandray, here in the middle of the Loire Valley was a proper garden that reminded me of how utterly wonderful it is to be a gardener and how reassuring it is to find solid inspiration in my adopted country. Whatever happened with this trip from here on in, I knew I had peaked with La Chatonnière even if it didn't produce wine – but I wasn't going to tell Tom that.

Sadly a rogue thunderstorm cooled the reverie and I had to go. Ahmed was sorry to see a fellow gardener leave prematurely but we both knew it was mighty good for the land to get watered from heaven. There is nothing like it, not even in bottles.

The rain drove down hard and fast and the drive to Angers was slow and dangerous. Huge lorries hurtled past each other blinding everybody else whilst windscreen wipers struggled to keep up.

Angers, a big Loire river city protected by its thousand-year-old fortress, is home to the famous tapestry *The Apocalypse*, which was ordered by Louis I of Anjou and made by Nicholas Bataille in 1375. It is reputedly one of the oldest known examples of the art and Angers remains one of the world centres of textile design and manufacture.

That may well be, but a look around the galleries near the hotel in the centre of town produced the same old provincial second-rate stuff. There must be some anti-art gang going around Europe wholesale selling the same run-of-the-mill nonsense. It is 'Railings Art' that you find at weekends all over cities, in small town galleries and on the walls of dreary bars. Dedication is no substitute for talent, and outside of a commendation for at least trying, these over-coloured, badly composed wrecks of art should be shipped en masse to the Saatchi scrapyard.

Wearied by the day, the gardens at La Chatonnière, the long drive and the disappointing artwork, I headed for the core of the city, found a brasserie, took up a ringside seat and ordered a large whisky with a beer chaser. Apart from the 'seen-it-all' old waiter there was no sign of anybody much over twenty-five, and most of them younger. There is something about young girls wearing socks that have inten-tionally been sunk to hang around their ankles that suggests dropped knickers, I thought, as I grabbed for the olives and nuts. The background noise of the city was quite invigorating after the silence of the countryside. The big bikes screaming off into the traffic, the honking and hooting and the beat of the people. I had with me a book on the genealogy of the Kings of France, and then underneath in much smaller writing, 'and their wives'.

Most French people nowadays seem happy without a monarchy. It was a position so abused that perhaps in their hearts they feel well rid of it. Maybe the old aristocracy, the fading princes, dukes, counts and barons, still lament the changes that a republic brought but with the continuing line of irrepressible presidents glued in place they just have to go with the flow. It has never occurred to me to think of kings and queens whilst living in France. I observe the continuing fan club of Britain's Royal family with ever-decreasing interest. Whilst the French press love to mock the Windsors I see little of the soap down here and care less and less about what Prince Harry wears in a nightclub.

I tried to concentrate on my French history but the book was heavy and on that evening in Angers it wouldn't stick to my mind. It was too much to take in, especially when it was such a buzzy spot. At the table across from me sat a dad, a mum and a little boy of about eight. The little chap was doing all the same kind of things that my little chap of eight does. The harmony, laughter and contentment amongst the threesome made me weep for my own broken accord.

But the city centre was jolly with its cafés, children's carousel and generous municipal planting. As I strolled along the pavement going towards the hotel for dinner, I

was looking at the lacy hydrangeas that imaginatively decorated the bus stop when I crashed straight into the bulk of
a huge man with his Great Dane. Actually it didn't look
that great, especially as it moved to viciously attack me.
They both looked like something out of a YMCA video and
the dog, obviously thinking I was about to rape his gay
monster-master, snarled and pulled dementedly on his
short chain-linked lead. They both had studs round their
necks, he had 'Fuck You' on his knuckles and the dog had
'Fisting' shaved out of his glistening coat. My relaxing
evening was suddenly all going horribly wrong. A few
moments ago I had been a contented middle-aged Scot
minding his own business in the leafy square of inner-city
Angers with hardly a care in the world, or at least tem-
porarily, and now here I was gazing into the face of a greasy
overweight belligerent psycho and a militant and
contentious Dane. It was a terrible, sinking moment of decision. The man stared at me with undiluted hatred, saliva
gathering in the corners of his mouth as he slobbed his
weight from one pudding foot to the other. I just knew he
was going to knock me over and sit on my face. I speedily
figured that if the 'Fuck You' on his knuckles was written
in English, I had to try something quick in the mother
tongue.

'Excuse me, I'm so sorry I wasn't looking where I was
going. Oh hi! Are you English? I'm here shooting a TV
commercial for Renault and we are casting for extras right
now. You'd be absolutely perfect. It's 2,000 euros a day for
three days. Here, let me give you the number of the casting

office, I'll tell them you'll be calling.' I was talking far too fast and the dog was clearly well into imagining what I was going to taste like and kept pulling with a fighting determination to get at his snack. The deep-set eyes in the flabby face of my opponent loosened their regard just a snitch; he had heard what I said, understood it, or at least the 2,000 euros a day bit, and backed off a little.

'What's your name, sir?' I enquired earnestly.

'Rhino Cerus, two words,' he glubbed.

'Great, Rhino,' I said. 'Take this card and call them in the morning. You'll be exceptional. Oh, and take Scooby with you.' I gave him a bogus number jotted down on the back of a wine shop card, suggested a time and told him to ask for Catarina in casting. I put my hand out to shake which he surprisingly took and shook, squeezed and teased, and I was out of there faster than is dignified for a gentleman of my impending age.

By the time I had showered off Rhino's clammy touch and put on some fresh clothes I was ready to meet my dining room reservation.

Dining alone is something I have become accustomed to during the last year, particularly during my Vine Garden quest, and it doesn't bother me. I just read, make notes and gaze out of the window and get on with it. However, waiting for my table in the hotel's restaurant that night, I realised it was going to be more of a challenge. The room was full and I had to hover awkwardly waiting for someone to 'sit' me. The dining room with its creaking old oak floorboards, its dark red walls and faded tapestries lit by bracket lights emulating Roman torches, its sideboards covered in thick linen and discreet china was no place to be on your own. It was a long minute before the *maître d'* came to my rescue and showed me to the only small table in the room, squeezed between three large round tables with at least six people on each having a ball.

Used to good but inexpensive practical provincial dining rooms where you could sit inconspicuously in a corner, this was quite shocking. I contemplated legging it quickly before the whole thing overtook me but as one waiter had made a big deal about moving my chair back whilst excusing me to the other guests and another had arrived to light the candle and pass me the menus, I was committed. I did my best to feel confident and important and settled down to ride it out.

It was quite clearly one of the city's hot spots for high achievers. The clientele all appeared to recognise their fellow diners. I was, it seemed, the only person in the place who didn't get kissed profusely or have my hand well shaken. Childish perhaps but this scenario seemed to personify my aloneness. There was nothing for it but to have a damned good, short but potent, feeling-sorry-for-myself session. I never was a travelling salesman or a company rep type. I have never preferred to be on my own, as I am naturally gregarious and like to share my wine. Of course, I realised I was simply getting on with a project and that, had I been happily married, the good lady would almost certainly not be with me, but that wasn't the point, I didn't think.

All around me groups of people at ease with their success and disposable incomes got down to having a cracking evening. I felt like a gatecrasher, but, fortunately, no one took much notice of me apart from an occasional quizzical glance; they were far too tied up with their own fabulousness. The tension was soon eased when asparagus, bacon and prawns arrived accompanied by some Château du Breuil Anjou, a frisky and fresh local wine.

The table to my right, I discovered with assiduous eavesdropping, was occupied by four formidable Americans with a mild-looking Frenchman in tow, hired, I supposed, to show them the sights, help with menus and generally negotiate them around the region. The lady whose elbow had been flirting with my wine glass was being asked what she would like next.

'I dunno, I just want something like cheese,' she said.

'I am sorry, *madame*, but we don't have lychees.'

She then took off her cardigan and the sleeve fell onto my asparagus. She dragged it away without looking at either it or me, but I didn't lose a bite, thank goodness.

Americans appear so confident. They don't have that British self-doubt as far as I can make out. One American guy who came to see me years ago about working together showed me his portfolio and before each page was turned he would say something like, 'Alex, you're going to *love* this.' Then when the photograph appeared I had already been programmed to think I loved it. None of that 'Sorry this isn't terribly good' or 'I'm not sure this is your kind of thing.'

The next morning, before returning to the Luberon, I had in mind to visit Le Parc Oriental de Maulévrier. At approximately 75 acres it is the biggest Japanese garden in Europe, built between 1899 and 1910 by the Parisian architect Alexandre Marcel. It is, by all accounts, a stunning example of the oriental art of landscaping, but I just couldn't summon the energy. I had already seen one Japanese garden in Beaujolais, I had been to the Chinese garden exhibition in Marseille and do you know what? I was looking forward to going home, being back in the office and living the Mediterranean life again. Things were looking up.

Chapter Twelve

The telephone rang late one night in early September. It was Georgie-Lou.

'Do you know about the Château Val Joanis?' she asked.

'The place near Pertuis?'

'Yeah.'

'I've heard about it often and have been meaning to go there for ages. Why?'

'Well, I was having lunch with someone today who just loves the place and as it's a *château* that produces wine and has a great garden I was thinking you ought to call in there. Shall we go together? I'd like to see it, too.'

'Good idea. When?'

'What are you doing tomorrow afternoon? I have to

make a delivery near Apt so I could pick you up at about two-thirty.'

'I'll be ready,' I said without looking at the diary. 'You know I don't live in the same place any more?'

'Is it difficult to find?'

'Not really but I'll fax you a map.'

Georgie-Lou arrived on time driving the little white van that bounded into the *hameau* and stopped outside the house like an enthusiastic terrier. She honked and I went to it.

It was a hot day even by September standards, with the temperature reaching the high thirties. Georgie-Lou was dressed in cycling gear with all-black skintight latex shorts and skimpy top, dark glasses and spiky hair. Her huge smile and kindly disposition probably wouldn't have got her far in Matrixland but it made me feel very responsive to her.

'Do you know the way?' I asked.

'I rang them so I have reliable instructions.' Her southern drawl lent authority to her words, and I sat back and let her get on with it. We talked a lot. I hardly knew her but by the time we arrived at Château Val Joanis I felt as though I was more than halfway there.

She had had a hard time in California without a father – a record producer who had abandoned the family – and a mother that had struggled to keep it all together. She had worked hard at university and had made plenty of friends, she said, but there was something singular about her. I couldn't believe that anybody who smiled and laughed so generously was going to turn out to be a manic-depressive, but I sensed that behind her ebullient persona lay a neediness.

'Are you happy down here being with Tom? Don't you get lonely?'

'I love Tom and he's very caring. He does his best to treat me like a daughter but sure I get a bit lonely. There aren't many single girls of my age around as far as I can see. Or I haven't found them, at any rate.'

'Or single men?' I said.

'No, single men aren't thick on the ground either, not of any age.'

'I suppose young people are going to migrate to the bright lights, big city.'

'I'm not into young guys. My last boyfriend was twenty-five years older than me.'

'Goodness,' I gulped, 'and what happened to him?'

'Oh, he turned out to be just an ordinary guy.'

'How disappointing.'

She looked at me with an unblinking stare, her mouth almost closed, and she seemed older suddenly. 'Yep. Another dud dude.'

The country house or *bastide* known as Val Joanis is located in the small valley that lies on the north side of Pertuis, less than half an hour from Aix-en-Provence, and is important not least as one of two remaining Roman villas to be found in the Luberon. In 1575 the building was home to Monsieur de Joanis, an ex-secretary to the King of Naples, and the house is recorded in the register by Cassini,

surveyor to Catherine de Médicis. Four hundred years later
Val Joanis belongs to Mme Cécile Chancel, who, in 1978,
set out to create a nineteenth-century garden combining
both the ornamental and practical, providing fruit and vegetables in a pretty setting. A few years later a major vine-
planting programme was under way along with the construction of a winery.

The long gravel driveway up to the house passes through
acres and acres of vine on one side and deep forest on the
other. Arriving at the house, you are directed into the shop
to obtain your ticket and think about all the 'gifts' you
might buy when you leave, not to mention the bottles of
Val Joanis wine. The walls are splattered here and there
with framed awards and certificates, laying confidence to
your purchases.

Georgie-Lou said she had told Tom that we were going
to Val Joanis, and he had agreed that the garden was worth
looking at, although, she told me, he felt that Beaupré had
better wine even if the estate was more classical. He was
right about this but, as it turned out, the less liturgical layout of the Val Joanis garden proved to be a delightful
antithesis to all the formality I had seen throughout the
trip.

The garden is presented on three terraces carved out of
the slope of the land and constructed in an area protected
from the legendary Provençal wind, the Mistral, by the
clever use of stone salvaged from a disused and depleted
Roman pool. We left the shop and arrived in a courtyard
surrounded by ivy-covered walls. Old vines in tubs

wrapped in *canisse* (split bamboo) decorated the centre and in one corner stood a vintage wooden table decorated with zinc baskets, miniature rustic garden seats no more than 30cm high, various pots, plants and carvings. An ancient stone archway in the wall led us out under a mulberry tree and on into the first terrace of the *potager* or kitchen garden. The impact was stunning, even though it was past its best by September. There was a formidable structure of wide, fine gravel paths with tall Mediterranean cypress trees striding down either side and criss-crossings the open space. Set back from the path edges, countless small balls of box bounced along in line and behind them minor meadows of flagging lavender. From the centre of these little quarters clipped pyramid yews of more than two metres high commanded the high ground.

This first level formed the main part of the vegetable garden, which, in the tradition of all French *potagers* had mixed the edibles with the decorative and practical. Everywhere *aromatiques*, thyme, verbena, lemon balm and artemisia popped up to help provide the kitchen with summer supplements. Herbs abounded: lovage, chives, fennel, celery, and that seducer of all cooks, basil, with its evocative aroma. There were rows of cordon-trained apples underplanted with swathes of rosemary, beds of red and green swiss chard, assorted-coloured cabbages and soft yellow lettuce. Unusual pairings of mahonias with potatoes, courgettes with roses, artichokes with caryopteris added to the folly. Vitex in both its white and blue forms existed as an acknowledgement to the site's history; the Romans used it to make crowns and decorate tables. In the middle of all this activity was a clearing with wire-framed chairs and table. To one side a giant cement snail with her offspring headed towards the safety of a pot; sometimes a small human would ride on her back. On the other side a small dovecot rose out of a bed of roses and purple sage in front of a charming little *cabanon* named after the *château*'s owner.

Down the slope on the eastern flank was a rose-covered arbour. Beneath cobbled steps a ramp run down the centre allowed easy access for wheelchairs, barrows and small tractors. From here we accessed the second level, another wonderland of colour and invention.

Clipped grey santolinas were contained by a low grill made from thin metal rods holding a rustic trellis. Periodically a pencil cypress imposed itself importantly on the crowd below and, from behind, the exhausted heads of the gold plate yarrow. Blankets of blue caryopteris pumped up the autumn colour with an occasional olive that had wandered in to lend a little of its famous grey-green foliage. Deep-purple buddleia, tobacco plants, erigeron, roses, rudbeckias, applauded the deep red apples that were trained up tall poles almost ready for picking along with scrambling white table grapes. With euphorbias and perovskias still hanging in there – who would dare say that a garden in late summer is lacking colour?

The old stone steps that lead down to the third and penultimate terrace are probably part of the Roman reclamation. They have impeccably worn treads with a smoothness of touch that is satisfyingly comfortable. The last level is an orchard of mixed players: jujubier, cotinus, crab apples, Portuguese laurels, ostrya, the Mediterranean hornbeam, and lagerstroemia, the summer lilac – a favourite with its late flowers and smooth twisting trunk – kumquats, tall standard abelias, catalpas, the Indian bean tree, cherries and figs. A row of enormous sycamores whose heads had been cut into squares sat on their trunks like huge cubes. Underneath the trees the lush well-watered grass showed off deep dappled shadows. Here was peace. We sat a while, relieved to be in the shade, and took in the landscape that dropped away beneath us down into the vineyards with the forest beyond, backed by the Luberon hills.

We talked a lot about the country we were in. Last winter there had been a splurge of bestsellers in France that talked about the country's decline as a force in Europe. These books, written by fully paid-up members of the intellectual elite, promoted the notion of a rapid descent in France's influence. There was, they said, a growing acceptance by parts of the French intellectual community that the French leadership is not something that Europe wants or France deserves.

Three of the books have focused discussion on the country's incapacities, rigidities and its role, they argue, in the context of the Iraq war, in dividing the western community and fracturing notions of Europe's potential unity. The titles, which translate to phrases like *France in Freefall* or *French Arrogance*, are merciless in these accusations of the ineffectuality of French foreign policy and the extent of the country's economic breakdown.

'The French hate change,' said Georgie-Lou, as we wandered the garden now. 'Most people do, but they refuse to accept that in the developing world France is beginning to slip behind, getting marginalised. Anyway, they don't exactly enhance themselves to Americans right now with their policy on Iraq, that's true enough. The States may be unilateral and imperial, but at least it is flexible and sort of open to change. By comparison, that is. You can't say that about France.'

'I guess not. Certainly it's very reluctant to give anything up,' I said. 'For example, it's always being discredited because of its advantages with agriculture, disregarding the rules of the EU as if they don't apply to them. Gets the British farmers up in arms. Actually I think to most Europeans, *l'exception française* – or the collective willingness to be prepared to cut the French a special deal at all times – is on the road toward extinction.'

'I think France loathes the United States more than it loathes the UK. It is cosying up to Russia just to annoy us,' she said.

'That's probably temporary, loathing the States, I mean. Maybe France needs a little shock therapy to help it bend towards modernity, but wouldn't it be terrible if it lost all its appeal because it started to toe the line?'

'It seems unlikely under Chirac.'

'I agree,' I said. 'It's amazing how strong his position is. France really is Chirac's country now. The fifth president of the Fifth Republic and his political allies reign supreme – from the Elysée to Matignon, the Assemblée Nationale to the Senate, the judges and the justice system. Not since Charles de Gaulle at the height of his power has France's destiny been so fully in the hands of just one man. Spooky.'

'Doubly spooky when you think that Monsieur Chirac was essentially elected by default – rather than by deliberate choice,' said Georgie Lou.

'Exactly. Even more curiously, all of this happens at a time when France desperately needs both economic and social reforms to modernise – and a thorough reshaping of its European policy.'

'In what direction will Chirac drive his stake, do you think?' she asked.

'Well, the man has a choice to make. Does he want to go down in history as the heroic defender of French farmers? Or will his legacy be that of a founding father of an enlarged Europe? If he wants to be remembered as a great EU moderniser, he has the chance. France could emerge again as a leading player in the new geo-strategic set-up of the European continent – or it could get increasingly close to the edge and drop out of contention.'

'So the whole country's position is in the balance?'

'Yes, I think it probably is, although I can't see it falling off the continental shelf. Whatever, you can be sure the old boy has a few tricks up his sleeve.'

'It must have been hard on him to realise that a lot of this French-bashing was coming from the inside and not just the outside as usual,' said Georgie-Lou. 'Guillotine those intellectual traitors!'

As we walked back through the garden I asked

Georgie-Lou what she was going to do after her year with Tom was up. 'Are you going to find a job in the wine trade in California?'

'I would rather lecture and teach than work in a wine store,' she said. 'Although there will be less people drinking wine if current trends are anything to go by. In the fifty years from the end of the Second World War up to the millennium, France's consumption, for example, is down 60 per cent. Whereas in the fifties, sixties and seventies, all cafés had licences to sell wine, nowadays a much smaller proportion bother to apply, and that's simply because the demand is so much lower. It is less dramatic in other countries but the pattern is similar.'

'Really? I didn't realise that. Why?'

'First because people are no longer drinking wine at lunchtime. The normal working lunch between executives is supported by water not wine. The production of bottled water has soared over the last twenty years. This even applies to an extent to dinner. Secondly, demand for *vins de table* have shrunk. People would rather have good wine or not bother. This is difficult for the small everyday producer. Mechanisation, better marketing, better equipment, disease control, and improved varieties of vines all make it hard for the local farmer to sell his produce. He is being pushed out by the richer, bigger wine-makers who are not only making better wine, thus better profits, but are also beginning to join forces. Moët in Argentina and Australia, Rothschild in California, Chile and South Africa. The potential marketing power of the big brands will squash the

minnows. It's the corner shop versus the supermarket syn-
drome. Thirdly, statistics show that more people are drinking spirits. But more importantly, people are becoming
increasingly body aware and don't want to shorten their
lives by killing their liver. So to answer your question, in the
future the wines that will be readily available will be of a
much higher quality, and the so-called wine lake will dry
up.'

'Doesn't that mean it will become an elitist drink then,
as not many people will be able to afford better wines?'

'No. The point is that because people will demand better wines, the producers will have to make it for less. They
will reach a wider audience which will compensate for nar-
rower margins of profit.'

'But if there are less people drinking wine then–'

'Less people drinking cheap, second-rate wine, more
people drinking fine wine.'

'Less overall?'

'Exactly. So, what do you think about gardening?'

'What about gardening?'

'What's the future of gardening?'

'Well,' I said, slightly nonplussed, 'it's a big subject.
There is growing awareness to the importance of urban and
municipal landscaping, conservation, promoting healthy
ecosystems–'

'I meant more in the private sector where you work,' she
interrupted, 'or at least in the home gardening that applies
to the regular garden owner.'

'Well, the contribution that science makes in enriching

our gardening experience is often overlooked. But it touches us all – modern rose-breeding, pest and disease control, irrigation regimes, commercial fruit and vegetable growing and countless other aspects of gardening we take for granted are only possible thanks to advances that have transferred more or less directly from the laboratory to the domestic garden as well as the commercial nursery. So it's reasonable to presume science will continue to help the gardener of the future. However, that said and in light of global warming, increasing EU regulations on chemicals and a developing awareness of our impact upon the environment and the effect our actions have upon it, do scientists have the right priorities for gardeners? Are they rising to the challenges we expect of them, or too arrogant in imposing unwanted solutions to unrecognised problems? Answers on a postcard, please.'

'It's kind of a luxury thing having a garden, isn't it? All that private dirt.' Georgie-Lou was looking at her surroundings and fanning herself with the Val Joanis brochure.

'It might be a privilege to own land that you can cultivate, but it is not a luxury to actually garden or be a gardener. You won't keep a real gardener down just because he or she doesn't have an expensive bit of real estate. You'll find people growing things out of old cans on window sills, avocado plants in their bedroom or runner beans around fire escape railings. In fact, a lot of people have a garden of some sort.'

'You can tell that from the amount of garden stores there are. Every supermarket has a garden corner of some sort.'

'Extended peace-time, not talking Middle East here, ensures that the leisure industry is expanding. Gardening and fishing are allegedly the two most popular leisure activities so gardening as a commercial concern is sitting pretty for the moment at least. The need for good garden design has seeped into public consciousness with new parks and playgrounds. People are staying at home more so the backyard becomes an increasingly important leisure space. Lifestyle magazines, television programmes and various journals are all pouring out the message. People nowadays have snazzy little gardens for entertaining in that only a few years ago would have done for the washing-line and the dog only.'

'Does a yard add much value to a property? I mean if you spend thousands of dollars on it will you recoup when you sell?'

'Yes, if the expenditure is in line with the overall property value. It's an emotive thing, decorating. If you put gold taps in your bathroom you probably won't get your money back; equally, if you spend a fortune on say mature trees you can't expect the full return. What is indisputable is that it will swing a sale for you. That is, if there are two similar houses for sale in the same location, the one with the better garden will attract more offers.'

'Do you like conservatories?'

'I like the idea although it is worrying how people persist in copying Victorian designs in Britain. Architects should shake a leg.'

'Maybe the Victorian style can't be bettered?'

'What a depressing thought. Anyway, the concept of

bleeding your house into the garden and being able to use it all the year round, especially in northern Europe, is sound. Don't see many of them down here though, do you?'

'Nope. What about the future for you? Will you stay in Provence?'

I hardly hesitated. 'Yes, I will.' There, I'd said it and meant it. 'It's my home now, my adopted country, and I love it.'

I don't think anyone would allow themselves to move to a country if they didn't like the inhabitants; certainly I would never have given myself permission to move to France if I hadn't liked the French. Any given country can seduce with its climate, rural bliss or ocean openness, with its food and its eccentricities, but if you want to live there it is the people themselves, their culture and take on life that you have to be able to waltz with.

A few weeks here and there does nothing to rub away the gloss, it's only when you commit, when you start living with them on a daily basis and share their lives and deaths, their marriages and babies, that a sound relationship can evolve. Involvement with a foreigner's problems is different from the involvement with a fellow countryman's. They say different things, believe and pray differently, celebrate and practise differently. France is not like Britain in nature, quality, amount or form as everybody knows – or say they know. Simply, it *is* different.

Britain and France have always promoted caricature opinions of each other with ludicrously unintelligent views that feed on determined misunderstandings, and they run through the two societies from the prime ministers down to soccer hooligans. But there is a bevy of us on both sides of the channel that adore one another. It is probably true that the historical alliances of the Scottish and French have warmed the hearts of the two parties more than anything that has ever been achieved with the English, but for two countries so accessible to each other it is hardly surprising that an Anglo-French fan club exists.

I have been involved with French people and their country for as long as I can remember. I like them enormously and that even includes the Parisians despite their reputation of haughtiness and coming from another plane. A certain arrogance and overconfidence can get under your teeth but overall I'm drawn towards people who don't seem to care much about anything other than themselves and nobody does it better than the populace from the capital.

My first serious love affair was with a French girl. We were both eighteen and declared undying love for one another at the top of a deserted moor on the Isle of Man. Her father was the French Ambassador in Rangoon, which made him sinisterly unapproachable, and whilst he was on duty Katherine would live with her grandmother in Paris attending school nearby. I would visit and we would kiss behind the curtains in case Grandma discovered me. She never did.

For half a decade I went to Paris every spring and autumn with another girlfriend whilst she stormed the catwalks for the collections. She earned a fortune and kept a small studio on the left bank. For a few weeks each season it was as good as it could get. Young, happy and rich in a city that offered so much.

My first wife was French. But that wasn't very surprising, for her, at least, as she seemed to have a thing for British and Irish men. Her first husband was English. I, her second, was Scottish. Next came a Welshman who died riding his bike too fast into that good night. Now she is married to an Irishman.

Years and years later here, I am living full-time France. It had been an unqualified success for the first seven years but after last winter – the winter of discontent – it had seemed as though I had had enough of the place. My marriage had collapsed and the thought of being some kind of solo sailor on a French tide left me cold. I was fed up with the lack of English-based culture, worried about the education of my little boy, even tired of fighting the relentless climate. On top of which I had had the uphill struggle of finding a new home that needed to be in the area to ensure easy access to Theo, because of my work and because the thought of moving far away was too daunting. Worse still, at that point I was not even sure that I did love the French so much after all. I was trapped and had nearly lost sight of 'that little tent of blue'.

I debated the possibility of real change with myself, but, as I did so, I soon realised that going back to England was not on the agenda. The cords had been severed and a retro move was unimaginable. I had gone from there, moved on. Perhaps America, I thought then, but where exactly? In any case, what a performance. It was quite likely we would fall out with each other anyway. The Caribbean perhaps? I envisaged a pretty beach hut with some exotic plants and warm water. I would need to be near an airstrip so they could fly me out to Miami if I was very ill. Or what about Croatia? Everybody's going there now for their big expensive second homes. I could do what I have done here and organise the landscape. But political unrest might upset the wheelbarrow at any moment. Australia probably wouldn't have me even if I wanted Australia. Canada might be too provincial. South Africa? Worth a thought.

Curiously, all the time these places were being juggled, Provence was settling itself back into my psyche. It seemed to take no notice of my considered wanderings, just melted down and waited for me to realise that this was home. As the summer had worn on through a haze of warm weather, exceptional castles, wines and gardens, the bad taste had given way to a new wave of passion. France had regained its colour but importantly it was the Vaucluse that had really called me back to where I once belonged.

Provence is a particular place. It is quite different in character – physically, geographically, politically and emotionally – from the 'mainland'. Being Mediterranean, it is a harsher place to live than say Burgundy, Bordeaux or the Loire. The Latin personality is more flamboyant here than in their northern fellows and, being both coastal and rural, it produces a wider set of characters. Remember that Provence was totally separate from France until 1481 when, following the death of King René, the states of Aix recognised Louis XI as the Count of Provence, effectively annexing it to France. Within that strange human desire to make a nest, to create a secure corner, to decorate and make a friendly abode, I knew now, after a year of doubt and uncertainty, that it had to be the Luberon.

If I had been doubting the wisdom of staying in Provence, in France at all, then one midsummer's evening the cloud lifted itself up and stopped trying to suffocate the life out of me. The weight suddenly got lighter. I had moved into my new house, which, bar the usual snagging list, was blissful. It was a place to call home, and it was smart and well organised. One section had been dedicated to offices, the rest was domestic. It had cost more than it should have but it had a shine that made me smile. Even the little hooligan, who had seen it in its dilapidated form and had solemnly declared it unliveable, dirty, smelly and 'like, gross', marvelled at the transformation and immediately confessed that he wouldn't have thought it possible. He had his own quarters, which pleased him no end, and he even agreed to sleep in the spare room. Well, for most of the night anyway. With the divorce behind us, the ex-Mrs and I had settled into an agreeable friendship, made possible, she said, 'because it's so much easier not having to live with you.' Where we would go from here was unpredictable but I felt calmer than I had felt for a year. All things considered, the move had worked out pretty well.

Soon it would be time to set off for the very north on the last part of my journey. Champagne was to be the final trip. Tom had a contact at Moët et Chandon who, he said, would tell and show me as much about champagne as I could possibly want to know, including its own gardens. 'Unsubtle choice, I know,' he had admitted cheerfully, 'but it's a giant and there's no other wine brand like it in the world. Besides, you'll love the Orangery.'

As I sat on my newly completed balcony, an old long-legged mongrel trotted past silhouetted against the fading light. He stopped to sniff, looked up to see who was saying good evening to him, wagged and widdled and continued on his way. Beyond, I saw Theo coming up the lane towards the house on his bike, pedalling for all he was worth. Little legs pumping like over-excited pistons, a determined but happy grin on his adorable wee face, he caught sight of me observing. He waved and called out, then pedalled harder. He was happy and so was I.

I rushed down and ran towards him, hauling him off the two-wheeler and hugging the living daylights out him. It was going to be fine.

Chapter Thirteen

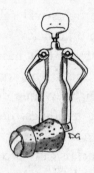

The approach to Epernay from the south gives no clue that one might be entering a vine-growing region. The flat lands happily supported end-of-season asparagus with its clouds of blown hair, shaved wheat and barley fields, carrots, spinach, various salads and greens, even blackcurrants (for the *kir royale*?) but no grapes. Even as you enter the city the only hint of anything bubbly going on came from the names of the streets – Rue Jean Moët, Place Eugene Mercier, Rue Jean Chandon – but for somebody familiar with the spreading acres of vine-growing in the other wine-producing regions it seemed ominous. Almost as if it were all a sinister joke to lure people into the net. Perhaps champagne was a man-made by-product from synthetic combustibles? But the answer is as simple as it is obvious. It is only on the slopes behind and between Epernay and Reims that the grape can be cultivated. It is too far north for the fruit to ripen, so anything planted on the plains will be damaged by frosts and floods whilst anything planted on the ridges will be harmed by the wind. It is therefore only possible to plant on the gentle slopes of the surrounding countryside where the frosts will roll down the gradient and the rainwater drain off quickly.

Epernay is a small town that has arrived on the map because of the wonder that is champagne. The main street named, hardly surprisingly, Avenue de Champagne, is full of enormous spreading buildings that make Buckingham Palace look like a garden shed. The grandeur built on either side of the road stands classically proud and magnificently dominating the town landscape in much the same way that the factories and mills used to in Britain during the Victorian period of industrial prosperity. It is hardly surprising that champagne pours out of such elegant properties. In keeping with the hype, the brand that sparkles with success and creates an aspiring lifestyle product must be seen to have great portals of power and prestige.

Moët et Chandon, born in 1743, is the biggest tank of them all, with entire blocks of land dedicated to the production, bottling and selling of its product. It also has enormous research laboratories and teaching facilities. Next door, or about half a mile up the street, comes Perrier-Jouet and Pol Roger, which are equally modest and unprepossessing.

The huge gates of these empires are thrown open to visitors who, having paid a few euros for the pleasure, can roam the caves and cellars within. In the case of Moët this covers a staggering 18 miles. These secret labyrinths are fascinating. The subtle smell of chalk, the gentle trickle of moisture, the muted clinking of bottles being shifted, all mixed with the sound of echoing voices, tell the story of man and nature conspiring to make the world a better place.

Hollowed out of massive banks of chalk, the lowly lit tunnels endlessly criss-cross one another beneath the town of Epernay, each with its vaulted caves brimming with ripening bottles. They start their bottled life lying very nearly horizontal in their racks, then each week they are turned a little and made more upright: this is to allow the yeast to ferment evenly and then when it has died, to collect up near the mouth of the bottle. It is then removed by freezing a section of the neck, removing the cap, dislodging the block of yeast then introducing the cork. One man will turn 40,000 bottles in a week. If you think that the Champagne area produces some 300 million bottles a year that's a lot of turning.

Yeasts are responsible for the transferring of juice into wine during the first fermentation and for the wine's effervescence during the second in-bottle fermentation. In warmer climates this second fermentation does not happen because the yeasts die off sooner as there is no longer enough sugar for them to feed off. It was this discovery by Dom Perignon (1638–1715) that started the phenomenon of sparkling wine.

Champagne is made from a blend of grapes taken not only from the diverse districts of the champagne appellation but also from wine made over different years. When the oenologists declare a certain year to be a vintage they make an amount of wine from only grapes of the same season and keep it for about five years before releasing it for sale. Hence Vintage Champagne.

Moët, with its annual production of some 30 million bottles, is making more than twice that of its nearest rival, Veuve-Clicquot. However, it is a fairly academic comparison as they both belong to LVMH group (Louis Vuitton, Moët & Co., and Hennessey). While they share a parent company, each 'house' works hard to produce its own recognisable wine and is responsible for achieving its own goals.

Incidentally, of the 300 million bottles produced each year in Champagne, nearly half is exported, and the UK has the honour of being the biggest importer at 31 million. The US scrapes in second with a measly 18 million.

Moët et Chandon has immense wine-making expertise handed down over several centuries; it operates 543 hectares, some of which belongs to them and the rest from contracted growers who cultivate the vines with the utmost care. They wouldn't want to lose their benefactor through sloppy stewardship.

All this started with Claude Moët. Born in 1683, he presided over the genesis of one of the oldest companies in France. He was part of a family of notables that had been ennobled by Charles VII back in 1446. It was his brother, a wine merchant in Paris, that advised him to head for the Champagne region. He took the advice, settled in Epernay and quickly established the house known as La Maison Moët in 1743. From an early age Claude Moët involved his son and between them they built up an enterprise that was supplying champagne to all the royal and princely courts of Europe. The wine became a favourite amongst women championed by Madame de Pompadour, 'the only wine that leaves a woman beautiful after drinking'.

Described as being elegant, witty and literary, Madame de Pompadour swore by the champagne of Monsieur Moët, who happily sent at least 120 bottles for the court's summer sojourn at the Château de Compiègne. Her reputation for impeccable taste helped spread the fame of the house of Moët. Her choices influenced every member of her entourage. Thanks to this elegant figurehead, the wines of Monsieur Moët acquired an eager following of lady admirers that continues today. Women are one of the strongest-selling images for champagne: whether it is the sponsorship of fashion shows or the compounded social acceptability as an expressive alcohol for females, it trades unashamedly on its heritage, helped in no small part by the elegant flute from which it is sipped.

By the beginning of the nineteenth century the glamour of champagne was already assured. However, with the visit of Napoleon Bonaparte in 1807, it became written in stone. He was charmed by the talents and charisma of Jean-Rémy Moët, the grandson of the founder, and made Epernay an obligatory stop for the great and powerful en route to

Prussia. In 1816 Jean-Rémy's daughter, Adélaide, married Pierre Gabriel Chandon. These two prestigious names of Champagne ensured an illustrious future. Today, they are proud to say that a bottle of Moët et Chandon is enjoyed by someone every second of every hour, somewhere in the world. It's ironic to think that the next drink with bubbles to become so successful was Coca-Cola, followed by fizzy water in Perrier.

The French are understandably very possessive about keeping Champagne French. It fits in with their pride and resistance to change, and they unceasingly strive to prevent the use of any French place-name for non-French products. Champagne is as good a case in point as you will find. Champagne is in France, on France, under France and no one else can use it as a product name, even if the product is every bit as good, even if another country has a place called Champagne and grows vines. One of the most fascinating challenges to this narcissistic French characteristic emerged when a small village of 650 residents in Switzerland became a battleground for the European Union. This tempest in a bottle, as the *New York Times* dubbed the dispute, revolved around the use of the appellation of 'champagne' by villagers in Champagne, Switzerland.

The inhabitants of Swiss Champagne contended that it would simply not be possible for consumers to confuse their product – still white wine in a screwtop bottle, priced at around 5 euros (£3.50) a bottle – with its bubbly French counterpart. The French champagne-makers' association, the *syndicat de grandes marques*, argued that this was not the primary issue. They argued that 'champagne' is not only a trademark of France, a position embraced in European Union regulations regarding commercial property, but also part of the French identity. 'It's our patrimony and our collective trademark,' testified Daniel Lorson, a spokesman for the French producers. 'If we don't defend it, in a few years the word "champagne" won't mean anything.'

Both sides fought their corner arduously, of course, and it defies credibility to think that Swiss and French intransigence was motivated solely by economic interest. This was really local business interests making themselves known as national concerns and infusing the debate with an urgency that it hardly merited. Of course it also has plenty to do with national ego and identity, keeping the notion of 'Frenchness' both within France and abroad.

It is forgivable though. The very word has found its way into languages far removed from French. People who have never seen, let alone tasted, French sparkling wine use the word as an image. Writers, painters and musicians, jazz singers, rich young things and elderly statesmen all contribute to the ongoing invention of the image by using the wine to denote social status and, more significantly, the glories of France where it is seen as an embodiment of the national spirit. Who worries when Champagne actually became French, who cares if the French think that the wine resembles their intelligence with its sparkle; it has an authority and legitimacy not afforded to most commodities. It's a snazzy drink, fits the bill and is of no consequence to you and me beyond the pop, fizz and bubble. Whether it's the big bang or the silent kiss, the released cork whose famous shape has seen a squillion celebrations brings an effervescence to a moment that no other drink on earth can emulate. Here is bottled glamour and liquid charisma. *La Vie en Rose*. Thank you, Dom Perignon, for the phenomenon. Let's toast the blind old monk who discovered bubbles in his wine at the abbey of Hautvillers in the old Province of Champagne. He knew a good thing when he tasted it.

There are three separate gardens attached to the Moët et Chandon set-up, each completely different all in diverse locations. In the nineteenth century, Epernay's prosperous wine-dealers, including Moët, built production facilities and sumptuous mansions along the Faubourg de la Folie. This thoroughfare was soon renamed the Rue de Commerce and eventually became the Avenue de Champagne in 1925.

The first garden belonged to the original mansion and although small it served well as a sanctuary away from the tasting salons and entertaining halls of the interior. Enclosed by an ivy-clad stone wall it supports a naturalised pond surrounded by grass, ferns and rocks whilst being shaded by an imposing old saphora tree which has been privy to many high points in the growth of the Moët empire. Arguably the most august of these was the meeting in March 1824 of a band of heavyweights from the arenas of world power: Emperor Francis II of Austria; the Tsar of all Russia, Alexander I; Grand Duke Nicholas, Tsar apparent; the King of Prussia; the Prince of Orange, future

King of Holland; Prince Metternich; and our own Duke of
Wellington. Together they enjoyed a glass or two of the
increasingly famous champagne and no doubt discussed the
future of the world.

Between 1805 and 1817 Jean-Rémy Moët, with the
help of his close friend the miniaturist architect, Jean-
Baptiste Isabey, built two identical mansions on a site across
the road from his own residence inherited from his father
and now too small for his needs. Between the mansions he
created an orangery and a traditional French garden for
entertaining guests. The two small buildings face each other
across a gravel courtyard, at one end of which the ironwork
gates and railings divide the property from the street outside; opposite broad stone steps lead down to a lower terrace broken up by a formal rectangular pond that has low,
intensive 'Parks Dept.' planting. Riots of colour bombard
each other from borders that are planted twice a year. It is
similar to the planting seen in the royal parks of London.
Orange marigolds, pink, white and scarlet busy lizzies,
mauve pelargoniums, blue salvias, and red bergenias snarl
and spit at one another, vying for attention. From the centre of the borders march regiments of standard roses. The
Moët crest is shown on a slight bank between the water and
the orangery, planted with box hedging against a background of pink winter roses.

The orangery itself is impeccably maintained and
adheres to all the classical rules of such a building. Built to
the Georgian proportions of 9/16 it has three ceiling-to-
floor windows on either side of the central arched doorway.

A flat roof with a parapet is interrupted every few metres by a typical Grecian urn. The gravel is carefully raked each day and the whole thing looks like a cinema set filmed in Technicolor. At the time of my visit the orange trees that would be kept in this building during the cold season were still outside the main visitor centre and car park. They were a motley bunch that hardly deserved the grandeur of their winter quarters.

The last garden is about 5km away from Epernay up on the side of the valley near Hautvillers. Surrounding the little chapel where Dom Perignon is buried are the gardens which belong to a small house which must have originally been the home of the priest, but as the land now belongs to the Moët Chandon family, the chapel itself has only a fraction of the land to call its own. The gardens and little house are not open to the public and are found only by passing through an inconspicuous little iron gate off to one side. The area is divided up into 'rooms', the biggest of which is the labyrinth planted thirty years ago and using traditional yew hedging. Having long been a symbol of religion, the corridors of the maze represent the chaos of an unfulfilled life whilst the centre represents the core of all being, of tranquillity and peace fuelled by the blood of Christ. Which explains the old lichen-covered stone wheel used for crushing the grapes to make wine which was taken in communion. The interconnecting space between the maze and the terraces which overlook the valleys is a simple gravel expanse some 30m by 15m. It is lined with conical-shaped junipers in half-casks, underplanted with horizontal cotoneaster. It is not really a place to hover but to pass through on your way to either the little house at one end or to the formal three-tiered pond at the other. All is surrounded by vast expanses of grass with a curtain of beautiful old evergreens lending a monasterial atmosphere to the enclosure, but it is the view from the terraces out and over the sloping hills of vineland that really arrests you. It is spectacular, and must rate as one of the calmest spots in all of France.

That night I stayed in a wonderful comfortable hotel with the most eclectic accumulation of *objets d'art* imaginable. The owner was a collector of strange and wonderful things that included furniture, light fittings, sculpture and tableware. In the sitting room was a hard cork-tapered wastepaper basket guarded by a sculpted penguin wearing oversized wooden sunglasses. On the mantelpiece an alabaster clown wearing billowing baggy trousers sat dangling his legs over the edge, in the hall a multi-coloured harlequin made from papier mâché stood guard at the front door, and in the dining room a priceless art deco sideboard supported a range of figurines and lamps. Upstairs a little marble lady sat in a wooden chair with her hands folded round a petite book, in my room metal and leather furniture combined with orange wood cupboards, and outside on the landing a huge backlit pink paper rose filled a tall vase. It was a wonderland of originality and would make any subsequent hotels feel mundane.

The next morning I was looking at the cathedral,

thinking that its multi-spires looked like a spider plant, when a young American man approached me.

'Hi, d'ya like the church?'

'Sure,' I said, 'it's rather remarkable and in very good condition.'

'That's because it's a repro,' he said. 'It was rebuilt after the First World War.'

It transpired that the elders of the commune had decided in their wisdom that the terribly damaged cathedral should be an exact copy of what was there before. Many would argue that it was a mistake.

'I hate copies,' said my new pal. 'Many generations knew the old church and then it went poof – end of story. They had a great opportunity to commission something new, but what did they do? They spent a fortune replicating the old one.'

It hadn't even occurred to me that it might be a reproduction. Why should it? Any wandering tourist without architecture as a specialist subject was going to make the same error. But of course as soon as he told me I went off it.

'Don't tell the theatre is a remake, too,' I said.

'No, that's genuine,' he said.

Thank goodness for that because I was just thinking how wonderful it was with its glorious vintage façade with the carved stone depicting: Comedy with smiling masks, flutes and flowers; Tragedy with crying masks, armour and death; Drama with costumes, props, and disguises; and Opera full of musical instruments, gaping mouths and harps. It was as powerful and appealing to actors and theatregoers alike, every bit as calling as the cathedral opposite might be to good Christians.

The following day I was eating lunch in Reims where I met a middle-aged caterpillar who crawled out from beneath a curly lettuce leaf. Unperturbed by the heat of my omelette, he set about conquering the dizzy heights of the *frites* mountain. When he got there he settled down and started to share my salad. Our dining was interrupted by a call from the office.

'Your agent rang and asked if you would be interested in doing a coffee table book about Mediterranean plants that will grow in Britain.' It was Lélia my assistant.

'Don't think so,' I said. 'Besides, I'm sure it's been done already.'

'Should I say that?'

'Depends on who's doing it and how interested they are.'

'So you might be in principle?'

'In principle, but only if it can be done around new gardens, something different.'

'Oh. OK, I'll tell her. How's Reims?'

'Full of friendly caterpillars.'

Coffee tables are strange things. They are certainly practical when it comes to having a low, easily accessible place to put a bottle and some glasses on, or bowls of cocktail canapés, even coffee cups, but it is the underlying support act that is so revealing. The coffee table book. The object that quickly exposes solid information about the owner of the coffee table. Much intelligence can be drawn from the selection of books that get piled up on that bit of furniture.

There is a conspiracy about these books between the people who write them, publish them, read them and display them. An understanding that this special category will probably be 'photographically led', as the publishing houses like to put it, or possibly painting led, even illustratively led, but the text, the written, highly researched, technically correct words will be the secondary element of the exercise, and the captions – often written by an editor rather than the author – are invariably bland. People may find inspiration in the stylish presentation, but it is rare that these books are ever really read. That's another kind of book, one that would more likely be on the shelves of the office, study or workroom. More often than not, coffee table books are bought to be showed off.

Of course, everything in your house is a declaration of your taste and preferences. A wall without decoration is an empty space waiting for the confidence of commitment that will illustrate your position, custom, law or religion, but the big book on that table (little books don't really qualify) is a shorthand broadcast. More deviously, they may even be an attempt to project yourself as something more than you really are. These books are fanciful publications which play an ephemeral role in one's life. After a short time one is removed from display and relegated to a big bottom shelf somewhere, to be replaced by a new titillating subject that is topical and acceptable.

When we first came down to live in the South of France I made contact with Riviera Radio in Monte Carlo with a view to doing some kind of general interest gardening programme. I sent them a mock-up tape that included an interview with someone working in the field. Marseille Radio would have been closer but Monte Carlo Radio had a swing about it that not only sounded more glamorous but also meant a bit more of a day out. I got a pilot. A bit more than that in fact, as it was a pilot that would be broadcast. I chose as my interviewee an English-speaking academic lady who had lived in France for the last thirty-something years. She was sharp, drily witty and hugely knowledgeable on the subject of gardening. She had already published many coffee table books on gardening in Provence and the Côte d'Azure, amongst others. She is prolific and sells well. She is also a major gardening networker who if you stay on the right side of her web will be happy to help you meet the spider.

My opening question was therefore: 'What does it feel like to spend so much time and effort writing books that nobody reads?'

It was professional suicide, of course.

It was just before midnight and I was three-quarters asleep. The hotel in Reims, by comparison to the little treasure in Epernay, was dull and the room rang of the sadness of failing salesmen, multi-corporate middle-management desperadoes and dejected delegates from IT conventions. There was no hint of the scent of a woman, beyond the girl gymnasts that were competing dutifully on the little TV screen.

Coming from a hollow old warehouse in Glasgow this gymnastic 'Grand Prix' offered up an assortment of equipment that wouldn't have looked out of place in a Helmut Newton shoot. Hanging against a brightly painted blue backdrop, glitzy red nylon curtains were neatly offset by lines of fake terracotta window boxes filled with yellow chrysanths and silver-leafed cineraria. It might have been cheap chic if it hadn't been let down by the blazing strip lighting and the vacuity of the Tannoy system announcing the contestants followed by their scores. Our female commentator, however, clearly knew her sport.

'Here comes Fiona Gennel, only fifteen but already a veteran of the full pirouette,' she said admiringly, then, as young Miss Fiona flew through her movements, assured me that she had performed a 'beautiful interpretation with good clean lines, and had shown great depth and focus.'

Then it was the turn of a slightly older Beth Tweddle. 'Look at that separation! She's doing the splits in mid-air, changing the body shape and looping on her hands. The audience will respect her courage.'

When Cherelle Baxter fought through to the finals with her combination of skills that included a wonderful double-front away, we all held our breath for her grand finalé. Unfortunately she lost shape in the final bounce with a slight softness through the back. 'She'll lose bonus points for that,' said our voiceover maiden. But happily, a strong release with an inverted swing allowed her to pull out a

ast-minute full-twisted double-buttock punch and float
down to snatch the cup. It's a tough sport.

Through this oscillating mode of dreams and wakeful-
ness came the distant irritation of a portable telephone
ringing. Its persistence pierced the pleasantries of slumber
and shook me awake. It was cruel in its continuance and
ominous with its presence. You don't just pick a phone up,
kill it and put it down again if the call is coming through at
midnight or thereabouts.

'Hello?' I managed.

'Alex, this is Georgie-Lou,' said an empty voice. 'I'm
sorry to wake you but I have to talk. Uncle Tom is dead.'

This had happened to me once before. A friend had rung
me in the middle of the night to tell me that she was in a
morgue in Malaga identifying her husband's mangled body.
A couple of hours earlier he had been killed in a car crash
out on the mountain roads. There was nobody else
involved; he had simply misjudged the corner and hurtled
over the precipice. A car not far behind had seen the whole
thing and reported it. In the still of the night everything is
exaggerated and the punch harder because you did not see
it coming.

Hauled from the shores of a disordered consciousness it
was hard to give the moment all the perception it demanded. I must have asked what had happened. I was rushing
towards full awakeness.

'He had a heart attack during dinner last night. He was
dead on arrival at the hospital.'

'Were you with him? Where's Jiminie?'

'We were both with him and so was Laura.'

Laura was a neighbour whose French husband had helped Tom set up his vineyard.

'It was really horrible. He suddenly got up from the table, tried to say something and then collapsed. He just folded up and bounced off his chair. I don't know what to do. Laura has been organising people to deal with everything. The ambulance and doctors. I've never seen anybody die before.' She sounded strangely concave, as if she had distanced herself from the tragedy.

'Who's looking after Jiminie? Where is he?'

'He's gone to Laura's. He's completely spaced out.'

'Where are you?' I asked.

'In my room at the château, I'm really cold. Can you come here and help me? I don't want to be on my own, I don't know who else to ask.'

'Oh Georgie-Lou, I'm in Champagne. I'm hours away but I will come back tomorrow. I'll come as quickly as I can.'

'I can't believe he's gone. We had just spent a great day together, all three of us. So much laughing.' She began to sob.

I had so little to offer, and felt so inadequate. 'Get into bed and try to rest,' I said. Keep the phone open on your pillow. I'll do the same then you can talk if you want to. It's as close as I can get.'

'What about the phone bill?' she asked abstractedly.

'It doesn't count,' I said.

We lay like that for what was left of the night and, with occasional reassurances, her sobbing finally gave way to a rhythmic breathing. It was 8.30 a.m. when I heard her ask if I was still there. I was, just. The battery was running on empty.

As I dressed the next morning everything was different. All the travelling I had been doing these last months had been done with Tom in mind. He had set up the course and I had been a willing and eager participant. At all times I had been thinking about how much he was or wasn't going to enjoy such and such wine that I had bought on his direction, and of our wine-tasting to come. I had been carrying around a happy scenario wherein we were tasting together while I regaled him with stories of the wines I had found and the gardens I had seen. I had been looking forward to getting to know him better and, because he had motivated this tour, he had been much in my mind. And so had Georgie-Lou. I had thought a lot about her and young Timinie, too. Only sixteen with an abstract mother who passed him confusion and insecurity that was balanced only by a solid loving father who anchored his life and gave him a sense of purpose. All he had wanted to do was impress his dad with his shared love of wine. It was heart-wrenching.

My journey of discovering France was suddenly over but in a way it had happened in the perfect place. Champagne was absolutely the correct office for me to be in to deal with the drama and tragedy of Tom's untimely and sudden departure, and celebrate his life – what little I knew of it.

We had easily fallen in step with each other when we first met. I remember thinking here was a new friend and had looked forward to seeing more of him after this trip was over. I could see he was a sensitive man who had been broken by his failed marriage and who didn't have half the confidence he pretended to have. He was shy about his passions for publishing, wine, his son and, unexpectedly, for poetry. Mind you, he could never resist sharing a line or two. I remember this:

> A woman drew her long black hair out tight
> And fiddled whisper music on those strings
> And bats with baby faces in the violet light
> Whistled, and beat their wings.

When he recited those words he glowed with warmth. It was doubly poignant because he was such an unlikely ambassador for T.S. Eliot.

That evening I went back up to the little Dom Perignon chapel at the abbey of Hautvillers in the old Province near Epernay and took a bottle of the old monk's vintage champagne with me. By the understanding grace of God the small iron side gate was ajar. I stole onto the grand terrace behind the chapel, the terrace that belongs to the Moët et Chandon enterprise, and looked over the grape-covered slopes below. The dipping sun was soft on the ripening fruit and the few birds that bobbed on the breeze called in with an inquisitive note.

I shook the bottle, exploded the cork and cascaded the

golden wine all around me and over the balcony. When it had slowed I held it high, letting the last of that autumn day's light leak through the polished surfaces, and then I drank from the bottle to the memory of a man that had settled my turmoil and given me back France. He had introduced me to the idiosyncrasies of the vine-grower and eccentricities of the wine-maker. In so doing he had introduced me to incredible gardens and reinstated a sense of belonging that I had begun to doubt existed. My bottle metaphorically wasn't full and his list remained incomplete, but my inspiration was sealed. I needed to look no further for evidence that France was where I wanted to be. The tears that rolled down my cheek fell silently into the bottle. I placed it on Dom Perignon's grave, lit a candle and left.

Epilogue

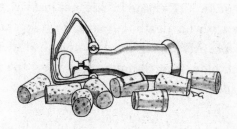

Tom MacArthur was buried in the Luberon. He had died a very wealthy man and his unambiguous Will made it clear exactly what was to happen to his estate. Jiminie was, of course, the main beneficiary. He now had a valuable property in the South of France, a very comfortable apartment in New York and enough investments to ensure that his life would be well pillowed, providing he wasn't torpid with the portfolio. Tom had also generously left Georgie-Lou a sizeable legacy, which showed us all the considerable esteem he had held for the girl from Atlanta. He had dictated that he wanted to have his ashes scattered over his *domaine*, to be 'used as a fertiliser for the vines to increase their potency!'

The gathering of friends and family were united in their loss but, under strict instructions from the boss, drank far too much of his homegrown red wine. It made us stagger and swear, argue and laugh. He would have thoroughly approved. Sadness at his demise and happiness at the memory made for a merry bunch that tumbled out of his estate that night. Merry, that was, except for Jiminie and Georgie-Lou. They couldn't celebrate his life, not just yet; they were still dealing with his death. I wanted to help them but it was impossible. My much-loved mother had died when I wasn't much older than Jiminie and I knew the raw hurt, the blunt sadness, the dried-out well of tears.

The end of Tom had signalled the end of my journey round France but it was also the beginning of my second term in office. I was ready now to kick off the next seven-year cycle in Provence, garden designing, writing, being a father and perhaps even blowing up with love again, providing, of course, I lived that long. Tom's death had alerted me to my own mortality, and although he wasn't the first of friends or acquaintances of my age who had thrown in the trowel, I had been living these last months so totally within his ether that it was like a fellow soldier getting the bullet instead of me.

Despite all the desiccation, I did not feel as emotionally impoverished as I had expected. I had thought that on top of Tom's death, all the horrors of separation, the trials of running a new home single-handedly and having to unravel a stack of work would come at me hard, and bruise with its force. In reality the relief of being able to unpack and set up house properly was liberating, and the story of uncorking the wine gardens had been a joyous one. I now had a fuller cellar than ever before and, most importantly, I was absolutely ready to work in the garden again – both my new courtyard garden and any gardens I might be commissioned to create. I had that peaceful, easy feeling and it was very welcome.

And so it was one evening in this state of relaxed animation that I was listening to the radio. A voice was saying forcefully: 'There is a need for us as a global community to address the grossly unequal distribution of wealth and power in the world that has generated murderous rage against rich nations in general, and the US and its allies in particular. The roots of terrorism lie in the concrete and growing problems of global poverty and inequality–' when the telephone rang.

'I'm going away for a week. I don't want to go back to California just yet, I want be on a beach.'

'Oh hi, Georgie-Lou. I don't blame you. Where are you going?'

'To Mauritius. I've bought a ticket for me and Jiminie.' Then she hesitated. 'Actually I've bought one for you as well so you pretty much have to come with us. OK?'

Surprised as I was, this was not a moment for dithering. I needed to be grown up and responsible, to handle the situation gently and straightforwardly. After all there was work to be done, affairs to be attended to and clients to be nourished.

'I'll go and get my swimming trunks,' I said.

Tom MacArthur's Vine Garden

NAME OF WINE	COLOUR	FROM
Château de Beaupré 1999	Red	Coteaux d'Aix-en-Provence
Baron Edmund 2000	Red	Fredericksburg, South Africa
Rupert & Rothschild Château de Beaucastel 1996	Red	Châteauneuf-du-Pape
Château Lafite 1999	Red	Pauillac, Bordeaux
Château Vignelaure 2003	Rosé	Coteaux d'Aix-en-Provence
Flint Valley 2003	White	Denbies, England
Ladoucette 2002	White	Pouilly-sur-Loire
Moët et Chandon Vintage 1999	White	Epernay, Champagne
Montrachet 2000	White	Côte de Beaune, Burgundy
Domaine de la Bongran Clos Vougeot 1979	Red	Côte-d'Or, Burgundy
La Chapelle 1999	Red	Hermitage, Côte du Rhone
Château MacArthur 2003	Red	Luberon (in memory)

Bibliography

Bulpin, T.V., *The Tavern of the Seas* (Sunbird Publishing, 2003)

Jones, Colin, *A History of France* (Cambridge University Press, 1994)

Phillips, Rod, *A Short History of Wine* (Penguin, 2002)

Pinder, Roger and Merton Sandler, *Wine: A Scientific Exploration* (Taylor & Francis, 2003)

Johnson, Hugh, *The Story of Wine* (Mitchell Beazley, 1989)